Top Deck Daze
Adventures on the Frog and Toad

TO 'SCREW' AND ALL THE CREW
IT'S YOUR STORY

First published 1999 by Halbooks Publishing
Copyright (©) Bill James 1999
Re-printed 2001 (twice), 2002, 2003, 2004, 2005, 2006

The 2011 revised edition is published by Kokoda Press
PO Box 43, Enmore, NSW 2042, Australia
Re-printed 2013, 2015 with an extra 8 pages in the colour section, 2018

This work is copyright. All rights reserved. Apart from any fair dealing for the purposes of study, research, criticism or review, as permitted under the Copyright Act, no part of this book may be reproduced by any means, electronic or mechanical, including photocopying, recording or by any informational storage and retrieval system, without the prior written consent of both the copyright owner and the publisher.

National Library of Australia Cataloguing-in-Publication entry

Author:	James, Bill (William M.)
Title:	Top deck daze: adventures on the frog and toad / Bill James; Illustrations by Bill Leak & Warren Brown.
Edition:	Rev ed.
ISBN:	9780977570423 (pbk.)
Subjects:	Top Deck Travel—History.
	Bus travel—Anecdotes.
	Tour guides (Persons)—Anecdotes.
	Backpacking—Anecdotes.

Other Authors/Contributors:
   Leak, Bill, 1956-
   Brown, Warren, 1965-

Dewey Number: 910.4

Edited by Robin Appleton (2001) and Scharlaine Cairns (2011)
Cover illustration by Warren Brown
Cover and text design by DiZign Pty Ltd (2011)
Printed in Australia

To purchase further copies of this book, visit your local bookstore. The book is stocked and distributed by Peribo.

Top Deck Daze

Adventures on the Frog and Toad

Bill James

ILLUSTRATIONS BY BILL LEAK & WARREN BROWN

ACKNOWLEDGEMENTS

The social gatherings of old friends who provided anecdotes for this modest opus were as much fun as the actual events the book describes. Special thanks to Timmy Oliver and James Kemsley (now sadly deceased), *raconteurs par excellence*, for sharing their recollections at regular get togethers with Mick Carroll, Peter 'Filthy' Browne, Andy Morgan and Denis Quinn. Others who kindly gave me their time and contributions included Mark Atkinson, Peter Baily, Trevor Carroll, Dick Cijffers, Alan Collingwood, Greg 'Wombat' Ettridge, Dave 'Dinga' Evans, Chris Greive, Chris Jones, Rex Julian, Bob Kennedy, Greg 'Five Eights' Lloyd, Murgha Mack, Bruce 'Moose' Maloney, 'Diesel Dave' Morse, Brian 'Dillon' O'Sullivan, Lew Pulbrook, Dave Reed, Ellie Reed, Graham Sewell, Jeff Skinner, 'Kessa' Ware, John 'Grilly' Wells and Mick Wiles. Thanks also to Bill Leak and Warren Brown for their fabulous drawings. Tony Sattler and Simon Benson helped with advice and editing. Thanks also to Alan Halbish who was the original publisher; to Diana and Peter Murray of DiZign for the wonderful layout of the 2011 edition; and to Lew Cody, Dave Reed, Lew Pulbrook, Trevor Carroll, Tim Oliver and Peter Yates for the updated Honour Roll and photos.

CONTENTS

Prologue vi

Part I Getting Started 1
1	Troppo in Morocco	(North Africa 1973)	2
2	Back to the Future	(London 1973)	26
3	Budding Businessmen	(Morocco 1974)	35
4	Declare Misère	(Europe 1975)	52
5	In Silk Road Mode	(Asia 1975)	68

Part II Things are Getting Bigger 113
6	Doubling the Deckers	(London 1976)	114
7	The Seventh of the Seventh	(Pamplona 1976)	122
8	Dodgy at Dover	(London 1976)	148
9	Blunder Down-under	(Australia 1977)	157
10	Boom or Doom	(London 1977–78)	174
11	Fare's Fair	(Australia 1978)	193
12	Pissed on the Piste	(Andorra 1978)	198
13	Randy in Scandi	(Scandinavia 1979)	216

Colour section (24 pages of colour photos)

Part III Getting Too Big 233
14	Worry Warts	(London 1980)	234
15	Sales Tales	(London 1980)	245
16	Martyrs on Charters	(Europe 1980)	254
17	Mates in the States	(USA 1981)	271
18	Wise Enterprise	(London 1982)	284
19	Rex's Rorts	(Russia 1982)	290
20	Conference Nonsense	(Sydney 1982)	306
21	Strine Steins	(Munich 1982)	315
22	Pay Day	(London 1983)	324

Epilogue 337

Honour Roll 340

The Top Deck Fleet 349

PROLOGUE
BRISBANE, NOVEMBER 1995

'Are you damned blind as well as …?' the motorcycle policeman yelled through the open window of the ute, checking himself in mid-sentence, but I knew immediately the unspoken word was 'bald'. We were eyeball to eyeball, and I could follow his gaze. Instinctively, I held my hand to my head and winced as I dragged the ever-diminishing strands of hair across my pate. Bald? Well, more than a little thin, damn it. But blind?

'Absolutely not!' I retorted with venom. 'Hell, I just didn't see you, the pace you were travelling. Where did you come from?'

It was hardly a case of culpable driving and the policeman knew it. The motorcycle was now jammed hard against the kerb, inches away from having been sideswiped as I'd changed lanes to make a left-hand turn off Brisbane's Story Bridge. I'd been going too slowly, if anything, while the policeman had been speeding unnecessarily and veering to the left to overtake me on the inside lane.

The patrolman backed off just a little.

'Okay, okay, but just watch it next time, will you? And use your side mirrors. That's what they're there for.' He stood right back now and eyed the dilapidated, ancient, bright blue Holden with suspicion. He looked back at me and given the condition of the vehicle, noted my incongruous attire of collared shirt, tie, and navy blue jacket slung across the front seat. 'Where are you heading?'

'The Stock Exchange Building, at the Riverside Centre … and I need to be there … now.' I studied my watch with exaggeration.

'Uh, haa? Doing it a bit tough on the markets, eh?' Obviously he thought I was a master of the universe, down on my luck. I could have explained but it wasn't worth the effort. This was to be the biggest day of my commercial life. Our company, Flight Centre, of which I was a director and shareholder, had applied to list on the Australian Stock Exchange. The other directors and I were due to meet that morning with two of the city's leading stockbrokers, Morgans and Wilson HTM. Would they be prepared to underwrite the float? Their support would be crucial if the deal was to proceed. The stakes were huge. The company would soon be worth more than $700 million and as we founding directors would still hold eighty per cent of the shares ... well, it was just too much to contemplate. My gut churned at the very thought of it.

I'd woken late, hung-over, and feeling decidedly ill, too late to order a taxi, and now this, to further spoil my day of destiny. I'd borrowed the ute from a mate I'd been drinking with till the early hours. It had been a get-together of some of the old Top Deck Travel crew, the bus tour company that Graham 'Screw' Turner, Geoff 'Spy' Lomas and I had founded in London in 1973.

'All right,' the policeman relented. 'I won't book you on this occasion, but just keep your wits about you in future and remember, double-check your mirrors before changing lanes or turning.' I said nothing in reply and just nodded acquiescence, thankful the brief ordeal was over. Hesitantly, the policeman turned to walk to his bike but after a few strides, abruptly swung around. 'Before I go, could I see your licence please, sir?' he asked sharply. Instinctively, I reached for my wallet tucked into the inside pocket of my coat lying beside me on the seat. As I did so, a fleeting recollection of one of the previous night's stories flashed across my mind. We'd played out this charade so many times in those early London days. I wasn't going to be booked on this occasion, so why not play the game again, just one more time, for old time's sake?

'Oh, gee, I'm sorry,' I said, patting the empty pockets of my shirt and trousers, 'I must have left my wallet at the hotel. I left in a bit of a rush this morning.'

Top Deck Daze

'You appreciate it's an offence to drive a vehicle without carrying your licence, sir? What's your name and where do you live?'

'Lloyd. Err, Graham James Lloyd, that is. I'm an Australian, but I usually reside in the UK.'

'And what's your date of birth?'

'Seventh of October, 1949.'

'Just hold it there a minute please, Mr Lloyd.' The policeman walked over and picked up the hand-piece on the bike's two-way radio and identified himself to his base. 'Go ahead, officer,' came the crackling reply over the speaker, audible at thirty metres.

'I want an ID check, base. The name's Lloyd. First names: Graham, James. Date of birth: seven, ten, forty-nine.' Half a minute passed in silence, then the radio crackled into life again.

'Hold your suspect please, officer. Interpol has fourteen outstanding warrants for Mr Lloyd's arrest. We'll have a squad car down to you in three minutes.'

'No, no. Please. It's a mistake. I mean, it's a joke. My name's not really Lloyd at all. It's James, William James. Look, see, I have a valid New South Wales licence right here. Please, officer?'

'Save that one for your solicitor, Mr Lloyd. You'll have plenty of time to explain …'

PART 1
Getting Started

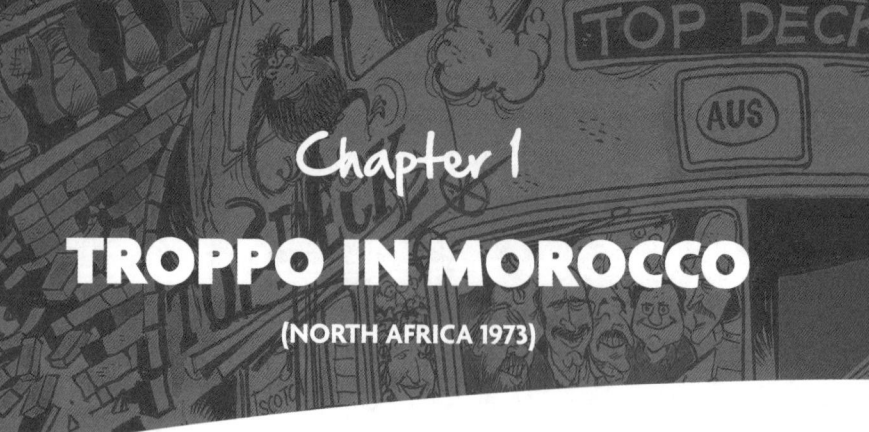

Chapter 1
TROPPO IN MOROCCO
(NORTH AFRICA 1973)

'No, no, Señors, I have told you five-a times already!' Manuel, the ferry clerk, was in an agitated, Spanish flap, holding his hands to his head in total frustration. 'It is impossible. Your autobus, he is over four metres. The ferry door, she is only three metres. You can see for yourself, and you can count, no? Four into three won't go. You must leave me alone now, please. Zere is nothing more I can do.'

There was similar depressing news at the tourist office, a garish pink and red, tube-shaped building on the Calle Juan de la Cierva. 'Yes,' this was the only ferry that made the one-and-a-half hour crossing from southern Spain to North Africa. 'No,' no other ports in Spain serviced the route at this time of year. 'No,' there were no alternatives.

For two weeks now, our group of seventeen had travelled from London via France and the Spanish Costa Brava and Costa del Sol to this, the port of Algeciras, in our big, green, Bristol double-decker bus named *Argas*, intent on ferrying it across the Straits of Gibraltar to our destination: Morocco. Now we had to accept that it was an impossibility. A ramp led up from the dock to the stern of the ferry and then a narrow deck led to a doorway through which the vehicular traffic embarked. Our bus was simply too big. We were never going to make it.

'Why do you want to go to Morocco anyway?' inquired the dusky, Spanish señorita behind the tourist office counter. 'Shopping in Spanish Ceuta, perhaps, but Morocco is a dirty,

Troppo in Morocco – North Africa 1973

backward country. You will not like it. Spend more time in our lovely country.' 'Screw' said nothing in reply but as he turned around, he noticed the dejected look on my face.

'Come on, Bill. I'll buy you a drink.' Screw's positive mood hadn't changed. 'Screw' and 'Spy' were the owners of the bus and the three of us retired to a bar near the port and sat, watched and drank in silence as the big ferry pulled clear of the docks without us.

I had only met Graham 'Screw' Turner and his mate, Geoff 'Spy' Lomas, some eight weeks previously at an Australian–Kiwi party in London. We were the same age (twenty-three) and shared similar interests and not dissimilar backgrounds. Screw, at five foot ten, was a few inches shorter than me, but much broader and was as solid as the proverbial brick thunderbox, the product of early maturity and hours in the gym training for school and college rugby and rowing firsts. A shock of straight, longish, blonde hair covered a broad, suntanned brow and his short, scruffy beard gave him the air of a viking chief on the lookout for a bit of rape and pillage.

My initial impression of Screw as a hard-drinking, indiscreet, swearing, man's man was, however, quickly tempered by the knowledge that he held a veterinary science degree from the University of Queensland and could hold his own with any scholar of note during our usual discussions on sex, politics or religion. Moreover, his views were clearly and uniquely his own while the rest of us tended to sprout conventional wisdoms inherited from parents or educational institutions, or from what we'd read the day before in Time or Newsweek magazines. My image of Screw was further confused when, after a long session on rough red, 'Vin Ordinaire', he was likely to either swear his head off or, depending on his mood, sprout poetry verbatim and with some eloquence, from the most obscure of texts. So, as a result of these eclectic talents combined with a gifted natural intelligence, easy-going manner and natural leadership qualities, he appealed to all who met him.

Top Deck Daze

Troppo in Morocco – North Africa 1973

Top Deck Daze

The nickname 'Screw' was a play on Graham's surname, Turner, and had been given to him by his mate, 'Spy' (so named because of his broad-brimmed hat and dark glasses), when they'd boarded together at Toowoomba Grammar. Their friendship grew at Emmanuel College where they'd resided as veterinary science undergraduates at the University of Queensland. Unlike Screw, Spy was a much more circumspect character. Of medium height with curly, mouse-coloured hair, he stared at you, expressionless, down a long, straight nose, his head held slightly back, adding to his air of aloofness. His guarded, poker-player's face would hold you in a firm gaze for some time as if any hint of a smile might alert you to the full house he'd been dealt until, perhaps, something you'd say might take his fancy and then a flicker of a smile would dance around his lips and, eventually, his shoulders would shake as he broke into a sustained, expressive, tension-relieving laugh.

You learnt to think before you spoke to Spy. He could listen in silence for some time and then, with a handful of well-chosen words, demolish your ill-conceived point of view in seconds. Consequently, I came to both admire and respect these newfound friends.

In addition to me, Screw and Spy had gathered fourteen other Aussies and Kiwis for this Moroccan jaunt from among their friends and acquaintances in London. After they had bought the bus between them, I had been the first 'passenger' to sign up for their trip, at a discount, and they had taken me into their confidence and generously treated me almost as a third partner right from the start. I'd helped with the fit-out of the double-decker with its sleeping bunks on the upper deck and its kitchen and tables and chairs downstairs (although a previous owner had already done the bulk of the work). All the other passengers had paid £100 each for their six-week journey with the promise of two weeks in Morocco. What were we going to tell them, now that it was impossible to get there?

Troppo in Morocco – North Africa 1973

The next day, the three of us went to the port to see if we had explored all the options. We went to every shipping agent in town and we were assured that there were no other vehicular ferries that could take us. We had run out of ideas and we settled into a bar by the docks and drank in silence for some time while the big ferry came and went again.

We were desperate to get to Morocco, but more time in Spain was hardly unappealing to me. I thought of Torremolinos. What an extraordinary melting pot of the world's youth, the drop-out capital of Europe and headquarters for every septic draft dodger this side of the Atlantic. And brother! Weren't those Scandinavian women something else? Bars sold beers at four cents a pop and then, at the bodegas, cellars with sawdust-covered floors, wine was doled out at five cents a litre. All seventeen of us had rolled up to a bar and ordered rum and cokes. The barman had lined up the glasses, lip to lip, and run the rum bottles up and down till there was barely an inch to spare. After all, the Coca-Cola was far more expensive than the rum. Screw was dismissive when I dared suggest we go back. Been there! Done that!

'Well, what about Portugal, Screw? We're going to the Algarve anyway, but this will give us time to explore right up the northern coast.' Again Screw ignored me and avoided further discussion on the topic. The more we drank the more I abused Screw for his pigheadedness and inability to accept the facts. We couldn't get to Morocco, and that was that. The more I appealed to him to see reason, the more he refused to talk with me. After a long and unpleasant lunch, Screw rose abruptly to leave.

'Spy, go and get the bus. Get everyone on board and be back here by five-thirty, but park out of sight on the Avenue Marina, then come and meet me back at the terminal.' Spy and I looked at one another and shrugged. There was nothing else for us to do, so we caught a taxi back to the campsite and rounded up the punters who were drinking by the pool.

We parked the bus as arranged. At five minutes to six, Screw came running towards us, jumped into the driver's cab, fired up

Top Deck Daze

the engine and hurtled the bus through the terminal gates, only slowing enough to throw a ferry ticket at the gatekeeper through the open window of the cab. Screw had only paid for a minibus but there was no time to discuss such technicalities.

The ferry was just about to depart again on its final sailing for the day. We zoomed around the terminal building and caught sight of the last car disappearing through the ferry's door while the whistle blew, signalling for the vehicle ramp to be hauled away from the ferry's stern. Screw ignored the frantic gesticulating of the stevedores as they jumped clear of the bus careering up the narrow ramp. There was a horrible grinding noise as the chassis scraped the lip of the stern and we came level with the deck. There was just enough room for the bus to perch on the ferry's rear deck, with the bus's top deck inches from the ferry door, and its back platform overhanging the ferry's stern so far that if you stepped off, you'd go straight into the Mediterranean Sea.

Troppo in Morocco - North Africa 1973

By this stage, the vehicle ramp had disappeared, the ropes were untethered, and with three loud shrills of the horn and a full head of steam, we powered out of the port, Morocco-bound, before it had really dawned on us what had happened.

Though minor in many ways, the incident had a profound impact on me. While I had willingly accepted defeat, Screw simply never entertained the idea of not making it to Morocco. The episode epitomised the power of his positive thinking and, on the other hand, highlighted my conservatism and narrowness of thought. I made a pact with myself that if the opportunity presented itself in the future, I would work with or near Screw in any capacity possible, as I felt I could learn and grow so much by simply being in his company.

These thoughts were still with me as I rose early on the morning of our seventh day in Morocco. With a punch of the starter button the old Bristol's six-cylinder diesel burst into life and I took to the wheel for the first driving shift of the day.

Eddies of cold air stirred in the rays of the newly risen sun. The bare earth, a rich outback ochre, camouflaged the bitumen road stretching interminably ahead. The familiar scent of beautiful big eucalypts, silhouetted against the cerulean sky, hung in the air. Was this really Morocco? The Sahara Desert? It was certainly the closest I'd felt to Australia since leaving there ten months before and a world away from the grey London winter we'd just escaped.

The whole situation seemed so surreal. What in God's name was I doing here, ten thousand miles from home, driving this

Argas *bogged in Tangier.*

Troppo in Morocco – North Africa 1973

English double-decker bus, of all things, in the North African desert? I looked into the face of a Berber woman standing by the road, staring at me, as the bus lumbered towards her. Her expression of total disbelief reflected my own thoughts.

The chilled air, in spite of the brilliant sunshine, wasn't the only reminder of the blizzard that had engulfed us as we'd crossed the High Atlas Mountains. Snow was still clearly visible on the heights, away to my left. These huge, snow-capped peaks rising abruptly from the desert, on the one side, and the vast sand dunes away on my right, made up an incongruous landscape.

The previous evening we'd made our way up the Tizi-n-Tichka Pass at the peak of the High Atlas between Marrakech and Ouarzazate. Screw had been driving as we climbed and twisted through the forests to the treeless summit of the pass and the storm seemed to fall on us like an ambush. Disaster had been seconds away. We stopped the bus near the top of the pass. Sheer thousand-metre cliffs lay just beyond the edge of the road. Slowly, but with absolute certainty, the bus began to slide on the black ice on the road and we lurched towards the precipice. From my seat at the front of the top deck, the height

Not a good place to miss the bus!
Argas *crossing the High Atlas, 1973.*

seem magnified, and death certain. I closed my eyes as the bus swayed in the blizzard, teetering on the edge of the Earth.

With only centimetres to spare, the tyres had found some traction as the ice broke in the loose gravel and we crawled, agonisingly slowly, back to the centre of the narrow roadway. It had been a harrowing experience and alternate visions of death and deliverance haunted me as I drove that following morning.

I continued my driving shift till lunchtime and then turned north, towards the mountains again. We stopped at a café nestled below rough hills with ruined Berber agadirs above. A freshwater pool nearby had the romantic name of 'La Source des Poissons Sacrés'. The water, according to the café-owner, 'cured female infertility'. Spy wondered aloud if it might also act as an aphrodisiac and in any event, had no trouble convincing the girls to strip off and take a swim. It wasn't long before most of the guys were in the stream with the girls as well as if obeying the ineluctable laws of nature. They could have it all by themselves. I wasn't taking my gear off for anyone.

'A hundred and twenty pounds of dynamite with a one-inch fuse,' was how one girl had described

The massive cliffs of Todra Gorge soared 300 metres above the gravel track.

me following a recent, typically dysfunctional tryst, and I wasn't about to provide any smart aleck with ammunition for further derision. A few kilometres further on we entered the massive canyon of Todra Gorge. The narrow facing cliffs soared 300 metres above the gravel track that constantly forded the fresh-flowing stream. We could spot mountain goats and eagles above and the locals relished telling us that panthers roamed the hills beyond the gorge. As late as the 1950s the French Foreign Legion picketed the heights to discourage snipers from taking pot shots at tourists.

The following day we swam at Meski Oasis, named after a spring of the clearest blue water that flowed into an artificial pool, originally built by the Legion as a haven free of the dreaded African disease of bilharzia. The constantly flushing toilets and the open air showers were a refreshing change from the primitive campsites we'd endured so far. It was also relaxing to be away from the street urchins and hawkers who hassled you at every turn in the narrow alleys and souks of Rabat, Casablanca and Marrakech.

Spy assisted Screw in organising a traditional national meal. We ate *mechoui* (a whole roasted lamb on the spit), and *kefta* (spicy meatballs made from minced mutton served in a rich tarty sauce with eggs), washed down with copious quantities of good Spanish wine.

On our ninth day in Morocco we entered the medieval city of Fez, the ancient capital of the original kingdom. The square in front of the main gate was a bustling throng of hawkers, buses, taxis, cheap hotels and cafés. Immediately we stopped the bus we were approached by three locals purporting to be our guides. They were roughly dressed and very aggressive in their manner. One had a club foot. They spoke in quick, broken English that was hard to understand and were 'a sandwich short of a lunch' according to Screw.

'We are your guides. We are your guides,' they insisted. 'If we do not have your passengers to guide, Mr Screw, we will starve,' they wailed. An excited crowd of people, ten-deep, swarmed

Tracking Argas' movements, 1973.

Troppo in Morocco – North Africa 1973

around Screw and the bus as he tried to negotiate with the guides. 'If you do not employ us, we will plant chocolate (local slang for hashish) on your bus, and you will be in big trouble.'

Suddenly a pathway opened up through the milling throng and into their midst strode a handsome, jellāba-clad young man with what the military might call 'command presence'. He wasn't big in stature but he had the bearing of the rich and powerful. He spoke loudly and harshly to the three guides in their local dialect. An angry exchange followed, resulting in the guides standing their ground, but mute at last, with snarls twisting their faces as they glowered at the young man. The crowd also backed off and quietened, making more room for Screw.

'Let me apologise, Mr Screw, for this unseemly welcome to our city. There has been a slight misunderstanding. I am, in fact, to be your guide during your stay. This will be at no charge to your good self. Let me introduce myself. My name is Aziz Lebbar. This is my assistant, Habib Desheri. We are totally at your service.'

I stood back and watched Screw and Aziz talk. Both the same height, both the same build (though Screw was as hard and blonde as Aziz was soft and dark), both exuding the confidence of natural leaders, one unconsciously acknowledging the authority of the other. Screw readily agreed to engage Aziz's services and as we moved off, the three would-be guides began to hurl invective in our general direction. Screw, smiling, held up the palms of his hands indicating he couldn't understand what they were saying. To their credit, they switched immediately to English and displayed an easy mastery of the Australian vernacular. 'Go and get rooted,' they suggested.

A local Moroccan guide.

Haberdashery—one of Ali Baba's forty thieves.

Our punters went off to explore the old city on foot with 'Haberdashery' as Screw called him.

15

Top Deck Daze

'Come wiz me to zee Casbah,' he said smiling, greatly impressed at his own good humour. Meanwhile, Screw, Spy and I joined Aziz in his Peugeot for a city tour and a rundown of events for the next day or so. Tonight: A national meal, with free food and drinks for the three of us, of course, then later, when the rest of our group was safely ensconced in the campsite, we would accompany Aziz to Club 88 for a sample of the local nightlife. Tomorrow: Shopping for carpets.

After the national meal, Aziz explained that he understood we didn't have good clothes to wear to Club 88. Our entire wardrobe consisted of dirty T-shirts, shorts and jeans. No matter, he would provide us all with jellābas, the traditional neck-to-ankle, long-sleeved tunics worn by Moroccan men.

Club 88 was like a palace; all marble, soft lights, high-pitched music and a singer who sounded like a cat being hot waxed. All this was mixed with the smell of pipe smoke from the hash bongs and free-flowing whisky.

Aziz was a Fassi, a member of the rich merchant class. We were introduced to the pasha, the provincial governor, before we were escorted to our own table which was low to the ground and we sat, cross-legged, on mats and cushions. This was obviously the place to be seen in Fez.

The long-legged, mini-skirted girls were a far cry from those we were used to seeing in the streets. Women were usually covered from head to foot in a haik, a large wrap-around cloth, and a strange mask that made them look like they belonged to 'Batman's Fan Club' according to Screw.

A well-endowed but rather flabby bellydancer strutted her stuff on the dance floor below us, the only westerners in the club, playing up to us as if we were oil-rich barons. The done thing was obviously to poke a US five-dollar note in her panties or bra to show one's approval. For some reason, she took a set on me and fixed me with a lurid smirk. Urged on by the others, I held aloft a five-dollar note and I stood up to negotiate the four steps to the dance floor. My new jellaba was about five sizes too big for me and the end of it tangled in my thonged feet. I stumbled and fell headlong onto the dance floor.

Great cheering and guffaws emanated from the bar and as I was helped to my feet, the dancer ripped the five-dollar note from my grasp and stuffed it deep into her crutch to more yells and suggestive laughter from the bar.

Having provided the bulk of the entertainment so far and sweating from the heat and embarrassment, I was desperate for a beer, any beer, the colder the better. No such luck. It was whisky or nothing, and at US forty-two dollars a bottle, thank-you very much! Aziz made a point of ordering and paying for the first round with a great flourish. Having once been sick on whisky at a teen party, I couldn't stand the stuff. It was apparent though, that it would have been the height of bad manners not to share in the offerings, so I suffered and sipped in silence. 'Haberdashery' ordered the second bottle and it was soon clear that we were all going to have to shout a round.

We had little money, and nothing like US forty-two dollars between us, let alone each. Somehow, somewhere Screw slipped out for ten minutes unnoticed and returned with US dollars, at least enough to buy two more rounds but, fortunately, as the night wore on, Aziz was beyond any care for protocol.

We learnt that the whisky had come from the crew of a Sundowners tour bus that had recently passed though Fez.

'The last lot was expensive. They charged me fifteen US dollars a bottle,' Aziz explained. 'Too much. They rip you off those Sundowner boys. Tell them next time you see them. Do you have any to sell?' Unfortunately, 'No,' we didn't, but I could see the calculators whirling in Screw and Spy's heads. No, not this time, but you could bet your sweet bottom that if any of us passed by this way again the answer would be, 'Yes, as much as you can buy.' We gleaned that Aziz made money from many sources, not the least of which was supplying illicit alcohol to the clubs and bars of Fez, just like the one we were in, a forbidden practice in this strictly Muslim, supposedly alcohol-free country. Kickbacks from the restaurants where we ate, and various shops where we were led to buy, brought Aziz further financial rewards.

But all this paled into insignificance when we went to the carpet shop the following day. Up until this point, everyone on board the bus had given the impression of being paupers but after Aziz and his helpers had done their full spiel, it was like a buying frenzy. After two hours the passengers had bought thirty-two carpets, all of them very expensive. Aziz took the three of us out the back for coffee after the sale. He explained to us that we were to receive our commission for having brought him the customers. Wonderful.

We were to be paid in dirham, the local currency. Aziz doled it out in dirty, lumpy wads. We had absolutely no idea how much he had paid us, nor what it was worth. While he attended to more customers we did a quick add-up. Just over 4000 dirhams.

'How many dirhams to the pound, Spy?' Screw asked, 'Eighty, isn't it?'

'Well, if that's the case, we've got over fifty quid here, that's seventeen each. You bloody beauty.' That was three weeks spending money each! 'Here, give "Haberdashery" a tip,' Screw said, and slung him 400 dirham—what we calculated to be worth about five pounds.

It wasn't until we settled into a coffee shop twenty minutes later that Spy discovered his mistake.

'Hang on. I knew that didn't sound right. There's eight dirham to the pound, not eighty! That means we've got 500 quid here, not fifty!'

'You've got to be joking,' I gasped, but he wasn't. That was enough money to finance the entire six-week trip, and then some! 'And geezez Screw, you gave "Haberdashery" fifty quid, not five. That's more than a year's wages in Morocco. Talk about buying a friend for life.'

The punters, on average, had spent more than £100 each, a total of £1500, and Aziz's policy was always a third, a third, a third—a third to him, a third to us, and a third to the shop. God knows how much the poor women and children in the mountains, who wove the things in the first place, received for their efforts. But we could do little about it, except support the local economy as best we could, and so we searched for a tourist bar and that long, cold beer I'd been thirsting for since the previous evening.

It was after 11:00 p.m. when we returned to the bus at the campsite. I was surprised to find Marty, one of our passengers, still on board. My night was just finishing; his was about to begin. He was the youngest of our group. Nineteen years of age, intelligent, quick-witted and sprouting a mop of curly red hair, he should have still been at home, at university. From Sydney's North Shore, he'd dropped out of school and travelled to Europe a year after. Screw had met him outside Aussie House, in the Strand, London, and convinced him to join us on the trip. Marty was our dope expert. At home, that scene had passed me by completely. Despite my years at Sydney University in the late 1960s coinciding with Flower Power, Woodstock, the radical Student Worker Movement, anti-Vietnam War marches, riots, sit-ins, and the general hippie scene, I remained as blissfully naive of the drug scene as I had been on leaving school.

Just the same, I could recognise the pungent smell of marijuana anywhere. Every YMCA I'd stayed at in the USA en route to Europe seemed to reek of it. I was really shocked when I was offered a joint in Miami. It had about as much appeal to me as smoking dirty socks.

The offer of hash in this part of the world, however, was a different matter. Here, cultural values were turned on their head. We were used to a society that accepted alcohol but absolutely abhorred any form of illicit drug, even the non-addictive kind. The reverse was the case in Islamic countries. Alcohol was absolutely forbidden but the local Arab men frequented their coffee houses where they sipped the sweet black liquid and smoked reefers of what they called 'keef', a fairly innocuous mixture of tobacco and marijuana.

Top Deck Daze

Drugs were nevertheless strictly forbidden as far as tourists were concerned. Marty could testify to that. He'd spent two nights in a Marrakech jail, delaying our departure, while Screw had tried to find out who he'd have to bribe to bail Marty out. Marty had bought some hash resin from a local hood, Mahout, in the medina quarter. Of course it was a set-up. After Marty had paid a grossly inflated price, Mahout went straight to the police where he would have received a nice little retainer for the information. Later that day, the police raided the bus, taking Marty and his little cache to the local jail. The charade was completed when the police accepted a cash fine/bribe from us, in US dollars only, of course, for Marty's release. The local team consisting of drug seller/informer/police did very well for themselves — a scene played out, no doubt, to this day, with regularity, from Casablanca to Bangkok.

Thankfully the police hadn't searched too far. I had, under one of the bus seats, half a garbage bag full of keef. Mine had been a much better bargain than Marty's. It had cost me all of five US dollars. Don't ask me its street value in LA or London. Suffice to say it would have been heaps. To be truthful, I had scant idea of what I'd purchased at the time.

Earlier in the trip we had passed through Kenitra, wended our way through the Lac de Sidi Bourhaba Nature Reserve, and by nightfall, had found ourselves at Mehdiya Plage, a remote Atlantic beach just north of Casablanca. We'd intended to free-camp there. The girls on board didn't like the idea much. There were a few too many local weirdos hanging around the sand-duned foreshores in the dark. The bus had bunks upstairs, tables and chairs downstairs, folding into beds at night, and a well-equipped kitchen, but there were no toilets or showers on board, so we either free-camped by rivers or beaches where possible, or paid for campsites every second or third night.

After the girls ventured outside to find a safe spot for their necessary ablutions, 'Kessa' Ware came straight back and said there was no way she was staying here for the night. Screw

Troppo in Morocco - North Africa 1973

reckoned there wasn't much option. We had no idea where the next campsite might be; it was already getting on for eight thirty and we were all keen for dinner. Being the hero, I told Kessa I would lead the girls to a safe toilet spot.

About 200 metres down the road, we'd past a crude police post. Morocco had modelled its police force according to its colonial master, France. That is, the Gendarmerie is part of the military. At least in France the gendarmes are distinguishable by their dark blue uniforms and distinctive caps but in Morocco they are indistinguishable from the military. Indeed they are subject to military discipline, wear khaki uniforms and are located throughout the cities and countryside in a series of barracks and guard huts. It was one of these guard huts that we happened to pass at Mehdiya Plage.

Not the Marrakech Express.

I led the girls there and, sure enough, the tall, erect, officious-looking, olive-skinned Moroccan gendarme showed them around the back of the hut to a reasonably well-maintained loo, a rarity in this part of the world but just what we'd been looking

Top Deck Daze

for. As the girls queued up with anticipated relief, I walked with the gendarme back around to the veranda facing the road and paused as I looked up and gazed at the brilliant stars. The surf pounded away on the beach just beyond the dunes. Again I thought of Australia. You simply didn't see night skies nor hear sounds like that in Europe.

The gendarme turned to me, 'Une bonne nuit!' (A good night), he said. He was Moroccan of course but like most of his compatriots, spoke fluent French. I only had a halting schoolboy knowledge of the language but understood what he meant.

'Ah, oui, oui,' I replied 'Tres bonne,' nodding in agreement.

He then turned to me and said, 'Keef?' indicating that I might like to buy some dope from him. At that stage I'd never heard the word 'keef' and had no idea what on Earth he was talking about.

'Oh, Keith?' I said.

'Yes, yes, keef?' he nodded.

'Well, I'm Bill. Bill James. Pleased to meet you, Keith.' I shook his hand vigorously.

He was obviously taken aback by my apparent keenness to do a deal. Leading me immediately into the two-roomed hut and checking over his shoulder to see that we were alone, he produced the bag of keef from the back of a cupboard with a dramatic flurry. Comprehension finally dawned on my part, and the negotiations began.

I had kept quiet about my secret haul up until our stay at Fez. I now produced it for Marty's approval and wasn't disappointed. Marty had given me a couple of reefers on board during the last week but they'd had no effect on me whatsoever. I was happy for him to have the keef.

'Marty, marijuana is crap,' I said. 'It does nothing for you. You only smoke it because it's the in thing to do.'

'Yeah?' he replied. 'Well, help me with this.'

He produced the resin made from the pollen of the marijuana plant and a small smoking pipe. He handed it to me. I tried to light the resin ground up in the pipe and only managed to get a few puffs on each occasion before it went out. After ten minutes or so of puff, puff, puffing, I was about to give up.

Suddenly a wave of drowsiness overcame me, then my head seemed to be lolling on my shoulders with a will of its own. I began to have trouble focusing. I gazed at the stereo speakers. The loud rock music seemed to double in volume. The white wood of the speaker boxes had dirty hand marks on them and now these shapes took on the form of animals dancing to the music. Without speaking, I pulled myself to my feet and staggered upstairs to the bunk beds.

I drifted into and out of consciousness. The hallucinations enabled me to access all the stored images of my mind. Thousands of scenes from my past life flashed through my mind like the pages of a comic book being flicked before my eyes. It was as if my brain was undergoing an electric short-circuit, spilling forth memories from my subconscious to my conscious mind in split-second images. These hallucinations would come in waves, then my mind would calm.

Don't look now—Argas *perches on the ferry's rear deck. For the return journey, we were able to reverse on board.*

By half-past midnight there was a party on board. All the passengers had returned from the bars in town and had congregated downstairs. Music blared over the stereo. The Beatles were playing 'A Hard

Top Deck Daze

Day's Night'. As I lay on the bed I could hear only Paul's voice, then only John's, then only Ringo's drumming, then just the rhythm guitar. More time passed and I felt in control enough to venture downstairs to join in the party. I sat on the kitchen bench and when I was about to tell my story, I burst into uncontrollable laughter. I giggled and gurgled incoherently for twenty minutes before struggling back up to bed again to focus on the music. I drifted into and out of the conscious world till the early hours of the morning.

It was the first and only time I'd been affected by drugs in this way. In the cold, sober light of the following day, I had mixed emotions about the whole experience. While I had no desire to lose myself like this on a regular basis, the whole experience had been so extraordinary and so fascinating, I could easily understand why artists, musicians or the emotionally fragile could find themselves so easily hooked.

After two weeks in Morocco we were ready to return to Spain. Ceuta is an enclave on the Moroccan North African coast that has been held by the Spanish in what has amounted to a continuous siege since 1580, so you actually cross the Moroccan/Spanish border on the outskirts of Ceuta, before catching the ferry across the Straits of Gibraltar to the Spanish mainland. We pulled into the Port of Ceuta to await the ferry and with several hours to kill, the passengers went duty-free shopping for grog, cigarettes and knick-knacks at the Indian shops lining the port.

Screw, Spy and I found a bar in Ceuta at the Plaza de Africa to reflect on the last two weeks and on our chances of getting back on the ferry across to Spain. None of the other passengers really knew that we had been within a whisker of never making it to Morocco in the first place. Screw had not told them of all the drama about the seeming impossibility of boarding the ferry.

Who should greet us at the Ceuta ferry terminal but Manuel, the ticket attendant from Algerciras! He obviously made the journey regularly to supervise the ferry loadings. We expected

Troppo in Morocco – North Africa 1973

Slightly jaded? On the ferry, returning from our very first trip in 1973 from left: 'Screw', me, Steve, Bruce and 'Spy'.

him to abuse us for the way Screw had duped him by only buying a ticket for a minibus on the first journey, and because of the way Screw just charged the double-decker, unannounced, onto the rear of the ferry. No worries. Manuel greeted the three of us with smiles. Presumably, all was forgiven.

'I charge you for two buses this time. One on top of the other,' he explained, pointing to the bottom and top decks. We agreed without argument. Our sense of achievement of having actually made it to Africa meant the cost didn't matter. We returned to the bar to await our departure and recounted all our stories of the past few weeks. I apologised again, at length, to Screw for being such a pain in the arse at Algerciras on the way over. I had a feeling that we would be in business in some way, shape or form for a long while to come and I said that, whatever happened in future, I would never say, 'It can't be done,' again.

As it turned out, the deckers were to cross the Straits of Gibraltar for another twenty-four years and for the first ten of them, did so hanging off the back of the same ferry.

Chapter 2
BACK TO THE FUTURE
(LONDON 1973)

I'd only set foot in London two months before our Moroccan escapade. The memory of my arrival at Heathrow, the transfer into London along the M4, and my very first ride in a London double-decker, is still as vivid now as if it had happened yesterday. Mum and Dad had been staunch Anglophiles and my sister, Helen, and I had grown up in a house where Britain was still the mother country and Australia was very much an outpost of the empire. Being a fifth-generation Australian couldn't dispel the notion that London was a spiritual home, with names and places as familiar as the Monopoly board.

I was as excited as I could possibly be at the thought of all that lay ahead and I soaked up the sights and sounds of the amazing city as we crawled through the thickening traffic. I jumped off the bus on the corner of Cromwell and Earls Court Roads and after wandering the streets just gazing at the crowds, poking my head in pubs and bars, I found a cheap hotel in Nevern Square, as close to the heart of Earls Court as I could afford.

Bazza McKenzie was alive and well in the London of 1973. This was before the diaspora, when Australians spread to all suburbs throughout the huge metropolis, forced out by the flood of rich Arabs who over-ran and over-priced the West End after the oil price shocks of the mid-1970s. At the time of my arrival, Earls Court was still very much 'Kangaroo Valley'. Historically, this had come about because of one man, ironically a South African, Max Wilson.

26

Back to the Future - London 1973

Before the war of 1939 to 1945, Earls Court had been a genteel, wealthy suburb. In the depressed decade of the 1950s, when rationing of basic commodities was still the norm, the previously well-to-do families found the upkeep of their four- and five-storey residences nearly impossible. Many houses became unoccupied and fell into a state of disrepair. Max Wilson exploited this situation by being the first to establish backpacker style hostels/hotels for young tourists flocking to the capital from the colonies. Max established the Overseas Visitors Club (OVC) at 180 Earls Court Road near the corner of Nevern Place. He advertised the OVC in the daily newspapers of the major cities of South Africa, Australia and New Zealand and when the bookings rolled in, he took out more leases on more tenements and named them 'Aussie House' and 'Kiwi House', and so on. Membership of the OVC included several nights' accommodation as well as transfers from Southampton where the passenger ships docked, and the colonial enclave grew rapidly as a result.

Max set up a travel centre at the OVC and this, in turn, spawned the dozens of camping tour operators that flourished in the 1960s and 1970s. One of the first, Protea, opened its own office directly opposite the OVC, in Earls Court Road. The operators even had commission salesmen travelling on the ships from Australia, so passengers were committed to a particular tour company before their arrival in the UK.

For vast numbers of young Australians, New Zealanders and South Africans, the 'grand working holiday tour' of Europe was an essential finishing school before any thought was given to taking up a 'real job' and a 'real life' at home. You stayed for a minimum of two years. You shared a crowded flat in Earls Court. There were no restrictions then on Aussies working in the UK, so you worked in a pub or got part-time work in an assumed profession.

Gough Whitlam was the newly elected prime minister of Australia and after twenty-three years of conservative government, the economic outlook was excitingly buoyant.

Top Deck Daze

Unemployment was at three per cent, what an economist would call nil, so one simply gave up one's job and travelled with the very real expectation of returning years later having lost nothing in the employment stakes.

You could travel the 20 000 km from home in the traditional way, on famous ships like the Canberra, the Oriana or the Arcadia, that still plied the route from Sydney to Southampton. The ships had seen their heyday in the post-war period, bringing out ten-pound Pommie immigrants, and they offered cheap, return travel to the thousands of working-holidaymakers heading for the British Isles.

Or you could take advantage of the cheaper air travel with the advent of the wide-bodied jumbos that first took to the skies in 1970. Air travel had been the sole domain of millionaires since the dawn of the commercial airliner, but the jumbo assured mass travel became available and affordable to all.

You bought a one-way ticket. This wasn't just a holiday; this was a way of life for two or three years. You bought a VW Kombi van, a hand-me-down from a home-going Aussie, at the car yard disguised as The Strand outside Australia House, or you joined one of the dozens of cheap tour operators based in London catering for the colonial market: Autotours, Protea, Pacesetters, Penn, Transit, Contiki, Vikings, NAT, CCT, Sundowners ... You could walk down Earls Court Road at any time of the day or night and see them loading or unloading their punters. Some had upmarket equipment but most used Ford Transit vans piled high with camping gear and stores. They were crewed by a driver and courier who happened to get off the plane the day before you did, who couldn't read a road map, who lost you in every European city, and who, if sober enough, gave you a tour of the sights and read the history from the Michelin guidebook you already had open in your lap.

Nobody cared. The history and culture of Europe were mere backdrops to the real purpose of being there. Besides the travel you were there to make friends, party hard, go to theatres, drink

Back to the Future – London 1973

in pubs, eat cheap, and sometimes sleep, always in crowded bedrooms in crowded flats. At last you were beyond the reach of family and familiar faces and places. We were, after all, baby boomers, children of the 1960s — a time of social and sexual revolution, a time to throw off the shackles that had bound our parents' generation. It was a time to discover who you really were and what life was all about, in a way that today's generation, having been raised in a much more liberal society, has never felt the need to do.

I didn't know a soul in London. I retrieved a name and a phone number from my address book. Barbie Sim was the sister of my first flatmate in Australia. 'Yes,' Dave had written and said I might call. 'Yes, sure,' why not meet tonight. Come to a party in Fulham, a reunion from a Munich Beerfest trip? 'Hey, that's great! Thanks, Barbie. See you then.'

Barbie was a fabulous girl, buzzing with energy and fun, an instant friend, full of information, suggestions, ideas. What to do, where to go, what to see, where to work, where you might share a room. She introduced me to two guys who'd been on her Beerfest trip to Munich: Screw and Spy. We talked about school and university. I'd done economics during the same years they'd done vet science. Screw mentioned that he'd been working as a locum all around England and had recently been in Yorkshire. He'd been on a call to a local farm and passed an old World War II bomber airfield that was now a huge bus yard crammed full of old double-deckers. Screw checked it out. Someone had fitted out one of the buses with bunks, a kitchen and tables and seats and used it as a mobile home, but it was now for sale back at the yard.

Over copious steins at the Beerfest, Screw and Spy had talked about buying the bus, getting a group together, and taking it to Morocco. It was probably a crazy idea and they didn't really have enough money anyway. The weather turned foul in Munich and after five consecutive nights of soggy tents and sleeping-bags, they were ready to pack their bags, abandon the trip, and catch

Top Deck Daze

the train to London. By chance, as they drove into Camping Zeeburg in Amsterdam on the way back, they happened to pull up next to an English double-decker that was permanently parked in the campsite and served as an on-site van. They stared at the cosy campers inside the decker as they watched their own group pitch tents in the pouring rain. They looked at one another in silence. They *would* buy that double-decker Screw had seen in Yorkshire. What had seemed like a stupid idea at the Beerfest became a committed course of action once they returned to London.

Screw and Spy took a room in an Aussie flat in Mablethorpe Road, Fulham, and they became regulars at the fashionable 'King's Head and Eight Bells' pub in Chelsea where I had landed a live-in job. By mid-October 1973, they announced they'd become the proud owners of the bus. It had cost them £400 from their £1000 savings. They managed to find a yard for it just off the Kings Road near the famous Chelsea Football Stadium, within walking distance of the pub. Plans for the Moroccan trip, to depart at the end of November 1973, were concocted over beers in the King's Head. I was the first punter to hand over my money at the discounted mate's rate of £85. As the departure date for the trip drew nearer, I continued my job at the pub, but moved into Mablethorpe Road to share a room with Screw and Spy.

We needed transport so Screw, Spy, another mate Steve Brown, and I, put in £8 each and bought a beautiful, slightly used, 1961 Wolseley sedan for £32. We headed to the London Walkabout Club to celebrate, with·me behind the wheel.

'Go via Hammersmith roundabout,' Spy directed.

'Roundabout? What's a roundabout?' I'd never heard the word before. I screeched to a halt as a pair of headlights closed in on mine. Slowly the doors of the other car opened. Slowly the occupants put their hats on … their police hats.

'Wot's this then, eh? Ah, bleedin' Orstralians, are we? Orright, where's yer insurance and yer MOT (roadworthy certificate)?'

'My what?'

'Yer MOT, en wot are yer doing going round a roundabout the wrong way then?'

'A what?'

'A bleedin' round-about yer silly bugger. Wot's yer name and where do you live?'

'Bill James, and he lives at 9 Mablethorpe Road, Fulham,' Screw obliged.

'9 Mablethorpe Road, Fulham eh? We'll remember that.'

The police picked us up time and time again in the Wolseley. Sometimes, I admit, we did bring a little too much attention to ourselves—like Spy attempting to remove freeloaders from the car before driving home from the Tournament pub. Four people lined the front seat, six were crammed into the back, three in the open boot, and two lay on the roof. It had started to drizzle and, damn, the wipers wouldn't work. No problem. Dave Lee on the roof extended his arms and waved them back and forth over the windscreen. The bobby standing nearby wasn't impressed.

'Where do you live?'

'9 Mablethorpe Road, Fulham.'

'I'll remember that.'

At other times we were flagged down in broad daylight when perfectly well-behaved.

'Lovely motor yer've got 'ere. Good nick, too.' a bobby said as he lifted up the floor mat, poked the floor with his truncheon, and exposed the roadway beneath as a square foot of rust gave way. Again, details were taken and the inevitable question, 'Where do you live?'

'9 Mablethorpe Road, Fulham.'

'I'll remember that.'

Spy decided that this continued harassment by the constabulary could not be tolerated and that action must be taken. Plan A: The Wolseley required a paint job to tart it up. Plan B: We needed a driver who wasn't going to get into any trouble. For this, Screw and Spy hatched a deviously simple plan. Whoever happened to be driving the car would adopt the name

Top Deck Daze

'Graham James Lloyd'. This continuously recalcitrant but purely fictitious character would reside at 9 Mablethorpe Road, but would always, as bad luck would have it, leave his wallet at home. Plan B worked brilliantly. Indeed, Graham James Lloyd proved to be such a dear and loyal friend that, in subsequent years, he ended up taking out the lease on 9 Mablethorpe Road, acted as guarantor for the lease on two shops and assorted office equipment, secured the overdraft on our National Westminster Bank account, and provided us with glowing, written references. He was such an impressive character that we promoted him to Director when we formed our first company. Unfortunately he travelled a lot and was always overseas whenever someone in authority needed to see him in person. So many people declared themselves to be 'Graham James Lloyd' every police station in the West End opened a file on 'Lloyd G.J./Mister', 30 cm thick, and he came to top the bill as one of London's most wanted men.

The landlord of 9 Mablethorpe Road was an aristocratic Englishman by the name of Mr Ironmonger who happened to be our local member of parliament. Despite the fact we Aussies hardly kept the flat in good order, 'Iron-mongrel', as Screw called him, loved us for three good reasons: first, we paid the rent on time; second, he could increase the rent any time he liked; and third, he could kick us out any time he wanted to sell. Had we been local Pommies, none of these advantages would have applied. An archaic law gave unprecedented protection to local 'sitting tenants'. Aussies were not afforded such generous treatment. Consequently, Iron-mongrel would call us regularly, wanting to speak to his beloved leaseholder, the esteemed Graham James Lloyd. We simply ran out of excuses as to where G.J. Lloyd had disappeared to.

One night, much later, Iron-mongrel called into Mablethorpe Road unannounced and Screw and I entertained him with stories about what a great bloke G.J. Lloyd was and how sorry he'd be to have missed Iron-mongrel once again. Iron-mongrel obviously loved a tipple and his favourite drink was port. Screw apologised

Back to the Future – London 1973

that the only bottle we had in the house was a Cockburns. 'I say, old boy,' Iron-mongrel admonished Screw, 'That's pronounced "Coh-burns".'

'Well, fuh me,' replied Screw in his best ocker English, 'Whad da ya know? Ever been to India? Well get it in-der-ya anyway,' he challenged Iron-mongrel, and they clinked glasses and sculled the port in unison.

As regards our other plan for the Wolseley—that is, Plan A—the painting of the car, unfortunately proved to be far less successful. I ventured to suggest to Spy that our continued conspicuousness may have had something to do with his choice of colour—canary yellow—especially as the paint job had been done so professionally, with a hand brush on the kerbside outside the flat. But no, Spy would have none of it. The Wolseley looked spiffingly okay, according to him.

The departure date for the very first trip had been set as 19 November 1973, with Screw and Spy assembling a passenger list of fourteen, short of their target, but well above the break-even mark. This had been done largely by word-of-mouth with the help of a one-page handout advertising the fact that, 'Everyone sleeps on luxury foam beds!'—what the current marketing gurus might call our 'unique selling proposition'. The gross takings from passengers was just below £1400, excluding the food kitty which was an extra £3 a week, enough for three healthy meals a day. The bus had cost £400 to buy and £150 to modify. The cost of operating the entire trip would be about £300, so this left Screw and Spy with a substantial profit, even taking into account the initial purchase price of the bus.

We gathered excitedly at the Kings Road yard on the morning of 19 November, supervised the final loading of everyone's gear and with a crunching and grinding of gears owing to driver inexperience, lurched off in the direction of Dover in our very own Marrakech Express.

Top Deck Daze

ARGAS PERSICUS
SPAIN MOROCCO PORTUGAL
GO BY DOUBLE-DECKER BUS

This is your chance for the trip of a lifetime. In six fun filled weeks, you will see all of the exciting attractions of Spain. More — you will, for a time, become part of the Spanish care-free way of life. We spend an evening with a friend who owns a bar in a small fishing village. We visit a western movie town in the mountains before wandering along the Costa Del Sol.

You will be fascinated by Morocco — a land of modern times that cannot relinquish the past. You can be in a new shopping area, turn a corner, and, in an instant, be back two thousand years in time. Morocco has wonderful beaches, excellent surf, and incredible mountain scenery, that you will see as we cross the Great Atlas, climbing to seven thousand feet.

Back in Spain, after leaving Morocco, we stay in Seville, possibly the most attractive Spanish city. Along with Madrid, it offers a great deal of beauty and culture, not to mention the vibrant excitement of Spanish life.

Portugal offers Lisbon and the beautiful Algarve, with it's superb sandy beaches, caves and grottoes, almond blossoms, and pretty, white villages.

Returning through France, you will appreciate how Cezanne was inspired to greatness by the French landscape. Two days in Paris is time enough to fall in love with this gorgeous city.

DON'T MISS THIS UNIQUE TRIP!!!

* **NO CAMPING IN TENTS.** Sleep in luxury foam beds on the upper deck.
* **FULLY EQUIPPED KITCHEN.** Includes oven, refrigerator, hot water system.
* **STEREO CASSETTE RECORDER.** If you have "Marrakech Express.", please bring it.

ONLY £110 FOR SIX WEEKS!

DEPARTURE DATES.
MARCH 7	JUNE 3
APRIL 4	JUNE 29
MAY 3	JULY 29

BOOK NOW!
CONTACT: Geoffrey Lomas.
Graham Turner.
Bill James.
9 Mablethorpe Road,
FULHAM. S.W.6.
Telephone: 385/8499.

The deposit required is £15, with the balance payable two weeks before departure. Also a food kitty of £3 per week is required. Cheques should be made out to Geoffrey Lomas or Graham Turner.
BOOK NOW! PHONE 385 - 8499.

OVERLAND TO SYDNEY

Are you interested in the overland trip from London right through to Sydney? Departure is November 7, 1974. For information, contact us at the address above.

This typed one-page handout, the company's first brochure, of 1973, advertises the 1974 tours.

Chapter 3

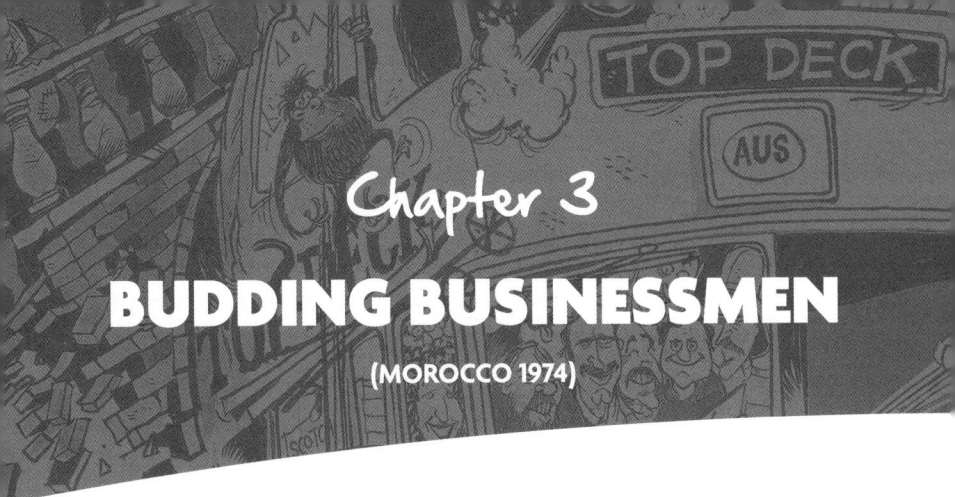

BUDDING BUSINESSMEN

(MOROCCO 1974)

I had given no real thought to what the future might hold, nor what opportunities such a venture might lead to. Not so Screw, who was always more than one step ahead. Before leaving London, he planned for a second trip to depart on 4 January 1974, after *Argas* returned from the first six-weeker. He'd placed an ad in the newly established *Australasian Express*, a newspaper founded by Colin Spears to cater for the colonial market in London which was starved of news from home. Screw had put Mablethorpe Road's phone number in the ad and told one of the girls residing there, Lesley Lovett, that she could have ten pounds commission for any person who answered the ad and booked on the second trip.

When we returned to London from the first trip, we learnt our first business lesson—incentives work! In the six weeks we'd been away, Lesley had booked seventeen passengers to go on the January 1974 departure. You beauty! Screw and Spy might have expected it but I, for one, was flabbergasted. This was really fantastic news and even someone with my limited nous could smell a good business venture when he fell over it.

I had become great friends with Screw and Spy in the short time we had known one another. They were unique characters and I genuinely admired them for what they had achieved, even at this early stage. Screw's 'crash or crash through' approach to life appealed to me enormously, given my subconscious desire to shake off my highly conservative nature. He was the most 'out-of-the-square' thinker I'd ever encountered and I had the premonition that I could learn so much from him by just being in his orbit, and have a hell of a lot of fun at the same time.

While I didn't have a financial interest in the first bus, *Argas*, the boys had generously treated me almost as a partner from the day I moved into Mablethorpe Road, so I now asked if I could join them formally as a financial partner. I offered to put up my own money to buy a second bus, which would cost about £300, plus whatever it cost to fit it out. This would be my contribution to the capital of the venture. The boys agreed and we shook on the deal.

I was now a fully-fledged third partner in 'Argas Persicus Travel'. This was a particularly apt and relevant name for a bus touring company and one which most people, especially new passengers, would immediately relate to. Screw, of course, had chosen it.

'What in God's name does "Argas Persicus" mean?' I asked.

'It's the name of a turkey tick, stupid. We learnt about it in vet science.'

'Fine,' I said, 'But what the fucken hell's that got to do with double-decker buses and travel?'

'Absolutely nothing,' replied Screw, 'But it's a great name, isn't it?'

By the time 4 January 1974 arrived, twenty-one punters had paid up to go on the second trip. That meant old *Argas* was fuller than a Catholic school but, most importantly, would run at maximum profit. I said goodbye to Screw and Spy as they took off from the Kings Road yard. I immediately set off by train for Yorkshire — it was time for me to put my money where my mouth was and buy the second bus. I headed for the bus yard 'W. Norths' at Sherburn-in-Elmet, not far from Leeds, where Screw had bought old *Argas*. I met David (who ran the business for his dad), Clifford the foreman, and Cunny the head mechanic. They all spoke with such broad Yorkshire accents I almost needed an interpreter.

Budding Businessmen - Morocco 1974

Row upon row of buses covered the entire defunct airfield. In addition to the thousands of buses still in working order, buses that were too worn out had been scrapped and their spares had been sorted and piled into small mountains of engines here, gearboxes there, and springs, diffs, wheels, clutches, brakes, you name it, everywhere else. The old hangers were fully-equipped workshops. The yard supplied buses and parts to all corners of the globe and I was fascinated to learn that Hong Kong and China were their biggest customers.

By the end of the day I had chosen a Bristol Lodekka. *Argas* was a Bristol, but this 'new' bus was a far more modern 1949 design, with the bodywork built in Lowestoft by Eastern Coach Works. The familiar red London double-deckers were Leylands or AECs but the Bristols, usually painted green, were designed for the longer UK country runs. The Lodekka was a standard length and width (8.25 m by 2.45 m) with a rear platform and stairwell but the external height was a 'lowbridge' 4.12 m. This meant it was 38 cm lower than *Argas*, and London double-deckers for that matter, and would be ideal for any low bridges and the like that we would inevitably encounter in many a foreign field.

The Bristol Lodekka (LD model) was first manufactured in 1953, and was perfect for our use. We bought more than fifty of this particular model.

Top Deck Daze

The interior was the same 'highbridge' standard as *Argas* and so comfort, as far as the passengers were concerned, was not compromised. This was achieved by fitting the gearbox conventionally behind the engine but offsetting the driveshaft to the rear axle to the side of the chassis, enabling the lower deck aisle to be sunken between the chassis frames. Like every bus that we ever bought, it had already done a lifetime's work carting commuters millions of kilometres around the highways and byways of Britain. It had a six-cylinder Bristol motor. I could have bought one with a more powerful Gardner motor but that would have cost an extra £100—well beyond my limited funds.

By the time I had a receipt for my £300 it was time to shut up shop. I had christened the bus *Grunt* and we retired to the local pub, the Half Moon, to wet the baby's head with more than a few pints of Tetley's, 'The beer they drink round 'ere.'

I slept on the bus floor and woke the next day with a rotten hangover and it was almost lunchtime before I set off for London. The sun, if it exists at all, sets early in an English winter and by the time I reached north London it was pitch dark and raining heavily. I had lots of time to think about what I'd done on the drive down from Leeds. My entire life savings equated to £600. I had spent £300 on the bus and was about to spend the remainder to fit it out, which left me with exactly—nothing. In the euphoria following the return of the first trip, the prospects seemed really exciting. Now, as I peered though the foggy windscreen into the choking traffic of Edgeware Road, tired, cold and hungry, and soon to be penniless, I seriously began to question the wisdom of what I'd done.

I still didn't know my way around London very well and had never approached the city from the north. I wanted to turn right onto the A40 to get to the yard at Chelsea, but missed the turn-off due to the shocking traffic and poor visibility. I turned right at what I thought was a reasonably major road. Wrong. It was a reasonably minor road that was getting more minor and narrower the further I drove.

Budding Businessmen – Morocco 1974

I was crawling along by now, holding up a huge row of cars behind me. The old London street was obviously not designed for double-decker buses. A large van came along in the opposite direction. It squeezed over to let me pass but with cars parked on both sides of the road, there was simply no room. Cars banked up behind the van as well and after a few minutes, a hundred horns were blazing. 'Oh, God,' I thought, 'I've spent every penny I have to dig myself into this hole.' I sat at the wheel, closed my eyes and held my hand over my face as the irate drivers yelled at me through the cabin window.

Somehow, I made it back to Chelsea and slept exhausted on the bus floor again. The next day I planned *Grunt's* fit out. The English winter of 1973–1974 was one of the coldest on record and the misery of the average Pommie was made worse by the industrial strife that racked the country as a result of the constant bickering between the Conservative Government of Edward Heath and the working-class unions. This culminated in the notorious miners' strike that brought the country to a virtual standstill. Power was rationed and many businesses simply closed their doors or only operated on a three or four day working week.

It was against this background that I set to work on the fit out, using the internal design of our first bus, old *Argas*, as a guide. I was such an inexperienced handyman I thought a Phillips head screw was a sexual position and the work was slow and laborious as I learnt by trial and error. The Bristol Lodekka, in its original form, had a rear platform and stairwell and two rows of seats on either side of an aisle, upstairs and down. My first job was to strip all the seats, then enclose the back platform and fit a lockable door.

Upstairs was then to be fitted out with wooden, triple-decker bunks that could sleep fourteen. At the front of both the upper and lower decks we reinstalled some seats to face one another with wooden tables in between. The tables were designed to detach from the walls and fill the gaps between the seats.

Top Deck Daze

From 1973 to 1997 hundreds of thousands of young funseekers 'top decked' through Europe, the USA, Asia, and Australia in buses outfitted like this one.

Too bad if anyone snored! Snug living, top-deck style, in triple-decker bunks. Viewing deck at front.

Budding Businessmen – Morocco 1974

Additional foam rubber mattresses over the lowered tables and aisle centre-boards resulted in three triple beds (one upstairs, and two down) to provide a sleeping capacity of twenty-three, at a squeeze. As our average loading would be about fifteen, the arrangement proved quite comfortable.

Half the downstairs area, at the rear, was a fully-equipped kitchen with benches, sink, running water, stove and oven that ran on camping gas. We enclosed the base of the seats to form storage lockers and with some additional upright cupboards, each person had the space equivalent to a small suitcase in which to store their luggage.

There was a tank for running water for the sink but no provision was made for toilets or showers and the idea was to use regular campsites or to free-camp wherever possible. The camping fees were, of course, based on numbers so it became common to try and fudge our passenger count as often as possible. Punters would hide under mattresses or in lockers and magically appear when the comings and goings of visitors made it impossible for the camp-owner to keep tabs.

I took off on the third Moroccan trip in early March 1974 with Steve Brown as my driver and me doing the couriering. Steve had been the second passenger, after me, to book on the very first Moroccan trip. He was a tall, ginger-haired Tasmanian, trained as a fitter and turner and so knew his way around diesels, a great asset for someone as unmechanical as I was. As far as I was concerned, the workings of a motor were still shrouded in a brocaded cloak of mystery. Although he was younger than Screw and I, about twenty-two going on forty-two, he displayed a maturity beyond his years. Sober when I was drunk, thoughtful when I was indiscreet, considerate when I offended, reliable and loyal when I was nowhere to be seen, I could hardly have asked for a better offsider. Steve had wanted to join the army but had been dissuaded by his parents. This was a great shame. With his tall bearing, handlebar moustache, immaculately pressed khaki clothes, polished boots and great sense of personal discipline 'he

Steve 'The Bombardier' Brown

was the very model of a modern major-general', or perhaps a wing commander. We gave him the name of 'Bombardier' Brown.

When we got back to London from this, the third trip, Spy had returned to Australia. His mum had suddenly fallen ill and he'd felt obligated to go home and be of what assistance he could. Screw and I decided to form a proper Proprietary Limited Company, 'Argas Persicus Travel Proprietary Limited,' and we held fifty per cent of the shares each.

Budding Businessmen - Morocco 1974

I did two more Moroccan trips during 1974. The first one could have been a disaster. There were sixteen girls, two other guys, the Bombardier and myself. It was one of those situations where we had about half-a-dozen stodgy types who would have been a real pain in most social situations but right from the start, one of the girls, Liz, insisted that everyone go out on the town as one. Liz was travelling with Stephanie, a friend from university college days. Although slim and slight in stature, these two could out drink any man I'd ever met. They simply badgered the other girls until everyone agreed to go as a group and of course, once they were all together, everyone had an absolutely fabulous time.

Because of Liz and Stephanie's love of life and their positive influence on the group, we all had one of the best six weeks any of us could remember. I asked Liz to keep in touch with me and come on some more trips later that year, or the next. She agreed and in the meantime, she took off to do some more travelling around the UK and Ireland. Liz's family could trace their ancestry back to the time of Richard the Third and Liz joined her cousin Alan in tracking down old family castles and manor houses, many of which still bore the family name and crest. Like many other Australians, Liz also did a stint on a kibbutz in Israel.

If the trip on which I'd met Liz could have been a disaster, then the next one was. The passengers fell into two main camps—a religious New Right versus a Gay and Lesbian Leftist Alliance. A minor, male-dominated, beer-swilling Philistine Party, with whom I inevitably identified, held the balance of power. The Right, of whom some members had had their sense of humour surgically removed at birth, was headed by a Julie who was having a year off before taking her final vows for the nunnery. While everyone lounged around in T-shirts, shorts and jeans, Julie always dressed in blouse and skirt.

The Left, headed by several punters of indeterminate gender, made fun of Julie. The flesh-coloured, lift-and-separate Playtex was a source of constant comment. I tried to make peace between

Top Deck Daze

the groups but had neither the patience nor the personality to succeed. At times I felt like Beelzebub incarnate.

This trip was one where Murphy's Law seemed to prevail. We had a slight prang with a Citroen in Paris, which simply went to show that you couldn't trust French cars with weird suspension and engines in odd places. Better still, never trust the French, full stop. The bus broke down in Barcelona. One of the girls on board, travelling with her husband, had a miscarriage and they had to leave the trip in Spain, then another of the girls was diagnosed as having a major illness in Malaga.

'Herpes,' Julie told me in the gravest confidence. I nodded my concern.

'What in the blazes is "herpes"?' I whispered to the Bombardier at the first discreet moment (these were naive times).

'An itchy fanny,' he divulged knowingly.

'Not that serious then?'

'It could be if her boyfriend gets it.'

When we reached Algeciras, I decided that as I wasn't going to enjoy the trip, I might as well make the most of any other

Crossing between the 'Pillars of Hercules'.

Budding Businessmen – Morocco 1974

opportunities that presented themselves, like making some money en route. How wise the Spanish were when it came to alcohol; definitely not a luxury item to be taxed to oblivion. On the contrary, surely it was one of life's necessities? Taxation-wise, it was placed in the same category as medical supplies. As a result of this far-sighted policy, I had made quite a good profit on previous trips by taking a dozen bottles of whisky from Spain and selling them at an inflated price in Morocco. Why not exploit the situation and do it on a slightly grander scale?

At Pepe's Bar on our last night in Spain, I ordered ten dozen bottles of Johnnie Walker. While the punters were in town, I spent an hour with the Bombardier hiding the crates in all the nooks and crannies we could possibly find. When we were just about to go, we did a final check and could only find nine dozen. We told Pepe he'd short-changed us a dozen, so Pepe sent five of his lackeys on board to check our claim. Sure enough they could only find nine and gave us an extra dozen. It wasn't till I was cleaning the bus in London four weeks later that I discovered the missing dozen. We'd hidden it so well we couldn't find it ourselves!

As we crossed the Straits of Gibraltar, I calculated the handsome profit the Bombardier and I would share, only to discover on our arrival that it was the Muslim feast of Ramadan. Not even Morocco's most recalcitrant alcoholic was going to risk the wrath of Mohammed by buying whisky during these holy times and even Aziz, for once, had filled his monthly quota. So much for that opportunity.

I did manage to offload all of two bottles to two Moroccan teenagers in Meski who said they were students. They were obviously from a wealthy family in Rabat as they'd travelled down for a couple of days in the family car. I got them to promise they wouldn't open the scotch till they returned home but they ignored me, gave the bottles a fair nudge that night, and managed to roll their car in the early hours of the morning a few kilometres out of the oasis.

Top Deck Daze

The cool water of the Source Bleu at Meski Oasis was one of our favourite stopovers.

To add to our woes, everyone on board had developed a bad dose of 'Montezuma's Revenge' (the runs) as well as throwing up a bit of berley for the goldfish in the spring that fed the oasis. We had pulled the mattresses out of the bus and just lay about in the shade of the date palms feeling sorry for ourselves. A sea of pink toilet paper surrounded the bus for a radius of 100 metres, a legacy of the previous night's torments. No one had been capable of making it to the toilets. Fortunately the locals weren't strong environmentalists, otherwise we might have been in big trouble. I'd thought about 'calling Bert on the big white telephone' before remembering such devices didn't exist in this part of the world, so simply chundered on the ground nearby like everyone else.

It was not a pretty sight that greeted the dilapidated police car that pulled up a safe distance from the bus. The windscreen wipers continued to work away at the dust-covered windscreen. Two swarthy, uniformed, sweat-caked, peaked-capped types with dark glasses carefully sidestepped their way through the minefield of pink loo paper.

Budding Businessmen – Morocco 1974

'Mr Bill?' they asked, and were pointed in my direction. I was lying on a mattress under a tree, weak from dehydration. I raised myself to one elbow. 'Mr Bill. We are hearing you are selling whisky.' I didn't have the energy to mount a defence. 'Please be advised that this is strictly forbidden. You could be jailed for such an offence. We will be watching you carefully from here to Ceuta.' Doubtless, in other circumstances, they would have mounted a thorough search of the bus but the risk of catching the dreaded lurgy obviously weighed more heavily than their sense of constabulary duty, and so they decided that a warning would suffice in this instance.

Okay, so we hadn't had a win with the whisky. But why not make the most of our opportunities with Aziz and maximise our commission on the carpet sales in Fez? I wised up the Bombardier on our tactics.

'When Aziz asks for the first sale, I'll put my hand up and buy a really expensive carpet. When the next person bids, you buy another really good one and after that, there'll be a stampede. It can get like an auction, a real buying frenzy. We can really clean up here. I've seen it happen before.'

For the next few days en route to Fez I did my best salesman's job on the troops, trying to drum up some interest: 'These are the best value carpets in all Morocco. No, not just Morocco, in the whole of the East …. Take them to London or send them home …. Double your money if you decide to sell …. The quality is guaranteed …. They're all beautifully hand woven.'

We met Aziz as expected, rounded up the punters and hustled them into the carpet shop. Out came the salesmen; out came the carpets and the intriguing stories of their makers. Out came the mint tea. Aziz was giving it all he had. His wonderful spiel came to its usual conclusion, '… and this is the Cave of Aladdin where you are sure to find the carpet of your dreams,' to which Julie rejoined, 'More like Ali Baba and the forty thieves if you ask me.'

Top Deck Daze

I ignored this remark with the contempt it deserved and bid for the most beautiful of the carpets at US$600. I smiled and turned to the Bombardier. Nothing. His face was mute. I waited for the frantic bidding. Nothing. Not a flicker. Despite the most impassioned beseeching of the salesforce and the most generous of discounts, not another carpet was sold.

I was US$600 down-the-gurgler, and no commission. I was furious when we got outside. Unreasonably, I took it out on the Bombardier.

'And where the hell were you? What about our plan? Why didn't you make a bid?'

'I was waiting for the stampede,' he replied, his blank expression adding to the sarcasm.

Relations between everyone on board soured further and the Bombardier and I did several night drives as we neared the end of the trip to try and get the misery over. This further riled the Mother Superior and the Leftists. On the last night out in Calais it had become customary for us to have a national meal and for the courier to extol the virtues of the punters and recount what a wonderful experience it had all been. Julie saw through my insincerity. Forgiveness, apparently, was not on the convent's curriculum. Julie rose to her feet and told the Leftists and Philistines what a horrible bunch they all were and how she hoped they'd all rot in hell, or sentiments to that effect, and with that, stormed off, back to the bus.

Now this sheer rudeness really stirred Bruce, one of my Philistine mates with whom I'd formed a somewhat clandestine friendship. Bruce was from out west; a hard drinking, mean shooting, National-Country-Party-voting type, but he'd displayed a deft hand at avoiding any form of controversy by keeping his views very much to himself. It was his first trip overseas and he'd quietly confided to me that he thought the rest of the world was a rather strange place. 'I couldn't agree more, Bruce,' I said. 'Bazza McKenzie was right after all. There are far too many foreigners overseas.'

Budding Businessmen – Morocco 1974

Typically, as we'd crossed the French-Spanish border, Bruce had asked me if we'd passed through the tick gates yet.

During the first week in France he'd complained about, 'The hopeless French plumbing.' On further questioning, he clarified the issue. 'These bloody Frog dunnies,' he said, 'Ya can't flush 'em properly.' I think I understood his problem. I explained bluntly that 'bidets' were just for washing your bum, and not for anything else, but I could tell by the look of disbelief on his face that he was none the wiser for my elucidation.

We'd all made good use of the French dunnies that week. Bruce had been on cooking duties. A strictly meat-and-three-veg mother's boy, he'd never seen garlic before in his life and put fifteen bulbs (yes bulbs, not cloves) in the mince meat for the spag-bol, thinking it must have been a variant of the onion or something similar — a reasonable assumption under the circumstances, I suppose. Consequently, we all had the foulest wind imaginable for a week.

As Julie stormed out of the restaurant at the conclusion of her tirade, Bruce was on his feet.

'Ya know what that damn woman needs, eh?' he asked of no one in particular, cocking his fist and forearm in the air. 'Yeah,' he said, nodding understandingly in our direction, 'And I'm just the one ter give it to 'er.'

I must admit I hesitated for a moment. There was no doubt Julie could do with a bit of love and tenderness, and Bruce wasn't such a bad-looking bloke in his powder blue, crimplene safari suit that he'd had handcrafted in 'Honkers' on the way over and had dusted off for tonight's festivities. But reason quickly took hold. Not even Julie deserved the subtle overtures of a drunken Bruce. I raced after him to the bus and was just about to climb the stairwell when I heard Bruce yell, 'I know what you need, Julie! A good poke with this!' obviously giving Julie a good look at his credentials. Julie let out a bloodcurdling scream.

I changed tactics. I flicked off the upstairs lights, hoping this might at least save Julie from the visual trauma. I raced

Top Deck Daze

back up the stairs only to find Bruce illuminating his loins with his cigarette lighter. As he staggered towards Julie's bunk he stumbled and scorched his pubic hairs. They were both howling and screaming now.

'Get this animal out of here,' shrieked Julie. I manhandled Bruce down the stairs and he kept hollering, 'This is what you need, I tell you. A bloody good dose of the old beef bayonet, ya hear?' After dinner, I said it was, 'My shout,' and I escorted Bruce and the rest of the Philistines on a late-night tour of the Calais bars until I was more than reasonably sure that the last of Bruce's amorous flames had been well and truly doused.

Rarely had I been happier to see fair England's shores as we docked at Dover the next day. I walked with the punters onto the terminal forecourt while the Bombardier drove the bus off the ferry. Customs told us not to board the bus because they intended to do a thorough search. This was to be expected, as any vehicle coming from Africa or the East was very much under suspicion, and for good reason. Although I would never have even contemplated bringing drugs or the like through a border, you could never be certain that one of the punters hadn't tried it and, of course, blame would always fall on the driver and courier.

What did surprise me was that, this time, the customs official was accompanied by a sniffer dog. We'd never had this treatment before and I must admit I was extremely on edge. I insisted on accompanying the two officers and the dog during the search and I caught Julie's eye as we went on board. It was more of a smirk than a smile, as if to say, 'I hope they bloody well find something.'

Despite much sniffing, scratching and pawing, the mongrel had found nothing of interest until he came to the very last bed upstairs—Julie's. Suddenly the hound went berserk. He leapt on Julie's tightly bound sleeping bag, barking, quivering and salivating with excitement. Great smug smiles lit up the faces of the customs officers as they nodded sagely to one another.

They could obviously see the headlines in the Times the following day, 'MAJOR DRUG HAUL IN DOVER. OFFICERS

Budding Businessmen – Morocco 1974

COMMENDED ON DETAILED SEARCH.' By this stage the continued barking and hysterics of the dog had alerted everyone in the whole dock area to the pending drug bust. The officers brought the sleeping-bag outside and a huge crowd gathered around them and the dog as they laid the bag out on the ground. I looked at Julie. Her smirk had long since vanished. In fact, she looked as terrified as I did.

Slowly one officer unzipped the bag, while the other wrestled with the dog as it leapt and strained on the leash. Finally, here it was, stashed in the farthest corner of the sleeping bag. Carefully, with arm fully extended for all to see, the officer held aloft the rarest of all contraband—a pair of Julie's dirty knickers.

The crowd now joined the dog in hysterics and fell about in peels of laughter. In the ensuing melee, the officer lost control of the dog who leapt on the offending knickers and ferociously mauled them to shreds. By the time some semblance of order had been restored and we got a final clearance to rejoin the bus and leave, there was no sign of Julie. Her gear was still on board when we cleaned the bus at the yard the following day. I guess she figured there was little need for worldly possessions in her future career at the Little Wounds of the Virgin Convent.

Chapter 4
DECLARE MISÈRE
(EUROPE 1975)

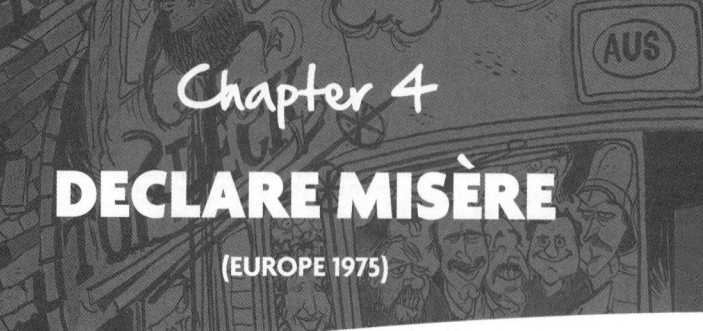

The only tours we ran through 1974, until the September, were eight six-week Moroccan tours on our two buses, *Argas* and *Grunt*, carrying a total of 120 passengers. Screw, however, always harboured much grander plans for the future. In August 1974, he produced our first-ever brochure—a single-sided, ten-page job with a yellow cover, with hand-drawn artwork and maps. It was simple and cheap but did the job required. It mapped out the remainder of our 1974 tours and the entire 1975 program. Screw had let his imagination run wild. He'd drawn up itineraries and departure dates for seven Moroccan tours, nine European, six Greek/Italian/Yugoslavian, three Russian-Scandinavian (planned as coach-camping tours), as well as shorter trips to the Beerfest, Pamplona, Hogmanay in Scotland, Tulip Time in Amsterdam, and T-Day in Venice.

Our first brochure in 1975 preceded our new name of Top Deck Travel.

The new brochure mapped out another first for late 1974, a

Declare Misère – Europe 1975

three-week Central European tour, planned to coincide with the Munich Beerfest. This meant our fleet needed to be augmented by a third bus, not just for this trip but for the expanded 1975 program. Screw managed to locate an already converted double-decker in Croydon, South London, which was supposedly up for sale. This was a real bonus as it meant we didn't have to convert a bus ourselves which, given our limited resources, would have been a major hassle.

Within days of this, Screw took off on another tour on *Grunt*, and with *Argas* already on the road with another driver, Mark Sullivan, I stayed behind to finalise the purchase and preparation of the new third bus. For several days I tried to phone the owner of the bus in Croydon. His wife said, 'Sorry', he wasn't available at the moment. With ten days to go, I still hadn't managed to make contact. The next day I phoned a half-a-dozen times, by which stage the wife was getting short with me and something told me all was not well in the kingdom. We already had eighteen fully-paid passengers and due to our growing expenses, not all of their money remained in the bank. There was enough to buy the bus, at a reasonable price, and finance the trip, but only just, and certainly not enough to refund all the punters' money.

On D-Day minus seven I drove the Wolseley to Croydon and located the bus parked on a suburban street outside the owner's home. It was just what the doctor ordered, perfect for our use. With no one answering the doorbell, I decided I should stake it out till someone turned up. I had few other options. I could get a bus from Norths but a fit-out might take four or five weeks at best. By nightfall, I had just about given up hope when Eric, the owner, pulled up outside. He apologised, but none too profusely, about reneging on his decision to sell.

'The bus has too much sentimental value.' What bollocks! He'd dingoed on the deal because he'd twigged to my predicament, figuring I was a twenty-four-carat mug, and he knew how to drive a bargain when he had the opportunity. He

Top Deck Daze

told me he'd think about it overnight and asked me to phone him the next day.

My offer went from £350 to £500, and then to £600, but still no deal. On the evening of D-Day minus four, I couldn't stand it any longer. I phoned him and offered him the outrageous price of £800, more than double the real worth of the vehicle. Okay, it was a deal.

So, with three days to go, I had my bus but still faced the prospect of working twenty hours a day to get it ready to accommodate twenty passengers. I arrived back at the Kings Road and waited for a break in the oncoming traffic to turn into Rewell Lane and then into our small yard. I was obviously causing a bank-up of traffic behind me and I didn't see the motorcycle cop pull up and come across to the bus. He pulled open the cab door, hopped up and yelled, 'What the hell are you parked here for?' I explained I wasn't 'parked here', but was trying to get into the laneway opposite. He hung off the bus as I drove into the yard. I got the third degree again and explained that I'd only bought the bus an hour beforehand and consequently there was no way the paperwork could be in order. Finally he asked me my address and name. Before I could answer, he held up the palm of his hand, 'No, no, no. Don't tell me.' A shockingly pained expression crossed his face. 'It's 9 bloody Mablethorpe Road, Fulham, isn't it, and I suppose you're bloody Graham James Lloyd?'

When I'd asked Eric for the roadworthy certificate for the bus, I'd noticed it was out of date. 'Don't worry about it anyway. You don't need one. It's not necessary for any vehicle fitted out as a mobile home,' Eric had explained, and then rabbited on about some old English law relating to gypsies' caravans and whatnot, and how the bus technically fell under this definition and, as such, circumvented all the normal rules and regulations relating to the vehicle's registration. I had taken note of the Act that Eric was purportedly referring to and repeated it all to the cop. He looked at me with total scepticism at the time, but wrote it all down in his notebook. Surprisingly, there was no follow-up by the police to this incident, and because we were never fined by the police in future, despite many run-ins, I came to believe that Eric's story had some validity.

The next few days blurred into one another but the bus was ready to leave on time, early on the arranged date. We made it to Dover. I drove the bus onto the Sealink ferry and while the punters went up to the passenger decks, I crawled into one of the upstairs bunks on board the bus. When I was finally dragged from the bed twenty-four hours later, we were breakfasting in the Bois De Boulogne campsite in Paris.

We took *Grunt* and *Tuft* (as the new bus was christened) to the Beerfest and then decided to have a quiet winter. Our crew numbers were growing and included the Bombardier, Mark Sullivan, Mark Sims and Greg 'Wombat' Ettridge. When Screw and I played rugby for London New Zealand, one of our back-rowers was a tall, lean, dark-haired Kiwi called Rex Julian. I told him about the deckers and our need for couriers in the New Year and asked him if he'd be interested. He was and he joined us in the New Year of 1975. It was the start of a long association—a very beneficial one for the company.

Another of our new couriers was a tall, slim, curly-haired Leeton lad by the name of Mick Carroll.

Mick was such an affable character, he had hundreds of friends and it seemed that half of Leeton's population came to travel or work with us at some stage (this was in addition to his 107 first cousins—good Catholics, the Carrolls). After a while it seemed that everyone I met was either from Leeton or from New Zealand. I became convinced that New Zealand's claim that its population was three million was a total farce. If it was, how come I met six million of them travelling around Europe?

All of us guys were fascinated by Mick's extraordinary luck with the girls. He seemed to have an endless succession of scrumptious lady-companions. Screw set about studying Mick's style to see if he could garner any clues that might assist his own endeavours in that direction. Screw finally concluded it

Top Deck Daze

MICK CARROLL

was Mick's prominent nose that was the secret of his success. Presumably Mick had no sense of smell and could breathe through his ears. There were no other apparent assets that could account for his remarkable popularity.

I had become great friends with one of Mick's Leeton mates, a Johnnie Wells. Johnnie, with a full head of jet-black hair and dark, piercing eyes, proved to be one of the most forthright characters I'd ever met. He'd been a budding rural newspaper and television reporter in Australia, a natural for such an in-your-face job, who could think of nothing more enjoyable than

Declare Misère – Europe 1975

a torrid discussion on the latest political or social issue to have grabbed the headlines on that particular day. Wellsie took no prisoners during these 'discussions'. You were either with him or agin' him; there was no middle ground.

'That's bloody outrageous,' he'd claim, if you dared to challenge his opinion, but there was always a twinkle in his eye and you got to know it was only his way of keeping up the sparring dialogue for as long as possible. His dark, hairy, Latin looks earned him the nickname of 'The Gorilla' or 'Grilly' for short. We became great friends and Grilly and I developed an act whereby whenever we saw one another, I'd grunt a gorilla type 'Oo, Oo, Oo' greeting and Grilly would reply likewise, with hunched back, swinging arms and pursed lips.

I was now keeping constant company with Liz and our friendship was getting 'serious'. Together with our widening circle of friends, our time in London between tours was just as much fun as our time on the road. The local pub has always been the accepted focal point for any social gathering in Britain, irrespective of one's age, gender, social strata or ethnic background, and it was no different for us expat Aussies in London.

We were fairly liberal in our patronage of the local establishments, to their great financial gain, as there were rarely fewer than forty in our party. We'd usually dine at one of the 'Pot' restaurants and then go on to the pub till closing. The Wheatsheaf, the Cock and the Norman Arms were popular, but the Golden Lion became our favourite. Besides the fact it served Aussie beer, rare for a London pub in 1975, it often hosted local bands like 'Buster Hymen and the Penetrations', but its main drawcard was a strip show on Sunday lunchtimes.

Invariably, the banter and ribald comments from the crowd were far more entertaining than the girls themselves. These Sunday sessions became such a regular event, the Golden Lion became know as 'The Church'.

One Sunday I arrived a little late for the Sunday service and having slept in and skipped breakfast, I grabbed a banana from a barrowman before entering the pub, not wanting to drink on a completely empty stomach. The congregation was well into its celebrations by this time and the first person who greeted me, en route to the bar for a refill, was none other than my good mate, Grilly Wells. Both of us immediately broke into our gorilla 'Oo, Oo, Oo' greeting routine, and Grilly, spying my banana, grabbed it from my hands, peeled it in one deft movement, stuffed the whole fruit into his mouth, and hurled the discarded peel over his shoulder with a great grunt of satisfaction.

Declare Misère – Europe 1975

Meanwhile, on the pub's stage, a stripper was in action, brewing up something of a trouser storm among the lads and, to the great anticipation of the congregation at large, was just about to unleash an enormous pair of maracas from her bra when she saw the banana peel land at her feet. Unfortunately, being of West Indian descent, she obviously interpreted the slinging of the banana peel as a provocative, racist slur. She stopped her routine in mid-stride, ripped the record she was dancing to from the record player, and marched off the stage in a great huff. As the crowd hushed in disappointed confusion, all that could be heard was Grilly's, 'Oo, Oo, Oo, more banana, more banana,' as he jumped up and down in front of me at the bar.

Unfortunately, the publican refused to believe the whole episode was entirely innocent and in an act of political correctness way ahead of its time, he clucked chucked us all out of the pub. It proved to be more than a socially magnanimous gesture on his behalf. It cost him forty drinkers every day for six months while we switched allegiances to the Norman Arms. The power of the faith is mighty however and forgiving those who'd borne false witness against us, we quietly resumed our Sunday services at 'The Church' without ever asking for absolution.

It was during this period of rather boring banishment to the wilderness of the Norman Arms that one Friday evening in early 1975, a friend of ours, Di McEwin, said she'd thought up a new name for our burgeoning business: 'Top Deck Travel'.

I don't know where Di got this flash of inspiration; it

Rod & Di McEwin. It was Di who thought up the name 'Top Deck Travel'.

seemed to come from right out of the blue. Maybe the lack of cultural entertainment at the Norman Arms forced us to think and converse a little more than we would have otherwise done at 'The Church', but Screw and I and everyone else just looked at one another in silence. There was no discussion.

It was such an obviously good suggestion it was hard to believe someone hadn't thought of it before. The weekend was taken up with discussions on the style of lettering we'd use and an appropriate logo.

We also changed the colour scheme of the buses. They were green when we had taken delivery of them, but we now painted them orange and cream, with 'Top Deck Travel' in black lettering on the top, side panels.

It was too late to change the name on our new, yellow-covered, 1975 brochure, but it didn't matter. Bookings were rolling in anyway, the majority coming from an £18 ad in the fortnightly Australasian Express.

Screw and I were on the road for much of the year with our alternating breaks in London taken up with top-up sales outside Australia House or anywhere else we might find an uncommitted Aussie. At night we were on the phone, making follow-up calls, or visiting potential punters.

That year I did our first-ever tours to Italy, Greece and Yugoslavia: four-weekers. Screw and I ensured, however, that we would be in Europe together in September 1975 for our most memorable trip of the year.

Venice, with its 150 canals, 400 bridges, and wealth of art, culture and history is one of the most magnificent cities in Europe. Its early history however, is not so romantic. It was once nothing more than a barren island in the middle of a swamp when, in the fifth century, it was settled by refugees fleeing the marauding barbarian hordes invading from the north.

To gain some sense of what it must have been like in those early days you can travel to one of the present-day Venetian districts of Mestre, on the mainland, and look across the water

Declare Misère – Europe 1975

to the island city in the far distance. The foreshores of Mestre consist of the original swampy land. Huge, well-fed mosquitoes come flying over in bomber formations at dusk. They are the only mosquitoes in the world that can short-circuit a mozzie zapper and still survive. The large industrial estate at your back will further dispel any lingering air of romance. It is here that Camping Fusina, the camping tour operators' choice, is located.

The experienced camping-tour crews were easily recognised by the fact that they wore long mechanics' overalls and boots, even in the sweltering heat, as protection from mozzies. The novices were conspicuous by their freshly printed T-shirts acquired from 'Goose', Neil Booth, an Aussie who became a resident institution at Fusina. The newly arrived punters were also easy to identify at the bar, soaked to the bone. It was custom for the newies to line up beside the wall of the shower block to have their photos taken, only to be doused with buckets of water by Renato, the camp-owner, and his helpers, who would be standing out of sight on the roof.

Tradition was also to be seen in the form of the famous 'burnt beam' overhanging the bar, where unsuspecting females' bras, or

Grunt *disembarking at Corfu on our first ever Greek tour.*

guys' jocks, were set alight to the cheers of the hordes, having been stripped off in the bar, of course.

Had you entered the camping ground in the September of 1975, past its famous sign which read, 'You Are Now Leaving Wogland and Entering the Republic of Fusina,' you would have been forgiven for thinking the barbarian army had assembled to again lay siege to the island city. At least 2500 colonials encamped over the sprawling 4 ha of the campsite. The parade ground was a full-size rugby pitch, goalposts and all. The mess and bar were open to all ranks, twenty-four hours a day, seven days a week. Red and white wine rations, in huge wicker-encased urns, were free, beer being the preferred beverage. There was even a Fusina police force that was entrusted with local law and order.

This was the famous T-Day Festival, an absolute must for any self-respecting barbarian on the European camping circuit. 'T-Day' stood for 'Tornado Day'. In the 1960s a tornado had flattened the campsite. The tour operators had assisted Renato, the owner, in rebuilding the facilities, and as a way of saying, 'Thank you,' T-Day was celebrated at this time every year. It consisted of a week of extraordinarily well-organised events. Competitions included rugby, greasy-pole-climbing, tug-o-wars, sitting-on-the-log-pillow fights, spaghetti-eating, beer-drinking, card games, and so on. You name it, it was happening somewhere. Nights melded into days. It was just one, big, week-long party.

Greasy Pole Competition Fusina.

Screw had planned the September departures so that we could all rendezvous for the festival. We entered teams in all events with little success, except for the 'Five Hundred' card

Declare Misère – Europe 1975

competition. Five Hundred was 'the game' in Europe. You played as a two-person team, and Screw and I entered the 128 team knockout competition. You were drawn to play another team on the first day and if you won the best-of-seven rubbers, you advanced to the next day's round.

I was no cardsharp, average at best but, through a combination of good play by Screw and the luck of the draw, we made it through to the semi-finals on day six. We only had to win this rubber and we'd be in the final, a hugely prestigious achievement. So prestigious, in fact, that I had a quiet night and turned up at the forecourt of the bar where the games were played, in a seriously sober and slightly nervous state. I was shocked to find Screw, on the other hand, still holding up the bar. He'd been there for the entire night. I sensed our chances of victory were slightly diminished. He was holding court in the centre of a circle of Autotours girls, clearly the drunkard of their dreams. He was slobbering spittle all over them while they were annoyingly attentive. I dragged him away, with difficulty.

'Whaddyatalkinabout?' he dribbled as he searched for me through foggy eyes when I reminded him of the competition and admonished him for his irresponsibility. 'Whad's all the fuss about, you old fart? I'm feeling fantastic.'

Our competitors were two big New Zealand boys, Wal and Graham, straight off a sheepfarm next door to Footrot Flats. The only thing missing was the Dog himself.

'What are we doin' this arvo, Waaaal?' Graham said at one point.

'I dunno, Graaaaham.'

'No ideas, Waaaal?'

'Not really, Graaaaham. Stay at the bar, I suppooose.'

'I reckon we ought'er go en see the sights in this 'ere Vienna place, Waaaal.'

'Ah, it's actually "Venice", Graham,' I added helpfully. 'You know, the place with the canals and the gondolas and things like that.' Graham looked at me inquisitively.

'Oh yeah, Venice. That's right. I reckon we ought'er go and see the sights in this 'ere Venice place.'

'Oh yes, Graham, you'll enjoy it immensely,' I said encouragingly, his suspicious look saying, 'That bloke gallops the lizard, I'll bet.'

The score was three/two our way at the end of the fifth. Screw sustained his drinking at the previous evening's pace and with the late morning sun at its zenith, I feared he wouldn't last the distance. As he attempted to pick up his cards for the sixth game, they tumbled from his hands, face-up on the table. He peered at them intently with his short-sighted squint, but there was no sign of intelligent life behind the deep-set blue eyes.

'Open misère,' he dribbled, with the big cheesy grin he gets on such occasions. 'Open misère! Christ!' I thought, 'That's it!' This was the hardest hand of all to win in Five Hundred. Instead of winning all the 'tricks' from your opposition, 'misère' means you have to lose all your tricks, and 'open misère' is even harder because you have to play with all your cards face-up on the table so that the opposition can see your every move. The benefit, of course, is that it's worth so many points, if you pull it off, you not only win that hand, you win the game as well.

We nearly won despite the fact that Screw had no idea what he was doing. The mob standing behind him virtually told him what to play, but Wal and Graham took it all in good spirits. Three all. Now for the Big One. There were tears in my eyes when Screw called, 'Open misère,' again, but I realised he was beyond playing another hand. We either won on this one, or not at all.

This game wasn't even close. We went 'out the back door' in a big way. Que sera, sera. We'd had a good run and come further than we deserved. We congratulated Wal and Graham and wished them well for the final. I dragged Screw to his feet intending to help him back to the bus, but no, getting the circulation going gave him a second wind. Besides, the Autotours girls were still at the bar.

In addition, great interest had been stirred by the fan-fared arrival of the local Italian road-cycling team. It consisted of twenty

Declare Misère – Europe 1975

young, dark, handsomely athletic riders and their attendant road crew. All of us guys crowded around to admire the beautiful bikes they had brought and, of course, the Aussie girls milled around the Italian bike-riders like bees to a honeypot.

This was to be the blue riband event of the whole festival. Renato, the campsite owner, stood on a table to announce the format. There would be five heats, each of about six kilometres, taking in two circuits of the campsite and a local road which, being a Sunday, was all but deserted. There would be four of the Italians in each heat and any of the colonials who wished to participate. The first three placegetters in each heat would go through to the final.

We were amazed the Italians were willing to let the colonials use their bikes, which were obviously very valuable, but I suppose it was a small price to pay for the hero-worship coming from the throngs of doting women.

Top Deck Daze

Screw pushed through the crowd and nominated for one of the heats. I reckoned he'd have trouble sitting on the bike let alone pedalling six kilometres. The heats got underway quickly, and barely half-an-hour passed before I joined the road crew to hold Screw upright for the start of his race, awaiting the starter's gun. The Italians were away in a flash, bums high above the seats as they powered down the road. Screw was among the stragglers at the start, sitting squat in the saddle, all power coming from his big thigh and calf muscles with no assistance by way of stylish riding.

We non-participants recharged our glasses and stood on the steps outside the bar to cheer the riders as they came through the first circuit. Screw had made up ground to about mid-field. I was absolutely stunned when later, he flashed across the line in third position! The Bombardier, Greg 'Wombat' Ettridge, another of our drivers, and I rushed to assist Screw off his bike. He would need to be lubricated for his crack at the final.

Screw's win in the final of the Fusina cycle race challenged credibility.

Declare Misère – Europe 1975

We knew Screw was in with a chance when he and three of the Italians broke away from the pack at the halfway mark. The finish came down to a one-kilometre sprint between the four of them, but Screw won clearly by several lengths. By the time the pack had come into view of the finish, all 2000 campers were engrossed in the race, and cheering wildly, and as Screw broke the tape we rushed down to chair him back to the stairs outside the bar. Celebrations were akin to a Formula One final, as Renato presented Screw with a gold cup while the placegetters sprayed the crowd with beer before we all retreated to the bar for the biggest night of the festival.

Screw's win in the final remains one of the most genuinely amazing physical feats I've ever witnessed, especially given the fact that he'd hardly slept or eaten for the previous six alcohol-drugged days. On many subsequent occasions I marvelled at his physical strength. I was not surprised when, five years later, he returned to Brisbane and played first grade rugby for Queensland University at the relatively old age of thirty. Uni was a grand finalist that year and the team boasted eight current Wallaby Internationals, including the then Australian captain, Mark Loane—ample testimony to Screw's physical prowess.

At dawn the following day, the last of the mosquito squadrons gathered for a final raid as, arm-in-arm with Screw and Wombat, I quit the bar. We staggered out to the stairs overlooking the campsite. I couldn't believe my eyes. Where, the previous evening, there had been row upon row of tents, campervans, cars and buses of all shapes and sizes, now, nothing remained. Only the litter of 2000 campers bore witness to the army's occupation. Slowly it dawned on me what had happened. The troops had heeded the call to battle from beyond the Bavarian Alps. This T-Day event had merely been a skirmish, a diversion, a curtain-raiser. The main battle was due to begin that night with a grand parade. It was the Beerfest, in Munich, and no self-respecting barbarian was going to miss it.

Chapter 5
IN SILK ROAD MODE
(ASIA 1975)

Liz joined me for several trips during late 1974 and early 1975, but it was a real spur-of-the-moment decision for us to get married when we did. We hadn't even shared accommodation in London for anything other than a couple of weeks, so it was hardly a well-thought-out move. I guess it was one of those situations where you have a gut feeling that you are doing the right thing—even though, logically, we should have given ourselves a bit more time. In hindsight, it was obviously the right thing to do, even though we would have appreciated more time together alone during the following few years. However, the new experiences we shared together became the basis of our ongoing friendship. I'm sure we would have become more set in our ways and, consequently, less tolerant of one another, had we waited for much longer than we did.

Despite the fact that we caught our families and friends off guard, we had everyone's support during our brief visit to Australia for 'the ceremony'. We only stayed a few weeks before returning to Europe to plan our next adventure.

I had met my match, and Liz and I returned to Australia in 1975 to be married.

Right from the time we were fitting out old *Argas* for the first trip in 1973, Screw planned to do an overland tour to Kathmandu. In fact, the very first handout for the 1974 Moroccan trips advertised an overland departure for November 1974. For various reasons, it never eventuated and we settled, after great argument, on a date for the following year.

The historic route through Turkey, Iran, Afghanistan and the Indian subcontinent has echoed to the march of Muslim Arab armies, Alexander the Great, Genghis Khan, Mongul and Mogul invaders, as well as trading caravans which gave it the romantic name of the Silk Road. It is still one of the great journeys of the world, and tough under any conditions. No overland operator had ever undertaken the trip in winter when much of central Asia, and especially the high Anatolian Plateau in eastern Turkey, is subject to Arctic-like conditions.

This was mere trivia as far as Screw was concerned, and he and I were at loggerheads about the date he'd selected: late October 1975.

'Winter's an impossibility,' I insisted. 'Just ask anyone who's been there.' Here I was again, saying it couldn't be done.

'You just said no one's been there in winter, so how can I ask them? Of course it can be done you pea-brained pygmy,' Screw replied, and so the argument raged. As usual, Screw won. The buses would be in greater demand in Europe during summer, and anyone doing an overland would prefer to leave in October, after the end of the touring season, and be home in Australia by Christmas. These were his valid reasons.

Screw would have been happy to set off with a map from the first set of services, but I embarked on some meticulous planning. I started by attending promotional sales evenings given by another operator, Penn Overland, at the Tournament pub in Old Brompton Road. Dick Cijffers, one of their couriers, was the presenter. I became Dick's most attentive, prospective customer. After my sixth film evening, Dick must have smelt a rat, but never let on. Gracious to the end, he gave me detailed answers

Top Deck Daze

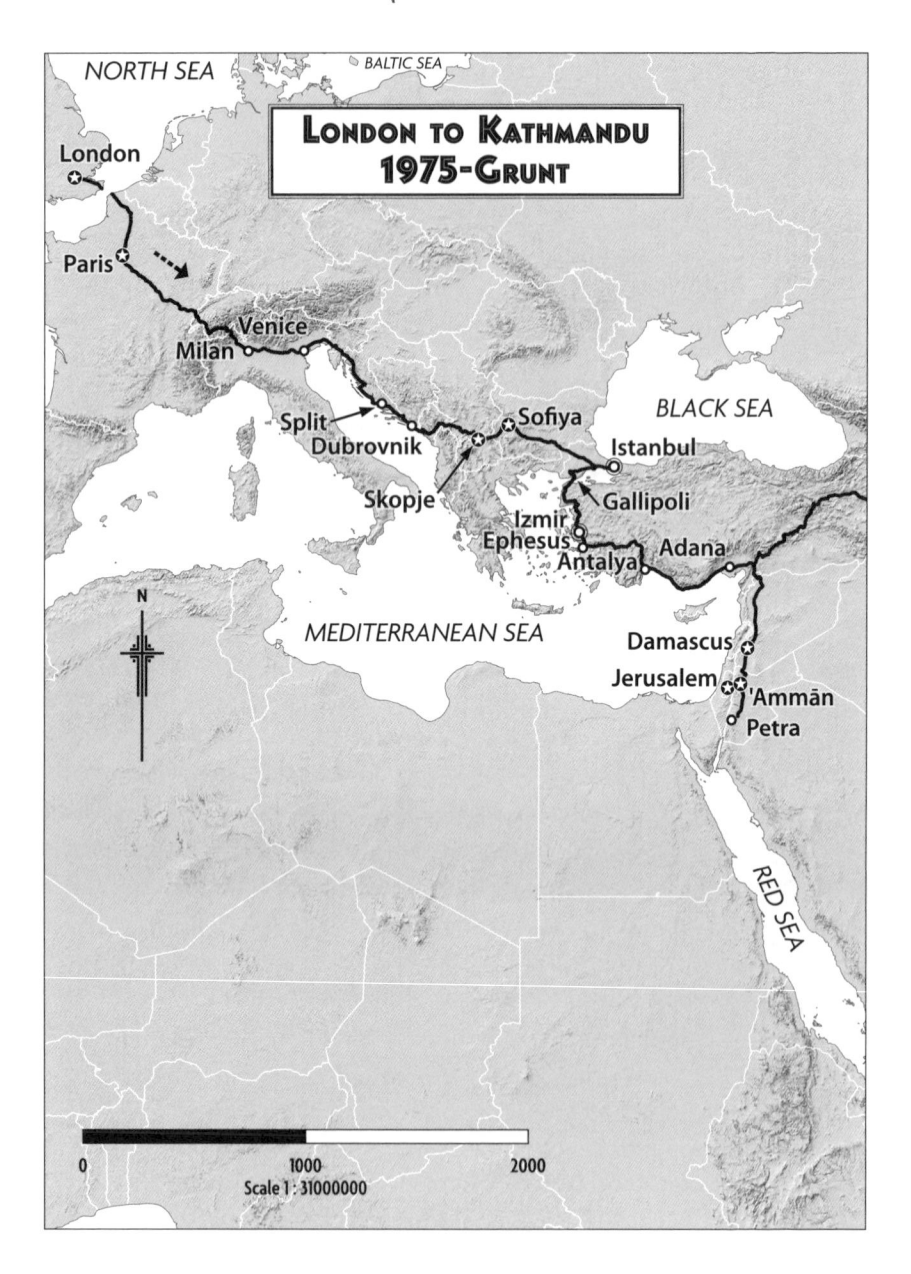

London to Kathmandu
1975-Grunt

In Silk Road Mode – Asia 1975

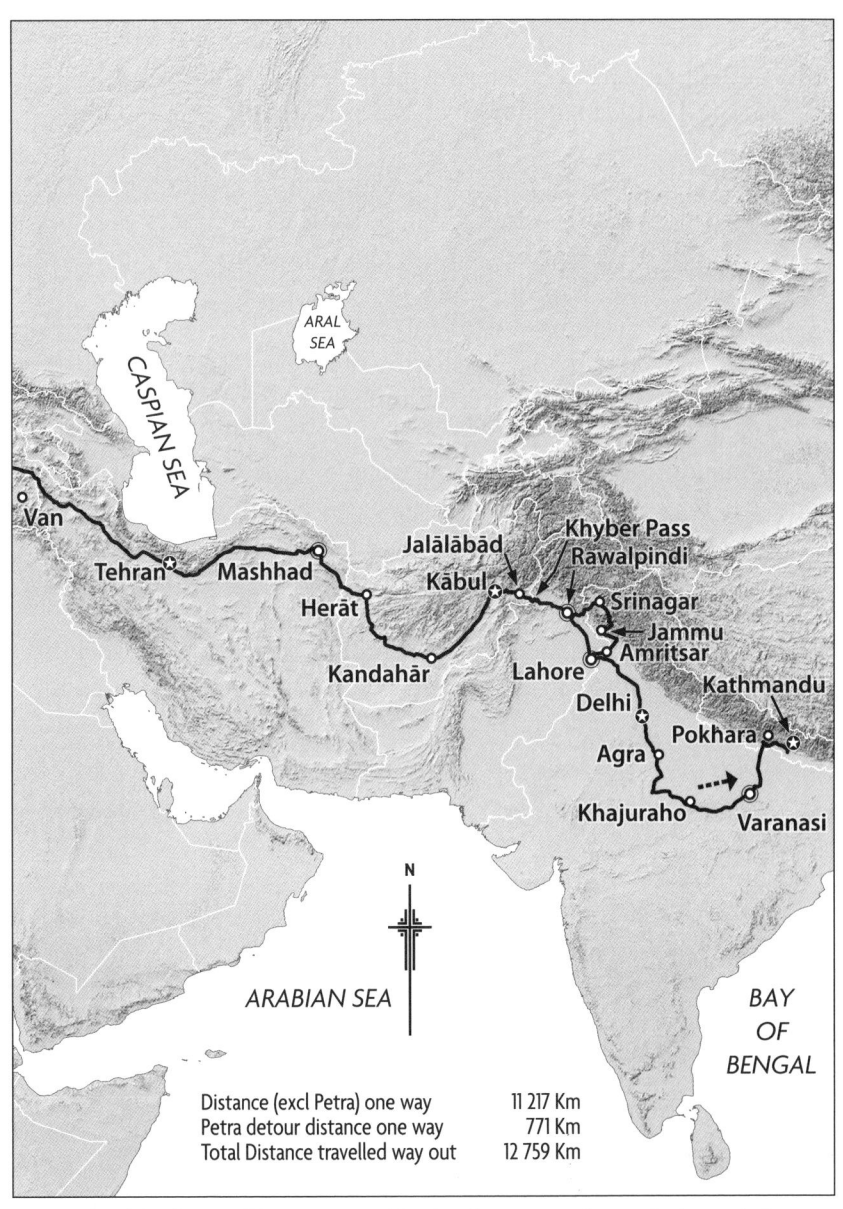

Distance (excl Petra) one way	11 217 Km
Petra detour distance one way	771 Km
Total Distance travelled way out	12 759 Km

I shouldn't have told Screw it couldn't be done—London to Kathmandu in a 1953 double-decker through some most inhospitable countryside—we set out in October 1975 in Grunt.

Top Deck Daze

to every question I could dream up and I'm sure he'd have been just as obliging had I come straight out and told him what I was planning. Dick went on to become a legend on the overland route, having first made a small fortune as a commission salesman at the Overseas Visitors Club, then couriering for Autotours and Penn, then investing in Indigo (and losing all his money because of a corrupt partner), then forming his own company Capricorn and, later, buying into Autotours.

With our customs document for the bus, called a 'carnet de passages en douane', special insurances, and all the other preparations I could think of complete, we set off in *Grunt* at 7:00 a.m. on 24 October 1975. Screw intended to fly home from Kathmandu and Steve 'The Bombardier' Brown and I would bring the bus back on the homeward leg, a five-month round trip.

We had fifteen passengers including Terry Gasner, Dave 'Dinga' Evans and Graham 'Pa Rug'. Fortunately for Liz, her good friend Stephanie (we all called her Steve) came on the trip as well. Not only was Steve great company, she had an in-depth knowledge of history and current affairs which greatly added to

Grunt in Florence Italy 1974.

In Silk Road Mode – Asia 1975

our understanding of, and interest in, the countries we visited. Another passenger was our good friend Johnnie 'Grilly' Wells.

All of us had toured Europe, so we made our way as fast as we could through France, Italy, Yugoslavia and into our first Eastern Bloc country, Bulgaria. The campsite in the capital, Sofia, was our first experience of socialism at work, or should I say not at work. There were at least twenty staff hanging around the campsite doing absolutely zilch. We were shocked at how poor everyone was and at the lack of goods in all the shops, which was in stark contrast to our western consumerist ways.

We had packed a cardboard carton full of plastic tubs of margarine but the box was damaged and the marg was going off, so we decided to chuck the lot in one of the camping ground garbage bins. Next morning we were in the campsite restaurant. I noticed they had shiny, new sugar bowls on all the tables. They were our empty marg containers, all nicely washed and polished, of course! They wouldn't have wasted something as valuable as that!

Because of the amazingly favourable exchange rate, everything was dirt-cheap so that night we went to the most exclusive, expensive restaurant we could find. The champagne and caviar were magnificent but when the waiter tried to serve the meal silver-service style, there were stifled, embarrassed laughs around the table as he kept fumbling with the spoon and fork and the food kept piling up in little mounds on his silver tray. In the end he gave up the charade and just shovelled it onto our plates with the back of his spoon in one gooey pile.

Turkey was foreign territory for all of us and so we slowed the pace of our travels. The Turkish Government had transferred to Ankara in 1923 but Istanbul, once known as Constantinople, was the historic capital of the country. A walk through the steep, cobblestoned streets of the old city with their overhanging porticoes and fountains inscribed with Koranic texts, and the covered bazaar with its leather-toolers, clockmakers and haggling hawkers, was a step back in time.

Top Deck Daze

The 'Pudding Shop' cafe is probably regarded as a passé, hippie hangout today but in 1975 it was *the* place to be seen in Istanbul. Adventurers of all persuasions would pass through its doors and hold court at its tables, most at the end of their great Asian treks. On our last evening in the city we stayed there till 3:00 a.m. and having checked out of Camping Londra, intended to grab a few hours sleep before a dawn departure.

We walked back to the bus which was parked in front of the holiest place in all of Turkey, the Blue Mosque. Unfortunately I slept in and was still dead to the world in the downstairs bunks at seven o'clock when there was a furious bang, bang, banging on the windows and someone yelling,

'Move zee bus. Move zee bus. I demaaaand you move zee bus, nowwww.' Groggily I drew back the curtains. My nose was inches away from that of a Turkish army general's, and steam was snorting from his nostrils as we eyeballed one another through the glass. He wasn't alone. I could see what looked like the entire Turkish infantry paraded along the streets behind him. The German chancellor was due in town on a State visit (so we found out) and old *Grunt* was spoiling the view of their holiest Mosque. 'Move zee bus nowwww!'

I stumbled out of the doorway only to find the general circling a rather suspicious looking object. An empty Banger Mix box, from a sort of soya-bean sausage mince, quite evidently from our kitchen, covered the scene of a possible crime. Gingerly, he prodded the box with his swagger stick, confirming his suspicions as to what lay underneath, then looked accusingly at me. Sheepishly, I saluted the general and without the need for an order, or any attempt to claim innocence on our behalf, I cleared it away and we beat a hasty retreat.

We headed south-west along the banks of the Sea of Marmara until we reached one of the highlights of this part of the trip, the Gallipoli Peninsula. On the shelves in my room at home I had an old book that I'd read countless times since my primary school days, *Australian Campaigns of the Great War*. I felt I knew the battlefields better than the generals who'd overseen the campaign in 1915.

At first, the only evidence of the battle we could find were the remains of what appeared to be landing boats or barges in the shallow waters of the cove. We soon discovered the trenches, still clearly visible, especially in the New Zealand sector and at the top of the ridges that had been occupied by the Turks and their commanders, including that of Mustafa Kemal Bey, later known as Atatürk, President of the first Turkish Republic. At what I deduced to be Reserve Gully, a dry creek bed exposed one to two metres of earth. By just scraping with our hands we found the remains of hundreds of empty food tins, drink bottles with Australian markings, gun shells and a myriad of other memorabilia.

We decided to wake up early the following morning and go down to the beach at Anzac Cove to watch the dawn. A dark, eerie pilgrim's walk, it was an appointment with the dead. I imagined the smell of citrus fruit and olives, carried on the cold Aegean wind, blowing in from the direction of Lemnos, the island where the Australians had embarked before the landings. Insects rustled in the scrub. The moon and stars shone dimly through the trailing clouds, silhouetting the grim outline of the cliffs known as Plugge's Plateau and The Sphinx, which seemed to watch our every move from above and to our right. I trod softly, in case a false step might wake a sleeping soul. We paused where we had stopped earlier that day, at the headstones of the diggers at the Beach Cemetery, remembering their ages: seventeen, eighteen, nineteen … We had walked as a group, but the mystic aura of the surroundings, the very impression on us of the dead, urged us to go from their midst alone and we each found a place of solitude on the beach and waited for the first rays of the sun.

The significance of the fact that our next stop, the ancient ruins of Troy, was only a few kilometres away, on the southern shores of the Dardanelles, was not lost on those of us who shared

Top Deck Daze

a love of history. The sheer waste of young men's lives, the heroic but pointless sacrifices, seemed to be everything a Greek tragedy might demand. One could easily substitute the names of the young boys lying at Quinn's Post or Shrapnel Gully for those of the heroes of Homer's *Iliad*.

Further south we walked in the footsteps of St Paul at Ephesus and in those of the Crusaders whose castles still dotted the coastline. Crossing into Syria, en route for Damascus, we took a wrong turn and found ourselves at the heavily fortified Lebanese border. The civil war had broken out, just months beforehand, between the Christians and the Palestine Liberation Organization (PLO)-Muslim Alliance. We were not aware of it at the time, but we had just stumbled upon thousands of Syrian troops massing for an invasion, intending to restore some sort of order to Lebanon. They obviously hadn't planned on a double-decker bus being at the vanguard of their attack and some laughingly embarrassed soldiers escorted us back to the main road.

From Damascus we ran south, parallel to the Golan Heights, and the narrow highway became crowded with military convoys. We stopped to stretch our legs in what looked like the middle of nowhere. Some of us took photos and thought nothing of it. A kilometre further on we were descended upon by a dozen armoured personnel carriers. Machine gun-toting officers ordered me out of the cab. We had been taking photos of missile-launching sites, so we were informed, and I had to drive the bus under armed guard to a military compound. After an hour of reasonably civil questioning and a lecture on Middle-Eastern politics, we had to empty all our cameras of film and were sent on our way.

From Amman, Jordan, after a swim in the Dead Sea, we drove to the Israeli border. We parked and locked the bus, crossed the Allenby Bridge on foot, and made our way to Jerusalem by public buses, along with thousands of Jordanian workers who made the same trip daily. We went on a side trip to Bethlehem to see 'where Screw had been born'.

In Silk Road Mode – Asia 1975

Having done the tourist thing of 'swimming' in the Dead Sea we drove to the Israeli border from Amman, Jordan.

Our three days in Israel were fascinating, not only for the history but also for what we learnt about current politics. The Jordanians were surprisingly tolerant of Israel and the countries cooperated in many ways. There were no problems re-entering Jordan, for example. The Israelis simply stapled extra pages in our passports and ripped them out on our return, removing all evidence of our visit.

The attitude of the Syrians, on the other hand, was much more aggressive. We had wanted to travel to Iran via Iraq but visas were refused and so we had to make our way back through Syria. We knew we'd be in big trouble if the Syrians found out we'd been to Israel so we wised everyone up on what to do and say at the border. Screw and I gathered up all the passports and presented them to the Syrian immigration officer. As he was checking them off one by one, a small piece of paper slipped from near the top of the pile and gently floated to the counter

Jaipur 1983

BELCH Great Trunk Road

BELCH Jaipur 1981

BOOBS YHT932 with TaTa on overland 1978

GRUNT

GRUNT on Punt

LEMMING in Algeria

desktop. Screw and I froze in horror. It was a Jerusalem bus ticket, printed in Hebrew.

The Syrian official was concentrating on his work and didn't notice, at first. Ever so gently and casually, Screw reached out his arm across the counter, as if rolling his body to shift the weight on his legs. The palm of his hand just covered the ticket when the official averted his eyes from the passports and slapped his hand on top of Screw's. He rolled their hands over and there was the ticket for all to see. Ten hours of not-so-civil questioning followed and we seriously feared for our future before we were eventually set free and sent on our way again.

For the next three weeks we headed east, back through Turkey and then across Iran, Afghanistan and into Pakistan. Some days were full of adventures such as the one we'd just experienced while others were just long tiring drives, but we were never bored. The decker was fantastic for such a trip. On occasions we came across other overlanders doing eleven weeks of sheer torture, sitting in the back of a truck or cramped in coach seats all day, only to face pitching tents or sleeping in some flea-ridden hotel at night. The passengers looked at us longingly as we lounged around in the decker, sitting at the tables playing 'Five Hundred', discussing politics, or making ourselves tea, coffee or snacks on the run.

The stereo would blast away all day. If we played Steely Dan's 'Rikki Don't Lose That Number' once, we played it 1000 times. I still can't hear it without breaking into bizarre hip-grinding movements, echoing the chorus then yelling '… remember that time on the overland when …' Best of all were the bunks upstairs, where you could lie and read or nap if you were tired or not feeling the best.

Some of the passengers needed to update their tetanus and other inoculations en route so we chose to visit the main hospital in Teheran. The third-world conditions were a shock and everyone secretly prayed they'd stay healthy and never have to avail themselves of such services. The doctor turned

In Silk Road Mode – Asia 1975

out to be of Indian descent with the name of Veriswarmi. He appeared to be a bit on the debauched side, most unprofessional in his manner, and could hardly stop himself touching the girls unnecessarily. Inevitably he was called Dr 'VerySlimy' to his face. Liz needed to get a jab in the backside to complete her set of injections and having the reputation of not being the bravest of patients, was giving Dr VerySlimy and the medical staff a hard time. As the good doctor approached her for the last and largest of her injections, she turned to him with indignation.

'What's that?' Liz demanded, eyeing the instrument as he leered at her behind. She could hardly believe it when he answered with that old line, 'Just a little prick with a needle, madam,' and so could not resist the classic reply, 'I didn't say, "Who are you?" I said, "What's that?"' and without waiting for further explanation, she hitched up her pants and bounded out of the ward untouched, vowing never to return.

Neither Screw nor I was the slightest bit sick from the local food. Whenever we got the munchies, which was often, we'd pull up at roadside stalls and eat anything that was on offer, especially savouring the rancid jungle curries of Pakistan and India. The others on board would fairly heave when they saw what we were tucking into and would suffer more than indelicate, abdominal fissions if they tried to eat it. Screw and I decided to have a competition. I would award him points if he found and ate at the grottiest, most unhygienic, fly-blown stall, and vice versa. God only knows what we ate half the time but it always tasted pretty good to me. I can only assume our stomachs gradually built up immunity to all the bugs. The others, who were ever-so-hygienic, always seemed to be coming down with bad cases of Delhi belly.

Our first stop in Pakistan was at Rawalpindi, in the North Western Frontier Territory. We left the Bombardier in charge of the bus while the rest of us scouted the markets for provisions. When we returned, the Pakistanis were swarming around the bus like flies, twenty or thirty-deep. We all knew Pakistan was

Screw and I would pull up at roadside stalls and eat anything that was on offer. Oddly, the cautious passengers were the ones who fell ill.

overpopulated but experiencing the country for the first time was overwhelming. The bulk of the populace seemed to wander the streets from sun-up till midnight with nothing to do, and *Grunt* proved to be a highlight of their very dull day.

All the passengers were back on board when Screw and I returned and the Pakistanis, like the Muslims of Iran, banged on the windows and drooled lecherously at the girls, staring wild-eyed at their crutches. Meanwhile the poor local women scurried along the streets like outcasts, without faces or identity, peering

In Silk Road Mode - Asia 1975

Snot in Islamabad.

at the world like jailbirds through the bars of their *burqas*. So much for the values of these supposedly religious countries!

The Bombardier was playing sergeant major today. With his starched-collared khaki shirt, mirror-polished boots and ginger handlebar moustache bristling in the morning light, he cut a dashing figure as he circled the bus with his wallah stick. 'Wallah' is a local word used to describe anyone engaged in a specific occupation. For example, the horse-drawn taxi drivers were called 'tonga-wallahs' and, somehow, the Bombardier had acquired one of their long, birch canes.

Around and around the bus the Bombadier went with a thwack and a 'Stand right back, I say!' here, and a thwack, and, 'Get your grubby little hands off!' there, as he tried, unsuccessfully, to keep the Pakistanis at a respectable distance from the windows. Screw hopped into the cab to drive off and I called, 'Thanks very much,

Top Deck Daze

Bombardier. We're ready to depart now, sir,' and he jumped up, backwards, into the doorway with a swish and a thwack of the wallah-stick in fresh air, just for good measure.

The crowd was so thick Screw could hardly drive at walking pace. A long, brown arm snaked in through the window and drew back one of the curtains shielding the girls. The Bombardier spied the intrusion and believing he was rightly defending the girls' honour, lunged at it with an almighty whack. A loud, wailing, 'Ooooooh! Ahrrrrrrr!' emanated from the arm's owner. The Bombardier opened the back door and yelled, 'Take that you bloody little heathen!' to which the offending Pakistani replied, in the strongest of East End London accents and in the most aggrieved manner, 'Wot do youse expects a fella to do when he sees a bus from home?'

The following day, Terry Gasner and I were walking through the markets in Lahore when we were accosted by a well-dressed, elderly Pakistani gentleman, anxious for a chat.

'You are English?' he enquired.

'No, Australian,' we replied.

'Oh! Goodness gracious me! Have you heard the news from your country?' he said, holding his hands to the side of his face as he sucked in the air. We shook our heads in ignorance. 'I have been listening to the BBC World Service,' he continued. 'There has been a revolution. Your government has been overthrown. Your prime minister is no more!'

Terry and I looked at one another and then back at the old man.

'Australia? Have you got the right country, sir? Governments don't get overthrown in Australia,' we informed him.

'Oh, dear me, yes, yes, yes,' he said, wobbling his head from side to side, 'I am not being mistaken. Australia it is.'

We hunted around the markets and found some international newspapers. Sure enough, there it was. Gough Whitlam had been dismissed by the governor general. Not exactly a revolution perhaps but, in the eyes of the old Pakistani gentleman, it amounted to the same thing.

In Silk Road Mode – Asia 1975

We gathered more news as we drove to Delhi. We went straight to the Australian High Commission where we were able to vote in the 13 December election. The Australian officials invited us back to the High Commission that night for their version of Don's Party. We had all the Swan Lager we could drink and a wonderful smorgasbord of Aussie tucker as we listened to the results come in over Radio Australia. Most on board our bus were card-carrying Bolshies and we'd driven in from the campsite to rousing choruses of *The Internationale*. However, as the night wore on, the group's good humour soured and then turned to misery as it became increasingly evident that Fraser would win in a landslide.

I must say I wasn't that despondent. No one had cheered louder than I had at Gough's initial victory in 1972, but Labor's turn in office had been a bitter disappointment. I felt it marked a watershed in our history. Until then, Australians believed that, whatever their station in life, they could achieve all that they

There were no apparent road rules, these bullock carts meandered along the road, day and night.

wanted and needed with hard work and initiative. But Gough's welfare-state mentality changed all that. Now, everyone blamed the government for their economic woes. Everyone abrogated responsibility for their own destiny. The less-well-off regarded themselves as 'victims' of the system.

Meanwhile, 'Emperor' Gough and his 'mandarin minions' splurged the taxpayers' money on their own vice-regal splendour to the rancour of both True Believers and Liberals alike. I'd been a 'Red' at uni, but a few seasons in the capitalist classes had seen me ready to jump ship. I was starting to think more like Attila the Hun every day, but couldn't stand Fraser as a person and regarded him as a total economic wet anyway. Consequently, I was now uncertain of my own politics.

By the time we'd reached Delhi, Screw, the Bombardier and I considered ourselves expert drivers. By far the worst experience so far had been negotiating the suicidal car drivers in Teheran, but driving on the Great Trunk Road through India was another experience altogether. Driving in the day was bad enough but at night it was near impossible. Bullock carts, pedestrians, cyclists and elephants competed with the trucks for the narrow strip of bitumen.

The bullock carts just meandered along the road in the dead of night with just a kerosene lamp, if you were lucky, to alert you to their presence. On one night drive Screw nearly collected a bullock cart wandering towards us and skidded to a halt just centimetres from the bullocks' noses. He jumped out of the driver's cab intent on abusing the bullocky, only to find him sound asleep, lying in the cart—an obviously common state of affairs. Quietly, Screw turned the cart around, gave the bullocks a slap on the rump, and sent them on their way in the opposite direction. We'd have loved to have stayed around to witness the bullocky's reaction when he woke up at dawn. He might think twice again about driving while asleep.

The Tata trucks, on the other hand, careered along at breakneck speed, scattering all before them. Tata is the name of

In Silk Road Mode – Asia 1975

Belch came off second best in this encounter with a Turkish truck.

the prominent industrial family that manufactures the vehicles and they have a monopoly throughout the subcontinent. The truckies have a notorious reputation for dangerous and erratic driving, and we would invariably have to slow down and pull over to let them pass, as they would never give way. If you held your line, you could play brinkmanship with them. In slow traffic you would pull up, window to window, both drivers staring at each other, each willing the other to give way.

As Top Deck's tours increased in popularity over subsequent years, the drivers developed special techniques for just such occasions. Bryan 'Light Blue' Ramsey, record-holding veteran of umpteen overlands, favoured the bike-pump approach. He'd suck up a couple of pints of water in the pump and, from a metre away, squirt it into the Tata driver's face. You would still have to pull over to get by, but at least you did so with a sense of satisfaction.

Top Deck Daze

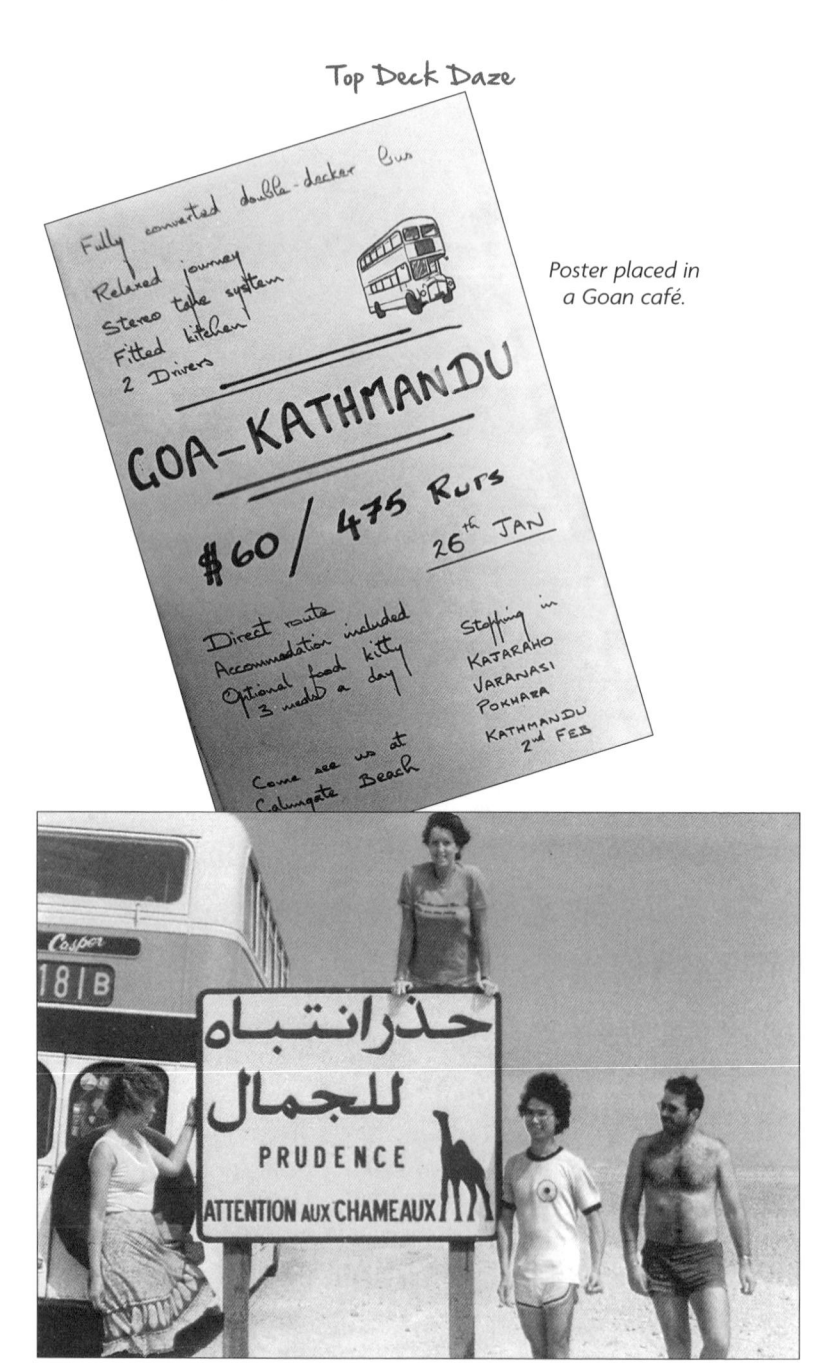

Fully converted double-decker Bus
Relaxed journey
Stereo tape system
Fitted kitchen
2 Drivers

GOA – KATHMANDU

$60 / 475 Rups

26th JAN

Direct route
Accommodation included
Optional food kitty
3 meals a day

Stopping in
KAJARAHO
VARANASI
POKHARA
KATHMANDU
2nd FEB

Come see us at Calangute Beach

Poster placed in a Goan café.

حذر انتباه
للجمال

PRUDENCE
ATTENTION AUX CHAMEAUX

Mark 'Ackko' Atkinson (far right) on Casper.

In Silk Road Mode – Asia 1975

Jeff 'Skin' Skinner favoured the Bombardier's wallah-stick approach until, that is, he observed the more technically advanced procedures of Bruce 'Moose' Maloney and Mark Atkinson. They would lob a lighted bunger into the Tata driver's cab with spectacular results. 'Skin' converted to this method until, one day, he scored an own-goal. He burnt his finger lighting a bunger, fumbled, and dropped the firecracker into his reserve supplies, and with the resultant explosion, managed to blow himself through the driver's cab window.

A day out of Delhi, the road narrowed and straddled a levee bank with water-filled rice paddies on either side. I was driving and a Tata truck and I came head-to-head. I wasn't budging as I had much further to reverse than he had and felt it only fair that he should be the one to pull back. The stalemate lasted several minutes until Screw appeared from the back of the bus and made his way towards the truck.

Screw isn't tall, but he's about five times wider in body and limb than your average Indian and, when the driver and his five

We didn't want to wait to see the seasons change, so we took the tools from the Nepalese workers and within an hour we had cleared a way for Grunt *through the debris left by the landslide.*

Top Deck Daze

mates lining the front seat saw Screw coming with a look of menace, they decided discretion was the better part of valour and piled out of the passenger side in a tactical retreat. Screw mounted the truck's cab, stuck it into reverse, and then let it roll down the levee bank until it was submerged to the mudguards in the waters of the rice paddy below. He walked back past me brushing his hands and without looking up said, 'Okay. You can go now.'

Two months to the day after leaving London, we climbed the last and most treacherous stretch of road leading up from the Kathmandu Valley in Nepal, only to be confronted by a massive landslide that might still deny us our goal of Kathmandu itself. The Nepalese workers were going about their task of clearing the road with about as much speed as a snail with piles and we were so frustrated at their lack of progress we literally shoved them aside, requisitioned their picks, shovels and spades, and formed a section of road wide and strong enough to allow *Grunt* to pass within an hour. Late in the day we entered the capital of the Kingdom of Nepal in triumphant mood.

We celebrated with a buffalo-steak barbecue in the grounds of the Withies Hotel, where we'd parked old *Grunt*, and had a traditional Christmas dinner at the Blue Star Hotel with all the trimmings including, according to the menu, 'mens' pie for dessert. Fortunately, it tasted more like fruit 'mince' pie.

We felt justifiably proud of being the first to ever drive a double-decker bus all the way from London to Kathmandu but, as we made friends with many of the foreign characters running various hotels and restaurants, we heard amazing stories of past adventures that put ours well and truly into perspective. We heard about Paddy Garrow-Fisher who, with a company called 'Indiaman', was reputedly the first-ever overlander. We met a Boris Voscavich at the Yak and Yeti Palace restaurant who had fled Russia after the war and with his new Scandinavian wife, towed a caravan behind his car to India in 1947. He told us that in 1969, four English guys had driven a genuine old steamroller

In Silk Road Mode – Asia 1975

over the same route from London. They drove a Mini Minor as well and used this to scavenge anything combustible for the roller's boiler. I doubted whether our effort could top that.

If we had tried to do what we'd done just one or two years earlier, it would have been impossible. The road we'd travelled via Pokhara and the Kathmandu Valley had only recently been built. Before that, the only way into Nepal was via the infamous Raj Pass and *Grunt* would never have made it. Still considered one of the most perilous roads on Earth, the pass, built by the Indian army, is hewn into the sheer face of the Himalayan foothills and falls 3000 metres to India's Valley of the Ganges below. The pass itself had not been open for that long. The original overland operators had chosen Calcutta or Bombay as their destinations and Kathmandu had only become popular in more recent times.

Sundowners and Penn still travelled via the Raj Pass. They left their buses at a small town called Birganj, just inside the Indian/Nepalese border, stopping over in the grottiest of hotels with the gall to call itself 'The Samjana Hotel for Healthy Living', and then took their passengers up to Kathmandu by local bus. When it came to collecting their passengers from Kathmandu for the return journey, they would have to charter two local buses. They would insist on two Nepalese drivers or two Indian drivers because if they got one of each, the drivers would race one another down the pass at the speed of gravity.

A week after our arrival, just for the thrill of it, we decided to travel down the pass from Kathmandu by local bus. At the bottom, we looked back to where we'd come from and the road simply disappeared into the clouds.

The isolation of Nepal ensured it remained a uniquely underdeveloped and distinctively different country. Until 1951 Nepal had been dominated by the Rana dynasty and since then, ruled with an iron fist by King Tribhuwan Shah and his descendants. There were no roads at all during King Shah's time so he had a half-a-mile of tarmac laid out and shipped a Rolls Royce up to

Top Deck Daze

Kathmandu in parts. On ceremonial occasions he drove up and down his little road, waving to the crowds.

There was a major flap when the newly crowned Queen Elizabeth II of England decided to visit Kathmandu as part of her world tour in 1954. Boris Voscavich had been imprisoned for some minor misdemeanour but was quickly pardoned by the Nepalese king to help with arrangements for the royal visit. The palace had no European-style dunny so Boris had a Royal Doulton shipped in, just in the nick of time. Plumbing for such appliances simply didn't exist, so four little boys were hidden on the palace roof and whenever She pulled the chain, it rang a small bell audible only to them, and the four boys chucked their buckets of water down the pipes. Presto. Problem solved.

Shah was succeeded by his grandson, King Birendra, in 1972, and was still held in awe by his subjects. On New Year's Day, 1976, a week after our arrival, the king was out for a drive in his Roller and knocked over and killed a cow which the Nepalese (being Hindus) believed to be sacred. This explained the headline in Kathmandu's main daily newspaper the following day: 'UNFORTUNATE COW COMMITS SUICIDE IN FRONT OF KING'S CAR'. As Grilly Wells, our intrepid newspaper man on board said, 'Never let the facts get in the way of a good story.'

I had mixed feelings about Kathmandu. On the plus side, it had an intriguing medieval atmosphere with winding alleys, squares full of pagodas and statues, intricate, erotic wood-carvings in Durbar Square and at Jagannath Temple. At the Monkey Temple the cheeky, belligerent little animals would jump up on your hip and rummage through your bags, looking for things to steal or eat. You could buy 'antiques to order' at Thamel, or just wander up and down Freak Street eating apple pies, chocolate cakes, or brown bread rolls—all local favourites.

One of the most fascinating and popular haunts was the 'Eden Hashish Shop'. This first-floor establishment displayed large glass jars full to the brim of hashish or *ganja*. The proprietor discussed

In Silk Road Mode – Asia 1975

the various merits of each crop as if he were a purveyor of fine vintage wines or cigars.

'The '71 was a particularly good year,' he would say. 'Please, ladies and gentlemen, take a seat while you try some,' and billowing clouds of smoke would fill the room as everyone puffed away on their samples.

On the negative side, despite all these attractions, Kathmandu was one of the dirtiest cities in the East with rubbish everywhere, rats lurking in gutters, and vultures hanging around the Bagmati River on the lookout for a feed. The Nepalese had the most horrible throaty chests, as if they were all afflicted with consumption. You didn't need an alarm clock in Kathmandu. Every morning at six the whole valley rose to the sound of 10 000 'Kerrrrrrrr, Spits' as they all cleared their throats as one.

In later years, when we sold Kathmandu/London trips out of Australia, the newly arrived punters would fly in 'green', straight from Sydney or Melbourne. What a culture shock, poor things. You could see the look of total horror on their faces as they tried to dodge the gollies and the crap on the footpaths and when they reached Withies Hotel and saw the dirty deckers still in 1000 pieces as the drivers rebuilt their motors, their looks simply said, 'Take me home to mother, please!'

Withies Hotel was so dirty even the cockroaches walked around on stilts, but it was the only hotel in town where we could park the bus in the grounds, making it reasonably secure. There was a guard hut at the gates where a 'security guard', of sorts, was supposed to keep watch. He lived in the most squalid of conditions, made worse by the fact that one of our rascal punters, Dave 'Dinga' Evans, would have several leaks through the doorway of the hut every night in his always-inebriated state, and the guard never detected the stench rising above the 'normal' squalid conditions in which he resided. There were never any other guests in the hotel so we commandeered it for our exclusive use, without any objection from the old owner whom we called 'Uncle' Arnu.

Top Deck Daze

Grunt *deserved a rest after the marathon trip, and the Hotel Withies was the only place in town where we could park in the grounds.*

Having farewelled Screw on his return to London by plane and having toured India and Sri Lanka independently, we regrouped in Kathmandu in late January 1976 to set off in our sturdy chariot for the return trip. We'd lost, but also gained, some passengers including Kessa Ware and her friend Lesley Russell. Kessa had been on the very first Moroccan with us and was our first London office manager when we worked out of Mablethorpe Road. Kessa was returning to the UK after a short visit to Australia.

We'd spent time exploring the major sights of northern India on the way out—Varanasi on the banks of the Holy Ganges, the temples of Khajuraho, the Taj Mahal and Fatehpur Sikri—so we made up time in the first week heading back by doing some long drives. We decided, however, to spend an extra day in the Punjab at Amritsar, holy city of millions of turbaned Sikhs. Their famous Golden Temple was easily the most beautiful of all I'd seen in the East. It was a delicate gold-leaf structure, standing in a huge, clean, mirror-reflecting pool with stark white marble

In Silk Road Mode - Asia 1975

We climbed the fabled Khyber Pass as we journeyed towards Afghanistan.

Looking towards Pakistan from 'Landi Kotal', the peak of the pass through the Hindu Kush mountains.

walkways all around. Inside, three fine-looking Sikhs were singing and playing enchantingly. It was the first time I'd ever felt an attempt at something meaningful was going on inside a place of worship. The interior was exquisite with designs of delicate flowers in marble and coloured stone with elaborately gilt-worked roofs and alcoves from which we could look down on the worshippers below.

If the Golden Temple looked amazing to us, who were used to fine homes and clean carpets underfoot, one can only imagine how the average Indian must have felt about coming to such a place when compared with the dusty, ramshackle dwellings in the streets outside. It was a good way to say goodbye to India but the visit was not without its usual injustices. As we were leaving the temple, a Sikh told Grilly Wells and Stephanie not to hold hands, frowning as if they were red-hot sinners. Liz overheard the exchange and turned on the Sikh with clenched fists and gritted teeth, but said and did nothing, other than glare at him. A Sikh had attacked her at one of the hotels we'd stayed in only two weeks beforehand and so she found this instance of apparent double standards particularly galling.

The backblocks of Iran.

In Silk Road Mode – Asia 1975

On leaving Pakistan we again climbed the fabled Khyber Pass towards Afghanistan. The Bombardier and I stopped to have our photos taken next to the monuments of various British regiments that had fought in the pass in earlier times. At one of these we ran into an elderly retired British colonel who had been posted to this region with the Indian army, just before World War II. He was out from England, visiting his old haunts for the last time, and had hired a car and driver from Rawalpindi. The Bombardier and I were spellbound with his stories. One of our passengers, Susan, who was terribly British herself, seemed particularly taken with the old gentleman. He cut a fine figure with his full head of greying hair, silver moustache and military dress which included a Sam Browne belt, riding breeches and leather puttees. If only he were forty years younger. She could just picture him on his trusty steed at the head of the parade, or perhaps dashing around the polo field.

'Tell me, Colonel,' she said with a longing look in her eyes, 'Was your regiment made up of British or Indian soldiers?'

'Well, actually, young lady, we had British officers with black privates.'

'Oh! How exotic!' said Susan dreamily.

The Entrance to the Kyber Pass.

Top Deck Daze

The road up the Khyber Pass, separating Pakistan from Afghanistan, followed a big, snow-fed river that shone many colours of blue and green in the late afternoon light. As the sun set, the rock-strewn hills and sky turned from crimson to pink, then brown, then ever darker shades of blue, until finally darkness and rain fell together. We'd experienced snow in Iran on the way out but this evening, as we climbed in altitude, it came sheeting down again—a foretaste of what lay ahead.

Kabul, the capital of Afghanistan, was covered in a curtain of white when we arrived and the backdrop of the snow-capped Hindu Kush made an impressive sight. We slipped and slid our way down the icy footpaths of Chicken Street and everyone overdosed on sugar at the cake shops. It was a time to stock up on new woolly socks, boots, coats, scarves and hats.

When I got back to the bus, some crazy local was dousing the outside with fuel and just about to set old *Grunt* aflame before the Bombardier, thankfully, took to him with his trusty wallah stick. We had no idea as to the motivation for the attack until someone explained that the bus was parked outside a holy mosque and, as such, had been 'defiling' the place. 'Balls to that,' I thought. *Grunt* was the nicest, most respectful bus I'd ever known. There wasn't a bad bone in her whole body.

We'd witnessed scenes of brutality in the streets in the form of police bashings and when two of our girls came back to the bus in tears having been hijacked by a leering, lecherous, extortive taxi driver, we began to believe the Afghanis were a mean and aggro bunch. Years later we had no trouble believing all the tales of terror from the region relayed to us by our crew. Wombat Ettridge (who'd been a driver with us since 1974 and who did several overlands later in the 1970s) witnessed the aftermath of a captive Russian soldier being skinned alive at Herat. The Russian invasion and subsequent civil war must have been a monstrous affair.

We'd been studying our maps and had decided on a different route home. Instead of following the main road through

In Silk Road Mode – Asia 1975

Afghanistan to Herat and across northern Iran (the way we'd come), we decided to head south from Kandahar, cross into the remote Baluchistan region of western Pakistan, and traverse Iran on a southerly route.

We stocked up on stores in Kandahar and as I opened up one of the cupboards on board, I noticed that it contained, in addition to a few old potatoes and carrots, a rather healthy looking mouse. I quietly closed the door and called the Bombardier and Grilly Wells to check and tell me I hadn't imagined it. I hadn't. Fortunately the lockers only contained canned food. When the others returned, I gingerly opened the door to have another look, but the stowaway had disappeared and a major search revealed no sign of him. I had no doubts, however, that he was still with us. He became the subject of much discussion. What nationality was he? Nepalese? Indian? Pakistani? British (God forbid)? And did he have a passport? A most intriguing situation!

We headed south into the desert wilderness. Afghanistan was like no other country we'd visited. Words like 'remote' or 'backward' failed to describe the reality. The lunar-like landscape was a dull, barren, desolate brown and devoid of trees or flora of any description. Carting wood for fuel was far more lucrative than running drugs. The slab-mud hovels afforded their raggedy-shawled inhabitants scant protection from the elements. We passed groups of plodding, bare-boned camels, their forlorn-looking masters bent forward against the howling, biting wind.

We took on board a handsome Afghani policeman who wanted a lift a short distance. Kessa and Susan were most attentive to his needs and in stark contrast to their earlier criticisms of the general male population, were very disappointed that he was so well-behaved. They offered him a bowl of our breakfast porridge and when they tried to explain to him what it was, the Afghani kept saying something that sounded very much like 'shithouse'. He only took a few mouthfuls so perhaps he knew more English than we gave him credit for. He didn't leave empty-handed, however, because as he waved goodbye he was chain-smoking a packet of Benson & Hedges that Kessa had given him as a present.

It was the Bombardier's birthday and 'Pa Rug' Graham and Susan baked a cake and some cookies for a celebratory lunch-on-the-run. About 2:00 p.m. the heavy rain turned into a deluge of biblical proportions. The desert was awash with flooding rivulets fording the road. It was almost impossible to see the way ahead but pulling over would have meant bogging *Grunt* to the axles.

To add to the whirl of worries in my head, almost everyone on board was hit with a mystery illness. One-by-one they complained of sickness in the stomach, dizziness, lack of muscle control and shortness of breath. At first I suggested it might be a leaking exhaust resulting in carbon-monoxide poisoning. At the border we pulled up under a large awning, aired the bus, and ensured everyone inhaled as much fresh air as possible, but their condition deteriorated. Perhaps it was food poisoning?

Fortunately I felt okay, but what was I going to do with fifteen stretcher-cases in the middle of the wilderness? In a panicky state, I gathered up all the passports and entered the customs hall. I was standing at the only desk, opposite the immigration officer, when Grilly Wells burst into the room. He was flushed in the face and his chest heaved as he struggled for breath and then with a wild, glazed look in his eyes, he inexplicably stuck one of his feet into the raging fire of the pot-bellied stove that stood in the middle of the hall. I was momentarily stunned at this extraordinary behaviour, but then took a flying leap and crash-tackled Grilly to the ground, rolling over his singed boot to douse the flames. More acts of sheer madness followed until I was sure I was dreaming, or watching some crazy Fellini movie.

It was like rounding up a bunch of loonies who'd escaped from the asylum, but I finally herded everyone on board as they bubbled, gurgled and frothed at the mouth. We were in No-Man's Land, halfway between the Afghani and Pakistani border posts, when *Grunt* finally bogged to the gunwales, refusing to budge another inch. I turned around to watch the demented

In Silk Road Mode – Asia 1975

nutters cartwheeling down the aisle when it struck me what had happened. They were drugged. High as kites. Off their faces. Stoned to the bejesus. They were the victims of either a joke gone horribly-wrong or foul play. For sure, someone had slipped a whacking great lump of hashish into the birthday cookies they'd been feasting on all afternoon. I wondered if ever, anywhere in the world, fifteen people had attempted an international border crossing while they were doped to the eyeballs and behaving like absolute fruitcakes. I suspected we'd just created another little piece of history.

One could hardly believe such a foul day and night could be followed by such a beautiful morning. The sky was a cloudless, brilliant blue and the air breathlessly still. Everyone rose with groggy heads but the symptoms of yesterday's afflictions had completely gone, adding irrefutable proof to the theory that hash was to blame. The culprit(s) must have been on board, but the significance of what they'd done was just dawning on all of us and they were too embarrassed to own up. We might well have ended up in the 'go-slow', never to be seen again.

It took us two hours to dig *Grunt* out of the mud and I was hardly in a state of equanimity when we confronted the Pakistani border guards. These crossings could take forever to complete. The Pakistanis required not one, not two, but seven copies of everything. You learnt one immutable fact when travelling: the more backward the country, the more red tape that entangles it. Whether suspicion had passed around about our drugged behaviour or whether they were just after bribes, I don't know, but they refused to let us go after all the formalities and several exhaustive searches were completed. Finally I gave the senior officer money and when he demanded more, I completely lost it. The Bombardier dragged me away as I hurled abuse at the officer, and he at me, and I just jumped in the cab and drove off. God only knows why he let me go. It was a crazy thing for me to do.

I calmed down as we drove to the first little Pakistani village of Chaman where we stopped for lunch. After all, it was a glorious

Top Deck Daze

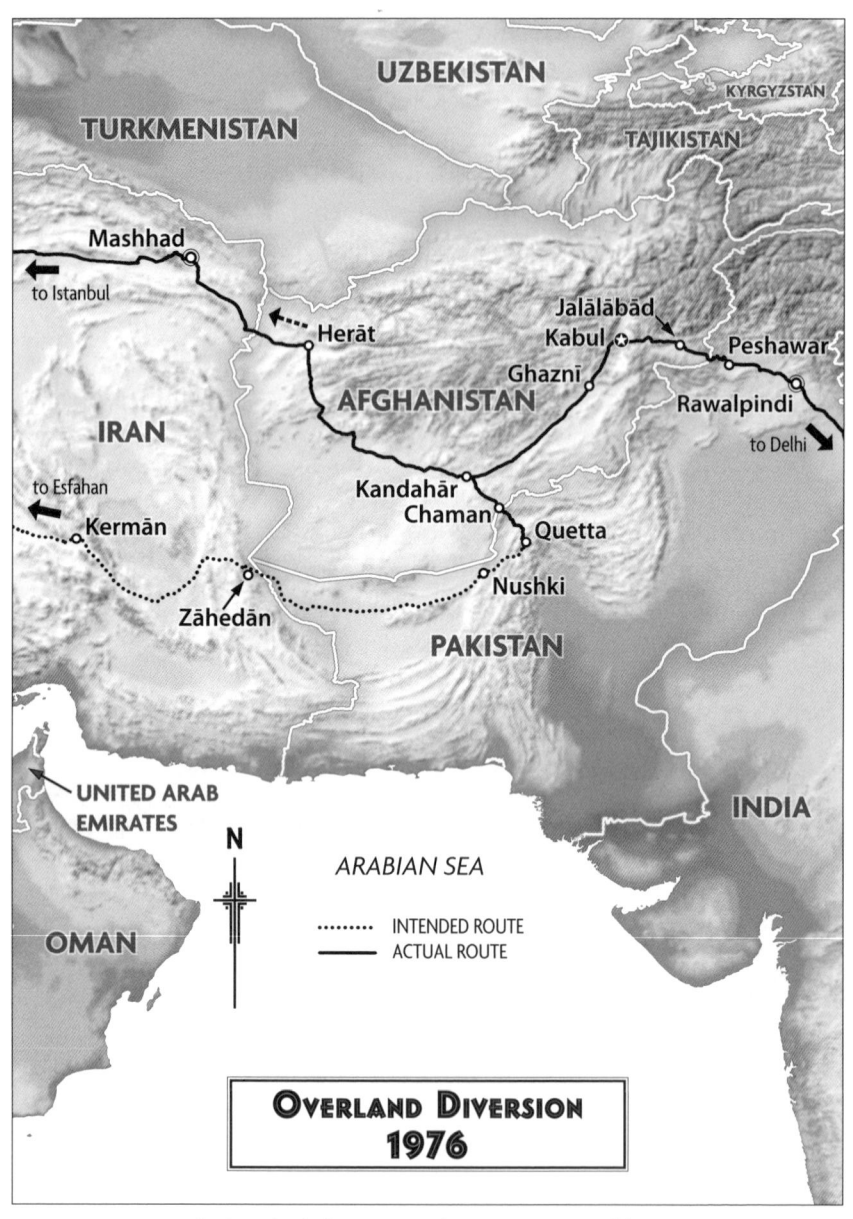

OVERLAND DIVERSION 1976

The best laid plans — our diversion was possibly wise.

In Silk Road Mode – Asia 1975

Woftam *Chitwan National Park 1983.*

day and by rights, I should have been in jail rather than sitting there laughing, sipping sweet tea and munching cake. No sooner had we left the village than the smile on my face was wiped well and truly clean away. The bitumen road simply ended at the edge of a twenty-metre-deep ravine. The road had been washed away. Completely! As far as the eye could see, to the shimmering mountain ranges in the distance, there was nothing—only boggy desert.

We all got out of the bus and peered down into the ravine, gouged by yesterday's floods, then stared into the distance, then looked back at the border posts we'd just come through. No one spoke. There was nothing to say, but we shared the same thoughts. No road ahead, and behind us, an abused Pakistani border guard, and no visas to re-enter Afghanistan.

An hour passed and still I hadn't moved. I just stood there, leaning against *Grunt's* front cowling, gazing into the distance.

'What a pickle. What a bloody pickle,' I kept saying to myself, and, 'Get out of this one, Bill, and you can get out of anything.' The same thought just kept clicking over and over in my mind.

Top Deck Daze

Crunch near Quetta.

The distant sound of an engine gradually brought me back to consciousness. A motor? Definitely, but from where? What kind? It wasn't on a road. There was no road. Where then? A speck in the distance grew larger. A truck? No. A bus! It couldn't be? It was. It wheeled, whined and wound itself over the boggy desert ground, going like the clappers. Pakistanis out the doorways ... Pakistanis out the windows ... Pakistanis, goats, and chickens, clinging to the roof for dear life. I simply couldn't believe it. I looked at the bus as it careered towards me, then looked down at the ravine, then back at the bus again.

'Okay, smart aleck,' I said to no one, 'You've come this far, but get over that (nodding at the ravine) and I'll really be impressed.'

The bus heaved, reared up, and then fairly plunged into the ravine at breakneck speed with ten ... twenty ... no, seventy Pakistanis at least, jumping out as it did so, completely lining the sides and rear of the bus as they manhandled it, yelling and screaming, without the slightest loss of momentum, up the nearside and over the lip of the road beside me. More yelling and screaming saw them back on board in the twinkling of an eye and off down the road they roared in a wheel-spinning spray of gravel and mud. I was more than impressed. I was awestruck.

In Silk Road Mode – Asia 1975

The Pakistani bus terminated at Chaman, within walking distance of where we stood. An hour later Grilly Wells and I were passengers on the same bus, heading in the opposite direction from which it had come, but to where we had originally intended to go, that is, over the mountains to the town of Quetta. We left the Bombardier in charge of *Grunt* and the other passengers, but we took all their passports with us. There was an embassy in Quetta where we could get visas, we hoped, so that we could return to Afghanistan. I was grateful Grilly had decided to join me. If I were General Custer at Little Bighorn, the last soldier I'd want standing with me would be Grilly.

Grilly and I travelled over open desert to the mountains where part of the road remained relatively intact but in other sections, nothing existed and we too became experts in the crazy pushing and shoving up impossible gradients, often failing and jumping clear of the bus as it spun in 360° circles to the bottom of massive gorges or mountain sides. The bus would then reverse a couple of kilometres or so to take another flying start as we stood halfway up the slopes, ready to rejoin the frantic pushing.

This region of Baluchistan was so remote that the Pakistani Government chose it, in later years, as the location for their nuclear-testing program. The Baluchis themselves were fierce, independent tribespeople whose kingdoms, or *mirdoms,* paid scant heed to the distant authorities in Karachi or Islamabad. There was no sign of police or law and order of any description. Men in the villages roamed the streets carrying long rifles and pistols of all shapes and sizes, with bandoliers of bullets slung crosswise over their shoulders. Except for their *shalwar kameez,* their baggy trousers and long shirts, and their turbans, it was a scene straight out of a Wild West movie.

We got the Afghani visas (with seven photos and seven application forms per person) in Quetta, having spent a whole day scouring the marketplace buying US dollars, as the embassy would accept nothing else.

Top Deck Daze

The ten hours of torture constituting the return bus ride to Chaman were punctuated by two acts of sheer madness. The first was mine. Grilly and I were cramped on piles of luggage at the rear of the bus with countless Baluchis. A precocious ten-year-old boy perched himself opposite me, just centimetres from my face, pulling faces and making irritating noises—annoying me as much as he possibly could, to see how I'd react. This went on for several hours until, finally, he elicited a response from me, but not the one he had expected—I gave him a healthy smack across his face. The knife-wielding, gun-toting, Baluchi elders glowered at us with such ferocity that Grilly reckoned he could almost feel the touch of cold steel on his throat. We held our breaths in the face of their ferocious, menacing glares, fearing for our very lives, until something of a smile broke out on one of the Baluchi's faces, as if he agreed with my disciplinary actions with the boy, and the tension of the moment, fortunately, passed.

The second act of absolute madness was by the Baluchi bus driver. Coming down the 2300 metre Khojak Pass at midnight, he caught sight of a white wolf in his headlights and raced it down the mountainside to wild cheers of encouragement from all the passengers, with the exception of Grilly and me cringing among the luggage, daring a peep every now and then as we careered like a luge down the icy, snow-covered road. The Man From Snowy River had nothing on this Baluchi dude.

Money talks a thousand languages and can settle a thousand arguments and, on 21 February 1976, we bribed our way back into Afghanistan for the third time. It took us a week to cross Iran and as we climbed up to the plateaus of eastern Turkey, past Mount Ararat of Noah's Ark fame, just below the Caucasus Mountains, we approached 4000 metres above sea level. The snow and ice had never left us but at this altitude, in the dead of winter, the cold was like nothing we'd ever experienced. The mercury dropped to minus 40° Celsius. It was almost impossible to function in these extremes. Fruit and vegetables turned into cricket balls. Water froze like wax dripping from a candle. Gas,

In Silk Road Mode – Asia 1975

Passing beautiful Mount Ararat where some believe Noah's Ark is to be found.

used for cooking, froze in the bottle. Toothpaste froze. Everything froze. Nothing worked.

We made a huge bed of mattresses downstairs with everyone huddled together and piled every available sleeping-bag and blanket on top of us in the hope that our body heat, fuelled by trouser coughs caught between the covers, would provide us with a semblance of warmth.

Not only was cooking impossible, we couldn't melt the ice to even drink! If there was no roadhouse or village at which to stop, we simply starved. We discovered the only way to get water, other than eating snow, was to locate a frozen creek, smash a hole in the ice with a hammer, and drink from a cup. It was pointless taking water with us because it would freeze in seconds.

We daren't stop old *Grunt* for fear we'd never get her going again. If we turned the motor off it would freeze and there was only one way of restarting it, a technique we learnt by observing the locals. You filled a tray or upturned garbage tin lid with sawdust, doused it in diesel, and set it ablaze. You then slid the fire under the engine and baked it, then slid it along the fuel lines, then left it to burn under the fuel tank itself. Diesel fumes,

Top Deck Daze

Göreme Valley, Cappadocia, Turkey.

unlike petrol, won't explode but nevertheless I could never quite get used to the sight of a raging fire under poor old *Grunt's* fuel tank for fear some mishap would blow the old girl sky high, so the Bombardier and I decided to drive in shifts around the clock.

At 3:00 a.m. one morning there was a delay due to a truck accident. Everyone else on board was sound asleep and I'd had nothing to drink for ten hours and was absolutely parched. I left the motor running, grabbed a hammer, and plunged into the snowdrifts beside the road, five metres deep, totally unaware that the ground fell away that steeply. I struggled to firmer ground and stumbled a hundred metres in search of a creek — I could hear it below the ice. I drank like a madman you see in the movies, only they're always lost in the desert, never in the snow!

On my way back to *Grunt*, still in the dead of night, the snow started to fall again and I disappeared over my head in the deep

In Silk Road Mode – Asia 1975

drift as I tried to make my way up the steep banks to the road. It was like quicksand. The more I thrashed about, the deeper I sank. God only knows how long I was down there—more than an hour at least. I was genuinely in a state of collapse when I finally reached the road. Had I failed to make it, I'd have simply vanished without trace. There'd have been no sign of me at dawn under the fresh snow. A frozen mummy would have been found by the side of the road in springtime, unidentifiable, and forever forgotten.

As we neared Erzurum, poor *Grunt* couldn't take it any longer. We'd mixed petrol with the diesel to lower its freezing point but it had the consistency of treacle and the motor just died on us. We tried to empty the water and antifreeze from the cooling system but we were too late and it froze and split the engine block like the lid off a can of sardines. I'd always been told that that was the end of a motor. You couldn't weld cast-iron because it would still be porous. You threw the motor away and got another one. Normally I'd have panicked in such a situation but after all we'd been through, I knew there'd be a way.

We got a tow into a small village called Pasinler. For everyone on board, except the Bombardier and me, the breakdown

Resourceful crews used various towing devices including an army M113.

Top Deck Daze

became the highlight of the trip. They spent countless hours in the one-and-only coffee house, by its raging open fire, drinking and eating to their fill, chatting to the locals in sign language or whiling away their time in the local Turkish baths — women in the mornings, men in the afternoons. On the odd occasion I visited the baths, I couldn't recall a more luxuriously indulgent experience. I literally wallowed in the piping hot pools or the hissing steam rooms, only to walk outside again to find my hair and beard frozen in seconds on the walk back to the mechanic.

The mechanic's shed was the size of an average suburban garage. *Grunt's* motor was thawed under a flaming fire, welded and patched with some form of strange glue while, in the meantime, we rebuilt the radiator and cooling system by hand from scraps we found in the shed. After five anxious days, old *Grunt* roared into life again — not perfectly, but enough to get us underway. After four days of non-stop driving, the Bombardier

'Fairy Chimneys', Cappadocia, Turkey.

In Silk Road Mode – Asia 1975

and I spent another ten hours in Arctic-like conditions, hands blue with frostbite and knuckles skinned to the bone, repairing the fuel pump and pipes, before we had a semblance of full power.

On the last day of March 1976, we crossed the English Channel, two weeks overdue. The overland was the most incredible experience of my life; a turning point in so many ways. It changed my views of the world, for the worse my friends would say, as I'm far less tolerant of third-world troubles, and paranoid about what I see as the ruination of our world, especially our Australian landscape. I became a rabid environmentalist and supporter of zero, better-still negative, population growth. I had been totally shattered by the devastation and rape of the countryside I'd observed from Calais to Calcutta. Flora and fauna had been totally exterminated in most countries while much of the route had covered vast tracts of once-fertile land that now lay as barren and bare as the planets that circle above us. Mankind was in plague proportions but seemed oblivious of this and its crimes of pollution. We pink and brown rats continue our hellbent destruction of the last remaining vestiges of the natural environment, keen to pass on lands and seas of human excrement to our future generations. Friends still dread my company at dinner parties when I get going on the subject after a few red wines.

More importantly, the overland changed my character. I'd lost my cool so many times I was embarrassed at the recollection of it, but I realised that all my cursing and fits of threatened violence had got me nowhere. Yet every problem I'd encountered had a solution, often falling into my lap from the most unexpected quarter. It took years for the full impact of the experience to seep into my consciousness, but I felt as if nothing I undertook in the future would ever seem to be such a big deal.

Top Deck Daze

L to R: Dennis O'Toole, Spike Cawthorn, Neil Armstrong, Kerry Ware, Moose Maloney, Tom the Pom, Dennis Brown Kenton, 'Weasel', Mario Bowman

The encounter with an elephant was on the Grand Trunk Road in India near Varanasi, the bus was Knackers but without Top Deck name on side since she left London at short notice.

PART 2
Things are getting bigger

Chapter 6

DOUBLING THE DECKERS

(LONDON 1976)

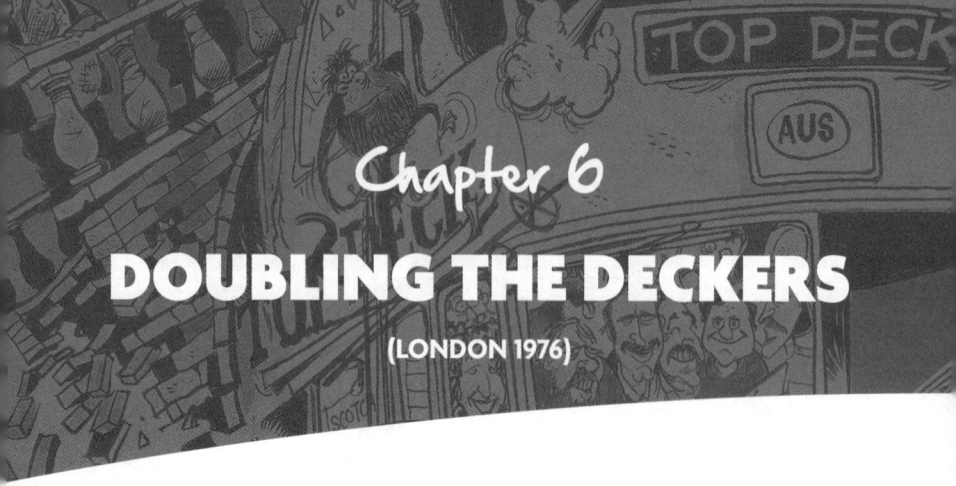

The overland represented the fulfilment of my own travel ambitions up to that particular time. Top Deck had reached a turning point. We only had three buses. We had seen and done so much and we could call it quits and still be completely satisfied with our achievements. We could return to a 'normal' life in Australia and pursue a 'normal' career. To expand from here meant that Top Deck would become a medium-to-large business, necessitating a total commitment from us for the foreseeable future. Holidaying in London was one thing. Working there full-time and forgoing an Australian lifestyle was quite another. Surely Screw wouldn't have studied so long and so hard to throw up a career in vet science? And what about me? Was there really a future in driving double-decker buses to the four corners of the Earth? What should we do? I contemplated these vexed questions in the mentally idle hours behind the wheel of *Grunt* as we headed towards London during the last few weeks of the overland.

If Screw suffered any such moments of vacillation, they were fleeting. I should have known. I'd always approached such situations with an archaic 'career-prospect' point of view, fretting over the pros and cons. Not so Screw. The whole thing was a game as far as he was concerned. His typical approach was, 'You're having fun, aren't you? Well, just do it.'

Prophetically, it was April Fools' Day 1976 when, on returning to London, I discovered that as far as Top Deck's future was

Doubling the Deckers – London 1976

concerned, the die had been well and truly cast. First, to *Argas*, *Tuft* and *Grunt*, new siblings had been born. Quadruplets, in fact, christened with the endearing names of *Snort*, *Snot*, *Slug* and *Belch*. For the third time, Screw had made what was to become a regular pilgrimage for us, to 'W. Norths' in Leeds. He had acquired a 'job lot': four double-decker buses for £1000. Our fleet more than doubled overnight. Just as importantly, we had taken possession of our very first shop and office, at 18 Dawes Road, Fulham, London.

The Hansom Cab in West Kensington was a regular hangout for many of the travel-industry people we'd come to know. One fellow we'd met there was a South African Jappie, Peter Baily, who with his brother Tim, ran an African overland company called 'Siafu'. 'Siafu' was the name of an African soldier ant. This was a similar idea to our 'Argas Persicus' turkey tick, but a tad more exotic and appropriate given the nature of their expeditions. Someone had joked that perhaps one day, 'Our turkey tick would go and eat their soldier ant.' It didn't work out exactly that way but our paths certainly crossed more than once.

Not only did we have buses and clients, but we had our first premises in London, at 18 Dawes Road, Fulham. Grilly Wells, Screw's mum, Iris (centre) and Kessa Ware.

Top Deck Daze

Siafu was operating long-wheel-based Land Rovers, carrying only a handful of passengers per vehicle. Business was tough enough as it was but when the price of oil doubled overnight in 1974, it was sufficient to put some of the smaller operators out of business. Siafu struggled on for a while but eventually was one of the casualties and it was their office we took over at Dawes Road. It was perfect for us, fully fitted-out with nothing further to be done.

Better still was the large amount of accommodation over three floors available for the overflow from Mablethorpe Road which had witnessed an endless parade of friends and acquaintances traipsing through the place, calling it home and just dossing on the floor. Mablethorpe Road was so crowded it wasn't a question of whether you got a bed; the place was full when you couldn't find a space to roll out your sleeping-bag. Suitcases lined both upstairs and downstairs hallways and the stairs, end-to-end. The situation was chronic.

Unfortunately it wasn't long before Dawes Road reached a similar state of overcrowding to Mablethorpe Road. Screw had triple-decker bunks built into the basement rooms, à la Top Deck buses. Not a square inch of space was wasted. A good night's sleep was an impossibility. Liz and I had to share the crowded rooms with everyone else. All the bunks at Dawes Road were quickly snaffled and I inherited the only unoccupied one. I soon discovered why. It was underneath a chute where, in earlier days, the building had received its supplies of coal. Dave 'Dinga' Evans, our ex-overland passenger, and his friends, would roll a dozen empty cans down the chute in a nerve-wrenching jangle after the last of the late-night wine bars finally closed its doors — just desserts for anyone wimpish enough to be in bed by 1:00 a.m.

Another eccentric, Joe 'Jag' Coelli, another of Mick Carroll's Leeton mates, knew the lines of every Monty Python script ever written and could quote them verbatim. Most nights, until 3:00 or 4:00 a.m., we were treated to a soliloquy as Jag paced sleeplessly up and down the kitchen reciting sketch after sketch.

Doubling the Deckers – London 1976

Finally, after a thousand disturbances, the populace might drift into some semblance of sleep only to thrust bolt upright in bed at the crack of dawn, awoken by the piercing shrill of a 'Kook-kook-kook-kook-kook' kookaburra call—a 'goodbye' from one of the mechanics off to work at our bus yard.

One major advantage of Dawes Road's location was its proximity to the Fulham Baths. For just a few pence you could luxuriate in the biggest of hot baths or the most ample of showers with large, warm, fresh-smelling towels to dry yourself down; a rarity in a country not noted for its love of personal ablutions.

One of the first residents to have made the move from Mablethorpe to Dawes Road was Ann Neeley's pet, Top Cat, aka TC. Ann was to be our first employee in the new office. TC was looking decidedly ill one night, hardly able to drag herself around. Her Whiskas and milk lay untouched on the basement

Joe Jag, Rev Head & Ackko.

Top Deck Daze

landing. Screw-the-vet was called on to give her a thorough check-up. The diagnosis? Gastroenteritis. The prognosis? Dry cat food for a day or two till the bug passed through her system. Next day TC went missing for a whole twenty-four hours. Poor Ann began to fret. Had the vet failed to identify a much more sinister ailment? Would TC be seen alive again? Ann was just mounting a neighbourhood search when the muffled sound of miaowing was heard from a cupboard under the stairs. It was TC okay, but she wasn't alone. Her six little newborn kittens were suckling away and TC was calling for some milk of her own. Some case of gastroenteritis! At least Screw-the-vet could rest assured that Top Deck Travel was indeed the correct career change for him.

The camping-tour industry, of which we were now very much a part, fell into two main camps — on the one hand the bigger European operators, and on the other the more adventurous African/Asian overlanders. The personalities were also divided. There were the English who usually saw their business as a purely commercial way of making (or losing) money. Michael Wood-Power ran Penn Overland. He publicised the fact that he came 'from a well-known family of Birmingham grocers', as if this lent some solidity and pedigree to the company. Vernon Reid owned Continental Camping Tours (CCT), though it was managed by a Kiwi, Geoff Phillips. Jeremy James, from the Midlands, established the very professional and successful Trek America and later established Trek Europa. Brian Lewis' Indigo, on the other hand, went to the wall when he was jailed for smuggling hashish. Paddy Garrow-Fisher's Indiaman was the first Asian overlander. Tentrek, Centrek and Minitrek were among the first European camping-tour operators. A company called Suntrek, based in Brighton, specialised in North Africa and used old double-decker buses with their roofs cut off, but they left the seats in the bus and camped in tents.

Then there was a whole raft of colonials, often motivated more by a sense of adventure than commerce. One of the first was a

Doubling the Deckers – London 1976

South African, Peter Hilne, with Protea Tours. Ken Brimmer ran Pacesetter. Ian Taylor, a Kiwi, Fred Shrive, a South African, and Mike Lloyd, formed Autotours which was managed by Vic Beck and later Graham Thomas. They carried tens of thousands of Australians, most of whom passed through the London Walkabout Club run by our Aussie friend, Bevan Aldridge.

Some operators were very professional and hugely successful like the Kiwi John Anderson, founder of Contiki. Others were major players for a while. Ian Johnson's Transit was the biggest operator before Contiki. Australians Brian Powell, Ron James and Kirk Cummins established Sundowners. Warren Sandral formed Nord-Afric Travel (NAT). Travers Cox ran Explore Worldwide. Lenny Howe, an ex-British SAS officer, established Vikings while fellow South Africans Peter and Tim Baily ran Siafu and Dick Cijffers ran Capricorn. Other prominent names were Norm Harris' Asian Greyhound and Merv Hannah's Atrek as well as Adventure International, Atlas Expeditions, Continental Greyhound, Exodus, Encounter, Frontier, Frontiercamp, Geoff Sturken Travel (GST), Hughes, Intertrek, Land Line, Mikes Treks, Nomad, Panther, Rene Dee Expeditions, Swagman, Transtrek, Trek and Tracks.

With seven buses and a London office, Top Deck had come of age. It was now a serious player competing with forty other operators, carrying a combined total of 50 000 passengers a year with a total turnover of £5 million per annum.

RAGS in Morocco

CRUNCH with WOFTAM

SNOT flooded Bridge India

PLATT COLOSSEUM

PIG PEN Paris

GRUNT Greece

BELCH at Carlsberg Brewery in Denmark

Chapter 7

THE SEVENTH OF THE SEVENTH

(PAMPLONA 1976)

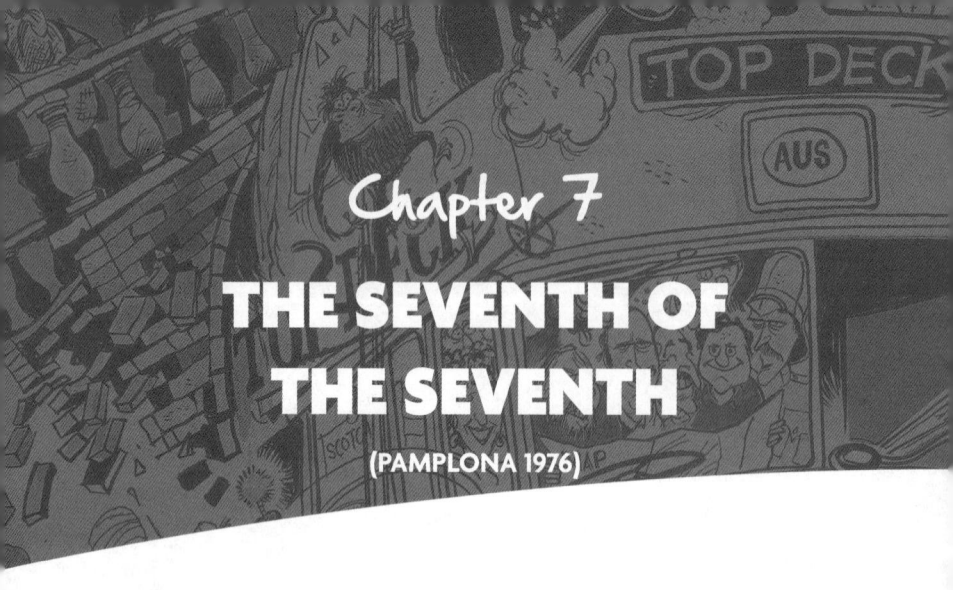

During 1976 an increasing stream of friends we'd known in Australia made contact with us in London. After all, we had what every budget-conscious traveller wanted in a new country—cheap digs in the centre of town and the prospect of cheaper travel to further foreign fields.

By far the most memorably eccentric of these visitors was a friend of Screw and Spy's called John Palm. Like Screw and Spy, he'd graduated in veterinary science at the University of Queensland but unlike them, he had continued to work in various practices around the UK. He invariably spent the breaks between his locum jobs at Dawes Road and so we had the opportunity to become good friends.

Palm was tall, lean and handsome, despite a thin, angular face and a rather prominent nose. He had a constant, mischievous grin and a mop of brown, collar-length hair that made him look like a cross between Mick Jagger and Lassie. John's purpose in life was to exhibit the most outrageous or unexpected behaviour in what might otherwise be described as 'normal' situations. The mundane boorishness of most people's lives was anathema to John. Normality was the enemy, something to be rooted out and smashed at every available opportunity.

Most people, even those among our own circle of friends, regarded this as nothing more than a gross example of attention-

The Seventh of the Seventh – Pamplona 1976

seeking behaviour, bordering on the psychotic. No doubt they were correct. But I, for one, was one of Palm's greatest fans. To me, he was an hilarious, walking, one-man show. I suppose his outrageous behaviour was a mirror-image-opposite of my own conservative character, hence his immediate appeal. I laughed uproariously at his antics which, of course, spurred him on to even greater extremes.

As a consequence of John's ongoing employment and hefty salary, he was always awash with money, just like all the Aussie dental fang-farriers we knew in London who made squillions by exploiting the National Health Service up to, and sometimes beyond, its legal limits ('Bash the Nash', as they called it). Palm drove a succession of the latest model cars like Aston Martin DB4s and XJ6 Jaguars, drank champagne at pubs when we drank beer, and always ate out. He was incredibly generous with his money and so, being a shocking tight-arse myself in those days, it provided me with another reason to seek his company.

There was only one area of Palm's behaviour of which I genuinely disapproved, indeed avoided at all costs, and that was his driving. To be a passenger of Palm's was one of the world's most harrowing experiences. Most people only ever accompanied him on one or two car trips in their life, me included. My first unsuspecting ordeal occurred when he gave me a lift to Heathrow to meet some friends arriving at Terminal Three. As far as John was concerned, the shortest distance between two points was a straight line, so he drove straight through roundabouts as opposed to around them, and over, across or along gardens, nature strips or footpaths, mattering little if they were crowded with pedestrians.

When we encountered a traffic snarl on Kensington High Street, John immediately turned right, across the oncoming traffic, into the pedestrian gates of Holland Park, across the park lawns, through the flowerbeds of the King George VI Memorial Gardens, and out the gates onto Holland Park Road, straight across the Holland Park roundabout and, finally, to my relief,

Top Deck Daze

to the relative safety of the barricaded A40. During the entire episode, he continued a casual, one-sided conversation on his exploits of the previous evening, hardly drawing breath, as I crouched below the dashboard in shock.

Months later, perhaps having suppressed the horror, or perhaps because I thought it may have simply been a bad day for Palm's chemical balance, Screw, some friends, and Liz and I, agreed to accompany him on a Sunday lunch trip to the country. We were chatting as he drove along in the heavy traffic on the Great West Road, still in the suburbs, when suddenly he pretended to take offence at some innocuous remark Screw had made.

'Okay. That's it,' said Palm, stopping the car, turning off the motor, locking the door, and storming off in the opposite direction while we sat there, speechless, stranded in the middle lane. After a delay suitably long enough to cause a major traffic snarl, Palm reappeared from nowhere and without a word, continued driving on our country sojourn.

The main street of the small but bustling town where we were to have lunch happened to have been made into a pedestrian mall. These were not common in Australia at the time and I could tell immediately that Palm, when he saw it, simply couldn't help himself. As our red Jag wended its way, slowly thankfully, along the market-stalled mall, barrow-keepers yelled abuse as they were gently nudged into their barrows of bananas or whatever and next, a rack of second-hand clothes collapsed on its seller, and so on, until we pulled up and parked in the middle of the mall in front of a typical English pub advertising ploughman's lunches.

The rest of us hurriedly slunk into the pub while Palm emerged slowly from his driver's seat, raised himself to his full height of six foot three and with a wide grin of satisfaction, surveyed the trail of chaos he had created.

As we hoed into our fresh cheese-and-chutney rolls and jars of Guinness, the police pushed open the front door of the pub.

'All right then, who owns this red Jag out here?'

The Seventh of the Seventh – Pamplona 1976

'He does,' we said in chorus, pointing at Palm.

Palm rose immediately and with a willing, lilting step, strode off with the police.

On his return to the pub, three-quarters of an hour later, Palm explained that he'd told the police he'd been brought up on a sheep station near Oodnadatta (he'd never been there in his life) and that he was terribly sorry, but he'd never seen a main street pedestrian mall before and had no idea you weren't suppose to drive down them. He finished his lunch with relish and it was obvious he would rest peacefully that night, secure in the knowledge that he'd had a most worthwhile day.

It was little wonder, therefore, that I broke out with a quivering case of the heebie-jeebies on receiving the news that Palm would be a passenger on my next trip, an eleven-dayer, departing on 3 July 1976, to Pamplona, Spain, for 'the running of the bulls'. Nevertheless, the trip was bound to be a good one. Just about everyone Liz and I knew in London at the time would be there,

Pamplona featured on the cover of our 1976/77 brochure. Grunt *(left) and* Argas.

including Stephanie, Rod and Di McEwin, Kessa Ware, and Ann Neeley, either with me and Mark Sullivan on *Grunt*, or with Rex Julian on *Snort*, or with Screw, who was due to leave a day earlier for Morocco on *Argos* but was going to Pamplona first.

We spent the first night in Paris and happened to have on board a young French girl, Francoise. Having just graduated from the Sorbonne, she was having a short holiday before settling into an English language college in London. Instead of frequenting the bars below Montmartre where we usually drank, Francoise suggested we go to the Latin Quarter near the university. She knew some genuine student hangouts off the Boulevard Saint-Michel. We readily agreed. Our previous visits there had been disappointing as it appeared to be nothing more than a tourist rip-off. Francoise explained that after the student riots of 1968, the university campus had been decentralised and consequently, most of the area's traditional bohemian and student inhabitants and their attendant bars and cafés had disappeared, forever altering the quarter's original character.

We had a fantastic night out and on returning to the bus, a party raged on board till the early hours of the morning by which time we were well south of Paris. Fortunately for me, Mark Sullivan had agreed to drive that night so I was able to join in the festivities.

Francoise had surprised me totally since joining the trip. She seemed to be a really well-educated young girl from a well-to-do Parisian family, but she used the foulest vocabulary imaginable, at least in English. She would come down to breakfast in the morning, for example, and say, 'Oh, I am zo hungry zis morning, I would love to suck a …,' or something equally vulgar. It got to be so bad that many of the other girls began to avoid her, wondering what on Earth possessed her to behave like that.

It didn't take me long to twig what was happening. Francoise was very attractive and consequently, as soon as she'd walked onto the bus she had been befriended by Palm. Palm was an aspiring French-speaker and as Francoise's aim during the next

The Seventh of the Seventh – Pamplona 1976

three months was to immerse herself in the English language, the two of them struck a contra deal. Palm would teach her English if she would teach him French. They ensconced themselves for hours alone on the front seat upstairs, deep in conversation. But of course, Francoise was getting the rough-end of the pineapple. While she was endeavouring to teach Palm perfect vocabulary and pronunciation, he was teaching her the crudest of ocker slang that would have made a shearer blush. So when Francoise, poor thing, had asked to 'suck a you-know-what', she probably thought she was asking for a bowl of cornflakes, or the like.

Francoise was eventually rescued, however, by another of our passengers, Ian Patrick, one of Screw's Aussie fang-farrier mates whom we'd befriended in London. Ian was also learning French and, thankfully, replaced Palm as her English teacher, which greatly improved the standard of her English vocabulary.

The tables were unintentionally turned on Palm when we went shopping for food and drinks during a brief stopover in Bordeaux. One of the girls had a head cold and bad nosebleed, and so wanted some tissues. Ian and Palm, playing the fluent interpreters, practised their translation, walked into what looked like a chemist shop and in their best French, said, 'Is this a pharmacy? Could we have some tissues, please? Someone has a bloody nose?' The pharmacist and his assistant collapsed on the floor writhing with laughter and after several minutes, were still incapable of serving the grossly embarrassed Ian. Palm, of course, knew he'd done something brilliant but for once, couldn't figure out what it was.

On repeating to Francoise what they had said to the chemist, she too rolled on the ground for several minutes before explaining that what they had actually said was, 'Is this a farm here? Could we have some tampons, please? Someone has a monkey up their nose.' 'Pharmacy' was mistaken for 'ferme ici'. Tampons are often referred to as 'serviettes', and the words for 'monkey' and 'blood' are very similar. Fortunately for all concerned, this put an end to the language laboratory on board the bus.

Top Deck Daze

Our plan had been to rendezvous with Screw and Rex on the other two buses in San Sebastian in northern Spain, spend the night there, and head on to Pamplona together the following day. Because of the excessive revelry en route, we were running well behind schedule. I happened to be driving as we passed through the French/Spanish border after midnight. I knew I would need Spanish pesetas that night to buy fuel and as all the money exchanges at the border were long-since closed, I kept an eye open for a hotel reception that might be willing to change my travellers' cheques. I spied a likely establishment and pulled the bus over.

The on-board party was still in full swing and I turned around and yelled to Mark above the screeching of the stereo, explaining what I was doing. He nodded, and I left the lights on and the motor running while I raced into the hotel foyer. No problems. They were willing to make their commission and within two minutes, I was back in the driver's cab. I turned again to Mark to ask if it was okay to go. He did a cursory, three-second head count, gave me the thumbs up, and I dropped the clutch and motored off in the direction of San Sebastian.

The road was long, straight and empty, and so I had *Grunt* on full revs. I'd been going a good ten minutes when suddenly Mark was shaking me by the shoulder and yelling at me to slow down and pull over. Mark had just been going up the rear stairwell of the bus when he saw one arm, then another, and then a head and upper body, coming through the top rear window. I screeched to a halt and was out and around the back in seconds, just in time to see a pair of boots disappear inside the top window. Darting around to the main door, I was confronted by the sight of Palm sliding down the stairwell headfirst.

When I had driven off from the hotel, Palm had been relieving himself against the back of the bus. As the bus pulled away, he'd run along behind, yanking up his fly, and, with a desperate lunge, grabbed hold of the spare wheel that was fixed to the rear panel. Over the next few kilometres he'd managed to drag himself up

The Seventh of the Seventh – Pamplona 1976

onto the wheel housing and into a standing position, open the emergency handle, and lever himself up, and into, the top rear window. How on Earth anyone could do this when the bus was stationary was beyond me, but at eighty kilometres an hour it defied imagination.

There was no point in me apologising or asking if he was okay because, by the time I had recovered from the shock, he'd resumed his seat opposite Francoise and was jabbering away in incoherent French.

It was too late for us to go to the Parte Vieja, the old city of San Sebastian, where the bars and restaurants cluster, and where we had agreed to meet Screw. Even our hardiest of passengers was glad when we pulled into the campsite for the night, located the other two Top Deck buses, parked next to them, and went straight to sleep.

Late the next morning, the three buses set out together, climbing up the narrow, winding road to the Navarra region of the Pyrenees Mountains, Basque territory, en route to the lovely old city of Pamplona. The passengers had all congregated over breakfast and intermingled on different buses as we set out. I was driving *Grunt*, bringing up the rear of the convoy. Palm had moved onto the second bus and was drinking with a group of friends standing at the back. He ducked his head out of the rear side door and waved at me, holding up his can of beer in a mock toast. I waved in acknowledgement. This routine continued over the next several kilometres with Palm, on each successive occasion, protruding further and further until, finally, hanging on with one hand and foot only, his whole body was out the door, and he waved his free arm and leg. Each time I was obliged to wave, laugh, and nod my approval of his antics.

I can only assume he felt the audience reaction had not been up to his expectations because Act Two consisted of him, beer can clenched in teeth, clambering inch by inch around the outside rear of the bus, fingers and toes perilously clutching the narrowest of railings, till he reached the rear wheel housing — for

Top Deck Daze

the second time in twenty-four hours. Securing one arm and leg as best he could, he swung around to face me, and again raised his can in salute. Again I laughed, nodded my approval, and waved salutations.

No sooner had Palm regained the safety of the rear platform when I saw a figure fall backwards, straight out the door.

His bus was negotiating a right-hand bend and, being an English right-hand-drive on the right side of the road (as they drive on the Continent), and an old-model Lodekka with a rear stairwell, the passenger door was open to the middle of the roadway. So not only did Palm hit the bitumen at between fifty and sixty kilometres an hour, he did so into the path of the oncoming traffic.

A Fiat swerved viciously to avoid him, nearly rolling in the loose gravel as it did so. Palm, beer can still firmly in hand, hit the road on his backside, bounced three or four feet into the air, rolled once or twice, and landed on his feet with a slight swagger and a swig of his drink. I was travelling a good six bus-lengths behind and so only had to break gently as I drew level with him. He swung himself into the doorway of my bus, stumbled up the aisle, slumped into a seat and immediately engrossed himself in conversation with Francoise's group. The whole episode had taken all of five seconds. No one else, other than the Fiat driver who presumably, like I, was suffering heart palpitations, was even aware of what had happened. If anyone from the bus that he fell from was missing him, they certainly didn't acknowledge it.

We stopped at the top of a wooded pass to catch our first sight of Pamplona, set on a plateau rising from a plain at the foothills of the Pyrenees. The orange city walls, the cathedral and church spires and assorted buildings bedecked with multicoloured flags and bunting, set against a sky turning deep blue from the approaching sunset, provided a magnificent panorama. Charlemagne, Ignatius Loyola and Hemingway had all seen the city for the first time from this very spot.

The Seventh of the Seventh – Pamplona 1976

The seventh hour of the seventh day of the seventh month heralds the start of the feast of San Fermin. The good saint became the patron of Pamplona when, 500 years before, he was martyred by being dragged by bulls through the city streets. Every year since then, the eight-day festival commemorates his memory with the *encierro*, the 'running of the bulls'.

The *sanferministas*, 'the runners', race huge, sharp-horned bulls through the barricaded streets of the old town to the Plaza de Toros. The action continues there with smaller steers with

Top Deck Daze

padded horns charging through the ranks of the now-assembled runners in the bullring itself. There could be five or six steers charging in different directions at any one time so while you may skilfully avoid the path of one monster, you are just as likely to step into the path of another. The locals, with a mixture of athleticism, experience, and Latin bravado, taunt the steers, and some even deliberately stand in their way and try and catapult over their heads in much the same way that the ancient Minoans had done in Crete. Others would sit in a triangle, right in front of the gates where the steers came charging into the ring. Bullfights are held every evening.

This is a festival of, and for, the inhabitants. Tourists are welcome, but nothing is staged on their behalf. The festival is more than just the *encierro* itself because every street, alley and square appears to be flooded with singing and dancing locals accompanied by drummers and bands with musical instruments of every conceivable description in a no-holds-barred, twenty-four-hours-a-day party. Everyone wears all-white shirts and pants with, appropriately, blood red berets and scarves.

There was a camping ground some distance outside the city but we wanted to stay close to all the action. Trying to coordinate the comings and goings of our crowd was equally difficult, so Screw and I decided we'd just park the buses beside one of the city's major parks. We managed to rent one room in a cheap hotel nearby so that anyone who wanted could shower or freshen up there. Otherwise everyone came and went as they pleased. Despite the altitude, the nights were too hot for sleeping inside so we just dragged the mattresses from the bus to under the trees in the park and slept there with no hassle from anyone. Oddly enough, one of our punters was arrested later in the week for having his shirt off. With all the crazy things that went on in Pamplona during the fiesta, it was an odd crime to pick on.

In typical continental fashion, the Spanish have long wine-quenched lunches, an afternoon siesta, and then come fully alive again at about ten or eleven in the evening. Many, irrespective of age, carry on throughout the night especially during the hot holiday period. We roamed from bar to bar, eating the tapas and drinking the local wine and sangria. The *Mejillon* Bar (Mussel Bar) became our favourite, only a short distance from the Plaza Castillo. We were familiar with its sister bars in San Sebastian and Bilbao and it became 'home base' for all the colonials in Pamplona. If it was too crowded inside the bar, people just sat in the gutter or on the cobblestoned street, drinking glasses of beer or sangria from enormous paper cups called 'catchi catchi'. Outside festival time, when things weren't so rowdy, the sangria would be served in huge, two-and-a-half litre, vase-shaped glasses. It was meant as a communal drink, to be held in two hands, then passed on to one's companions as a sign of friendship. Mussels, chips and assorted tapas were served in cheesy, white wine or hot chilli sauces. Delicious! Consequently, there were no set times for meals as the clock rolled around its twenty-four hours.

We were urged to go to the small, triangular plaza nearby to watch some crazy colonials try and commit harakari by climbing twenty feet or more up a statued fountain before swallow-diving earthwards in the hope and expectation that their drunken friends would catch them before they broke their necks. The Basques rarely, if ever, participated in these antics and no one knew when or why this definitely 'expat' custom evolved. Of all the nationalities we got to know at the Mussel Bar, the Rhodesian guys were definitely the craziest. The war of independence in their country, the future Zimbabwe, was still at its peak. Most of them had volunteered or been conscripted into the army. They'd seen all the horrors of war, faced death themselves countless times, seen mates killed or mutilated, and now faced the prospect of losing what they considered to be their homeland, their livelihoods, and everything their families had worked for. Doubtless these traumas accounted for the bird-brained buffoonery they exhibited at the fountain and elsewhere we encountered them. Occasionally a Basque would attempt to emulate the colonials' feats but not even the bravest, proudest,

Top Deck Daze

most inebriated local would follow the Rhodesians' number-one trick—diving off the fountain backwards. That really was beyond the Basque pale.

Inevitably, someone would come near to killing themselves and that's exactly what had happened the previous evening, so this night the Guardia Civil kept coming around to stop the craziness and disperse the mob. Everyone would drift away, for a while, but it wasn't long before some recalcitrant was up the fountain again and the brouhaha began all over.

Palm tried to climb the fountain on at least two occasions, but I managed to crash-tackle him and drag him back to the Mussel Bar before he finished off the job he had set out to do by falling off the bus.

The streets were filled with the most insane collection of people: men dressed as giants, walking on stilts with gross papier-mâché heads representing kings, queens, pirates and Moors, accompanied by squat little manikins that stalked the least-suspecting revellers and then squirted them with inflated pigs' bladders. Then there were the bands playing and marching. Bagpipes and drums, fifes and drums, trumpets and drums, bugles, flutes, accordions and oboes, always with drums, drums, and more drums. I don't know what gave the Pamplona drums their enormous power, but they echoed off the mountains and throbbed through the city at any and every hour. They played the *riau-riau* music and behind every band came men and women, and boys and girls, dancing the *jota*. When a band stopped to catch its breath or change tunes, all the dancers would crouch down on the cobblestones and wait in absolute stillness. The second the shrill music or beat of the drums began again they would all leap head and shoulders into the air and off they'd go again, bobbing and cavorting their way down the streets.

Well after midnight, we returned to the central Plaza Castillo where we'd seen a fireworks display earlier in the evening. We found the Aussies had taken over the Tropicana Bar, but I was intent on finding the hotel where Ernest Hemingway had resided when he'd come here fifty years previously to prepare his book The *Sun Also Rises*. After finding some Basques who spoke English, they laughed at my request, grabbed me by the shirt and pulled me into a seat.

'Here, here, Señor. The old hotel of Montoya. This is the very spot. These very chairs and tables are where he sat. Join us. Join us. Drink the wine.' They offered me their *bota,* a large two-litre version of the leather bag, filled with *Rioja* wine—the traditional way of drinking in Spain. I tried but inevitably missed my mouth and received a shower of red down my shirtfront for my troubles.

'Arriba! Arriba! Higher. Higher,' they yelled. The owner of the bota was about to demonstrate when his mate snatched it from him.

'Like this. You watch,' and he stood and held the bag at a full arms-length and, as he squeezed with the palm of his hand, the wine shot out in a long, flat, trajectory, hissing as it hit the back of his mouth and he swallowed in slow, even glugs.

Then the next Basque drank, then the next, all equally skilled. The bag returned, finally, to its owner and he, too, stood to demonstrate before realising it was empty. He sat, slowly and dejectedly, eyeing the nozzle of the bota as he turned it upside down, and watched the leather as it wobbled from side to side and the last drops trickled out. No wine. No demonstration. No kudos. No justice in the world. Such is life.

Soon Liz, Screw, Palm, Ian Patrick and most of the other Top Deckers joined me at the tables. We all mixed among the Basques. I complained to our new-found friends that we had all bought botas to drink from but all we could taste was wine fouled by the tar from the inside of the leather.

'Oh, that's because they are new, of course. First you must fill them with milk,' they explained patiently. 'Leave it in there for a day or two, then wash it out. That will cure it, for sure.'

Every now and then, the band at the rotunda played a song that sounded like the tune of Marty Robbins' song 'El Paso': 'Out

Brian 'Dark Blue' Coubrough was keen to demonstrate his skill with his new bota.

in the west Texas town of El Paso, I fell In love with a Mexican girl …' When it came to the end of the chorus, everyone in the entire plaza leapt onto chairs and tables and threw anything and everything they had high into the air and then tried to catch it as it came down. Drinks, coats, bags, hats. Even the grandmothers nursing baby children hurled them into the air with mutual squeals of delight — an 'all-together' Mexican wave. I guessed it had something to do with the Basque separatist cause. At last, I couldn't contain my curiosity any longer and persuaded my new friends to explain and translate the song. It went:

Eminent Señor Carrero Blanco,
Naval Minister of General Franco,
Had a dream that he might fly,
So the ETA blew him up sky high.

I knew something of the Basque cause. An Aussie friend of mine, Bob Kennedy, had spent the previous winter in San Sebastian and had fallen in love with the town and its people — so

The Seventh of the Seventh – Pamplona 1976

much so that he'd become a surrogate Basque and had regaled me with their stories at every opportunity. On his arrival there, in November 1975, there was delirium, drinking and dancing in the streets.

'What festival are you celebrating today, Señor?' Bob asked an old man, thinking he must have struck it lucky again in that lovely old city.

'Festival? What festival? This is better than any festival, my boy. Have you not heard? He's dead. He's dead.' Then the man grabbed Bob by the arms and waltzed him along the promenade by the beach. It was General Franco, of course, who had died.

Again we were told the Basque story with great fervour and passion as we sat at the tables in the Pamplona plaza. Franco, along with his old ministers like Blanco, had a particular hatred for the Basques of northern Spain. The Basques had sided with the Communist Republicans against Franco's Nationalists during the bitter, brutal Spanish Civil War of 1936–1939. Franco had engaged the German Luftwaffe to bomb, and obliterate, the Basque capital of Guernica in 1938. Guernica became the subject of Picasso's most famous painting. Neither side had forgiven nor forgotten respective atrocities. Thirty-five years of repression followed. The Basques had their own language, history, culture, and their own flag. It was illegal to fly it. Most tourists would have wondered why all the Basque fishing boats and many cars and shops were painted red, white and green. Subtle rebellion! The cruel Guardia Civil and ultra-aggressive Policia Nationale, recruited from the poor south and paid handsomely for their duties of repression, were nicknamed 'the greasers' for their evil acts and murky grey uniforms.

Repression created, as it always will, terrorism, or freedom fighters (depending on what side of the border you were born on), in the form of the ETA (a Basque Separatist organisation). One morning in Madrid, the infamous Carrero Blanco, hater of the Basques, turned on the ignition key of his car. The explosion blew his car and body five storeys into the sky.

Top Deck Daze

We heard many more yarns and enjoyed a most memorable night but by 4:00 a.m., despite the best will in the world, I simply couldn't stay awake any longer. I decided to return to the bus and sleep in the park. My friends bade me good night.

'Buen hombre,' the bota owner said, laying his hand on my shoulder. 'Good luck for the run in the morning.' The run in the morning? Good God, the run! Was that why we were here? Earlier I'd boasted long and hard about my intentions for the following morning. Now my bravado was drowning in a sea of beer and red wine. My last thought as my whirling head hit the mattress was, 'Bugger the run.' There'd be six more days to go. Why kill myself on the first morning?

I would have been happy to sleep till midday but at six-fifteen sharp, I had an insight into what Carrero Blanco must have experienced on that fateful morning in Madrid. I was blasted three metres into the air by the shrill toot of a trumpet, centimetres from my ear. All the bands and drummers were reassembling for the day and they amused themselves by walking through the parks, locating all the sleeping, has-been revellers — creeping up on their prey with a stealth-like tread, putting their trumpets or enormous bass drums next to an unsuspecting ear, then scaring the absolute, living daylights out of their victims.

'Come on. Come on. This is fiesta time, not sleeping time,' my private, terrorist trumpet player cajoled me. It seemed I had no option. Most of us boys found ourselves inside the barricades just before 7:00 a.m. My head was a fuzzy, foggy ball, ears still ringing from the trumpet blast. The Top Deckers had originally intended to run as a group but we were separated in the crush. I looked around for a familiar face but found none. I made my way as best I could along a street called Dona Blanca, away from the corral where the bulls start their run, towards the bullring, so as to make my run as short as possible — not necessarily a good move, so I found out later. There were far more nooks and crannies where you could hide in the early section of the run. Then I had a most sensible thought: 'Why run at all?' I'd only agreed to join in, in the first place, to avoid being called a wimp. Now that no one I knew was in sight, what was the point? Why not just be a spectator like most other sane people?

There was only a minute to go before the mayor let off a rocket, the *chupinazo*, with a sound like a cannon, signalling the start of the run. I attempted to climb the barricade but got the shock of my life when, expecting the locals to help me over and into their midst, they did the exact opposite. A hundred hands pushed me back. I tried to protest but they only laughed and started yelling at me in Spanish and pointing in the direction of the Plaza de Toros. I didn't understand a word they were saying but knew exactly what they meant. It was a rude way to discover the local custom of 'once you've decided to run, you run'—no chickening out at the last minute.

Then 'bang!', dead on seven, off went the rocket and a barbaric howl emanated from the sanferministas, echoed by the yelling and screaming of the spectators, and we all set off at a brisk jog. I reached a corner and turned up Estafeta, a long, narrow and slightly uphill section. After a delay of about thirty seconds, a second rocket sounded. I didn't know what it meant and paid scant regard to it at the time. Pity! It signalled that the bulls hadn't left the corral in a tight herd and would be more strung out, and so would cause more trouble than normal, if that was possible.

There is nothing like the fear of death to clear the mind. A plan crystallised in my now-functioning brain: Run as hard as you can towards the bullring; as soon as any nook appears, be it a doorway, protruding wall or the like, crouch and stay there till the brutes passed, then casually mingle with the throng.

No sooner had I conjured up the thought than just such an empty doorway presented itself to me. I flattened my stomach against its leading edge, with one eye peaking out in the direction of bulls. There was not long to wait. They were enormous brutes. This was no sham. It was unbelievable to see some runners actually waving their red scarves in the faces of the bulls as they bolted past.

Top Deck Daze

'Get out of the way you bloody fools,' I yelled instinctively, unheard above the melee. Then it was over as quickly as it had begun. I breathed deeply and all the muscles in my body relaxed, and just as I took one step into the alley, a running sanferminista tripped and sprawled headlong onto the cobblestones in front of me. Then I heard a cry, 'Otro! Otro! Another! Another!' and caught sight of the last of the toros, galloping along by himself, well to the rear of the pack. The bull almost trampled the prostrate runner before the bull himself had a thought: Why run? He slowed from a gallop to a trot, then stiffened his front legs and skidded to a halt.

Slowly, his head turned and he narrowed his big brown eyes as he focused on his quarry. I don't think the runner was hurt but, whether by training or instinct, he remained perfectly motionless, facedown on the ground with his hands over his head.

The bull turned fully and lowered his head. I'd seen this action in the movies, and caricatured on the Bugs Bunny Show for example, but this fellow's performance was Academy Award-winning stuff. The great lump of muscle on his neck was swollen tight and all his body muscles quivered. He took one or two paces backwards, then forwards, and lowered his head to charge, then inexplicably hesitated and turned his head from side to side to assess his audience ... and who do you think should come fully into his gaze? Me, cowering back in the doorway!

Fight or flight are the options of cornered animals. The former was hardly a consideration and so, again, instinct took over. I caught sight of a streetlight pole, three or four metres away, on the other side of the alley. I ran to it and scaled it with a dexterity that would have amazed me in other circumstances. I wasn't the only one up the pole. My head cushioned the backside of another runner who'd had a similar, but earlier, survival instinct. Minutes seem to pass while the bull dwelt on his options. Finally he lost interest in the fallen runner, turned on his heels, and trotted off in the direction of the yells now emanating from the bullring.

The Seventh of the Seventh – Pamplona 1976

For the first time, I was really conscious of the person on top of me and I now felt as if I was carrying the full weight of his torso. It was time to extricate my head from his primary orifice. I looked up into the face above me and a wide, silly grin covered its visage. 'Hello, Billy,' smiled Palm. 'Fancy meeting you here.'

Top Deck Daze

I'd seen bullfights in Mexico and Barcelona, enough to convince me it was a barbaric sport that should die, and the sooner the better. Bullfights were held every afternoon in Pamplona and in spite of my beliefs, on the fifth day of the fiesta, I found myself accompanying Palm, Screw, Ian Patrick and twenty other Top Deckers en route to the Plaza de Toros. About an hour-and-a-half before the fight, in various parts of the city, ancient Taurus Clubs (Clubs of the Bulls), each with its own distinctive uniform, assembled behind their individual bands. Auditions for the bands obviously placed low priority on musicianship but marked high for noisemaking.

Club members arrived in pairs, carrying large buckets filled with either cans of beer (the modernists), or overflowing with sangria (the traditionalists). They carried large quantities of long, thick, crusty bread-rolls, chockers-full of ham and cheese, wrapped in foil. The clubs marched in wild fashion behind their bands, carrying banners proclaiming their identity. They circulated throughout the city, picking up casual followers as they went who danced along behind. Palm and Screw paired us up with the noisiest, wildest-looking, most inebriated club they could find. The club accepted them like long-lost brothers. They could obviously pick their kin on instinct. By the time we all reached the bullring, hundreds of raucous followers piled into the plaza and sat with their adopted clubs.

Only one rule applied in the bullring: Each band must play as loudly and as long as possible in order to drown out all the others. The cacophony of noise echoing around the arena was so loud they were all championship material as far as I was concerned. In the interval between the second and third bullfights, the sandwich committee stood on their seats at the back row and hurtled all the rolls as high and as wide as possible. If you caught one you could feed three people for days. Then the drinks were passed. The modernists with their beer cans obviously had little trouble, but our mob were definitely sentimentalists—sangria drinkers to the last man and woman—and at least half their

The Seventh of the Seventh – Pamplona 1976

ration was poured over the heads of the crowd sitting below. Palm and Screw were like pigs in their very own sty. When the last of the sangria had been chucked and Palm and his new Basque mates began pissing into the empty sangria buckets, I decided it was time to bid farewell to the last of the poor bulls, so I gave him the thumbs up and retreated to the partial sanity of the Mussel Bar.

On the afternoon of our last day I went to a money exchange to get sufficient cash to cover us for the trip back through France. I also decided to go to the local newspaper office. It had a normal shopfront with windows that were plastered every day with the latest and best photos of the previous day's run. Rumour had it that there had been a death the day before, and some terrible gorings, and I knew the exact spot where it had all happened.

The critical section in the whole run is the narrow tunnel that connects the street to the bullring, near a place they simply call *Telefonos (or* Telephones). There is a slight downhill funnel section just before the tunnel, where runners and bulls are at their fastest, and there is no escape or sanctuary in the tunnel itself. If someone trips or falls, the runners simply crash into one another like a freeway pile-up and if the bulls happen to be just behind, well, it's a disaster, and apparently that's what had happened the previous day.

There were no photos of the pile-up but plenty of the bloody aftermath, and there, in the top right-hand corner of the window, was a photo of Palm and me up the pole. It was unmistakably us. There were the sanferministas, holding themselves back, behind the fallen runner — and the bull, hesitating, trying to decide whether to charge or return to the pack.

The crowd in front of the shop window was five or six deep and we were all straining for a better view of the photos. I was carrying what all road crew carried and referred to as a 'poofter bag' — a leather pouch threaded through my belt in which I had a large wallet containing my passport, bus papers, travellers' cheques and all the trip cash. I had an intuitive feeling something

Top Deck Daze

The bull is just deciding to forget about the fallen runner and to head off to the bullring. I can just be seen climbing up the pole on the right.

was wrong and, looking down, realised that the wallet was gone. The latch was open and the pouch was empty. An awful panicky feeling gripped my stomach. I'd lost everything! What had I done? I stared ahead trying to focus and replay my actions, attempting to recall the moment it could have happened. There were two Spaniards standing right in front of me and I just happened to notice one of them make a furtive glance at his mate. It was a purely gut feeling that this guy had just 'picked my pouch' as one might say. I trusted my instinct, grabbed him by the shoulder, spun him around, clenched my fist and cocked my arm ready to smack him on the nose with all I had. He reeled back with mock innocence, arms and hands extended as if to say, 'What's gotten into this idiot?' His mate adopted a similar pose. Out of the corner of my eye, I saw it, my black wallet, on the ground between their feet. I stared down at it, but still held the would-be thief by the scruff of the neck. Obviously he'd dropped the wallet the instant I'd grabbed him. I loosened my grip and bent down and picked the wallet up. They were gone in a flash. I turned to run after them when someone else in the crowd grabbed me by the collar and swung me around.

The Seventh of the Seventh – Pamplona 1976

It was a strong, sure grip and I was amazed to see that it was a white-haired old man who held me. He'd obviously seen the whole episode.

'Don't bother with them, young man,' he said calmly in perfect English. 'You have your wallet. Unless you fancy a knife in your gullet, better leave them be.'

On the seventh night of the festivities, attempting to make our way back to the bus in a state of total exhaustion, we were unwittingly swept up in a mob behind a band, along a long, narrow street when suddenly, on a signal from nowhere, except presumably from the hearts of those who were saying farewell to this riotous week, the music stopped, the singers fell silent, the noise halted, and even the drummers kept quiet. Everyone in the street fell down on their hands and knees and began knocking their heads on the cobblestones. From the deathly, eerie silence came one voice, then many, singing the traditional song:

Poor me, poor me! How sad, so sad are we.
The fiesta of San Fermin is over. Home to bed with thee.

It was time for some rest and recuperation. We decided to retreat to the large, temporary camping ground several kilometres outside Pamplona that we'd learnt about on previous visits. We elected to head there first thing the following morning and arrived at the camping ground at 7:00 a.m. The scene itself was not dissimilar to the one at Fusina on T-day, but with a slightly different backdrop. There were many hundreds of campers of every persuasion but by far the bulk of them were colonials. The vast wheatfield with mown hay trampled underfoot, and a fresh flowing stream meandering coolly and invitingly down from the golden, undulating hills held the prospect of a relaxing and enjoyable stay.

A closer inspection of the campsite proved that this was not necessarily to be. There were hardly any facilities and from the stench wafting from the few toilets, one could tell that they'd been blocked from day one. The bar area, with a broad, straw-covered awning, was now monopolised by flies fussing over hundreds of 'empties' littering the ground and the sleeping, recumbent bodies of several dozen of 'the lads' who were probably yet to see a bull.

As I continued my survey of the camp, I saw someone I knew walking towards me from the direction of a knot of campervans where, given the noise, there was obviously some action, even though it was still very early in the morning. He was a Maori and we had met and spent a night drinking together at La Ballena Alegre Campsite in Barcelona only the previous month.

He was a great guy and we got on well together. He was travelling in a blue Kombi van that had 'Animal Tours' handpainted on the side. We had run into this Kombi on innumerable occasions around Europe. There were always about four or five Maoris on board, but rarely the same ones. We deduced that the Kombi was communal property and was handed on from one new arrival to another. During the night in Barcelona I had learnt Maori-speak. It was relatively easy to pick up. You started and finished most sentences with an 'eh' and threw in lots of 'Brothers' in the middle and, in this way, you could have a conversation that went on for hours.

Pamplona campsite 1983.

The Seventh of the Seventh – Pamplona 1976

'Eh, Kelly, how are you, Brother?' He looked pale. Well not as dark as normal.

'Eh, Brother, I'm crook. Bloody crook! Too much to drink last night, eh. I've had enough of this place, eh. I'm going into town to see the bulls, eh?'

'The bulls, eh? Sorry Brother, you're too late, eh? It's all over for this year, eh?' Kelly and his mates had lost track of time. 'Guess you'll have to come back next year, eh Brother?' I suggested.

'Eh, Brother, I suppose so. It's a tradition, eh?'

Drinking red wine Pamplona-style.

Chapter 8
DODGY AT DOVER
(LONDON 1976)

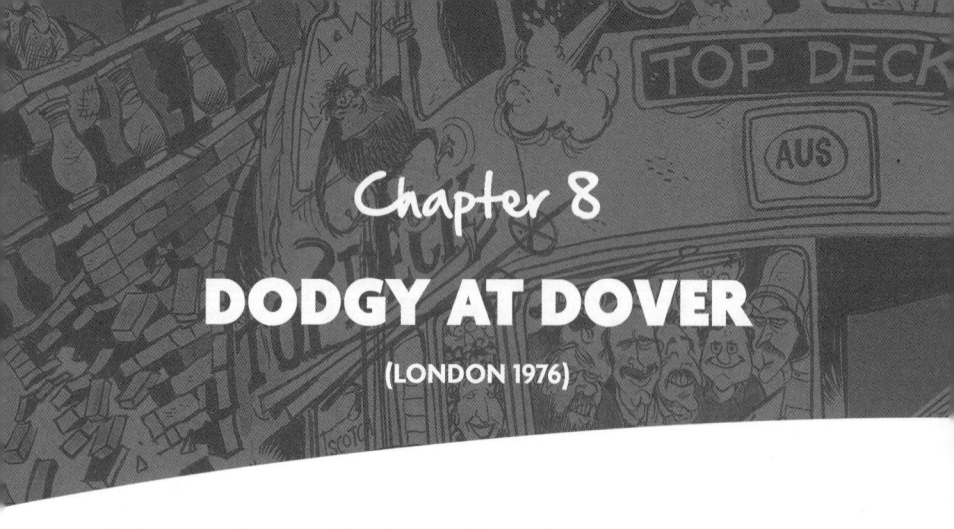

If you study a world atlas you'll see that a continental landmass stretches from the west coast of France all the way to the causeway linking Singapore with the Malayan Peninsula. In 1271, Marco Polo was the first to journey from Europe to Singapore, but did so by taking a land route north of the Himalayas into China, and from there by sea, via Singapore, back to Persia (Iran).

Today, you can certainly travel east by road as far as eastern India and Bangladesh (East Pakistan), but then you are confronted by the mountainous jungles of Burma (now Myanmar) and north-western Thailand. In 1937 and 1938, 160 000 'coolies' chiselled the Burma Road through the mountainous rock and jungle linking Burma with China to the north, but the east-west route remained a dream. If anyone has travelled from Europe to Singapore, or vice versa, in a motorised vehicle by way of the southern Himalayan route, I am yet to find history of it.

In a similar prelude to our first overland to Kathmandu in 1975, none of this trivia of history or geography, such as impenetrable jungles and mountains, mattered one iota to Screw when he decided to advertise a London to Sydney overland to depart on 7 October 1976. Just like our arguments in 1975, I strained and chafed at the bit trying to hold back the old line, 'It can't be done.' I argued that it was one thing to be bold and adventurous, but quite another to take money from punters under entirely false pretences, and so Screw and I reached a rare compromise.

Dodgy at Dover – London 1976

We agreed that the brochure would indeed advertise the trip, but with a four-day ferry journey from Madras (now Chennai), India, to Penang in Malaysia, and a flight (which was always agreed on) from Singapore to Perth. It was to take twenty-four weeks and cost £630 or $940 Australian.

We weren't the first company to undertake such an expedition. There may have been others, but David Smith from Hughes Overland had operated this itinerary since 1971. Hughes ran minibuses and had been one of the first camping tour operators ever to go into Russia.

We had enough bookings to take one busload all the way from London to Sydney, but the London/Kathmandu nine-weeker just kept selling like proverbial hot cakes. The remainder of our fleet was already committed to tours until the end of October, so we bought an additional bus and filled it, then a third bus and filled it as well. The overlands' popularity was no doubt due, among other things, to the departure and arrival dates Screw had insisted on. It appealed to all the Aussies and Kiwis because not only did they miss the dreaded London winter they were also due to arrive home in the weeks before Christmas—an ideal time to be reunited with family and friends after an extended time abroad.

Mick Carroll and Kevin 'Tiny' Olliff on the first bus, Dave Reed and Barry Innes on the second, and Guy Freeman and Brian 'Dark Blue' Coubrough on the third, were the hastily put-together crews. Tiny had done part of an overland as a passenger with another company, but none of the other boys had toured outside Europe. Dave and Barry were Rhodesians doing it tough on their working holiday as drillers on the North Sea oilrigs. They were spending one of their well-earned breaks in London when they stumbled on us drinking at the Cock. Being two likely lads, we press-ganged them into a more fulfilling career.

All available hands were engaged on general preparations and the fitting-out of the two new buses. Mick, being the most experienced and senior courier, took on much of the responsibility.

Top Deck Daze

Trip funds were always taken in the form of travellers' cheques. Credit cards were not commonly used in those days and were useless beyond Central Europe. Automatic teller machines dispensing cash were a thing of the future, so the procedure was to take a bank cheque to Thomas Cook in Kensington High Street, where we would be issued with unsigned travellers' cheques which would then be dispersed among, and signed by, the relevant crew.

It was going to be touch and go as to whether the buses would be ready to leave by the scheduled date: 7 October 1976. It wouldn't be the first time punters had been asked on the morning of departure to come back again in a few days because their bus wasn't ready.

Having outgrown our small yard in Chelsea, we had relocated the buses to a new yard at Richmond and the evening before departure, Mick departed there just in time to make Tommy Cook's office in Kensington before closing. The only transport available at the yard was a Kombi van belonging to Mike Stent. The van had only been bought three days beforehand in Amsterdam and so wasn't registered in the UK.

Screw and I and all the crew had agreed to meet Mick at Dawes Road at 6:00 p.m. so they could sign their cheques and have a final rundown on plans—a rare event in itself. We waited and waited. By 8:00 p.m. Mick had still not shown up, so the boys went back to Richmond to work on their buses well into the night. Mick's no-show was totally out of character for him. He was the most honest and reliable person you could find, so it was out of the question that he'd 'done a runner' with the £6000. As the time dragged on, therefore, I began to fear some form of foul play.

Financially, things were already serious for the company. We had collected £20 000 from the sixty overland passengers during the preceding six weeks. Top Deck operated with no financial controls or budgeting of any kind and like the vast majority of small businesses the world over, we survived on an ever-increasing overdraft without the formal approval of our long-suffering bank manager.

Dodgy at Dover – London 1976

The £20 000 had put our bank account into the black, for a while, but it didn't take long to lag into the red again. For starters, more than £5000 had gone to buy, fit-out, and repair the extra buses, including wages, and this was over and above the overheads and general running expenses of the business. We survived solely because of the cash flow provided by the up-front tour payments for yet-to-depart trips. Losing Mick was one thing, we would miss him dearly no doubt, but the £6000 he had with him represented the cost of getting the three buses all the way to Kathmandu.

At 11:00 p.m. we did what we should have done much earlier, and that was call the police. Could they help us, we asked? Did they have any knowledge of someone answering the following description: A tall, curly-haired, scruffily dressed, grease-covered Australian, in possession of £6000 of unsigned travellers' cheques, with no licence or passport, driving a Dutch-registered blue van, full of tools? The driver might possibly identify himself as either Graham James Lloyd or Michael Patrick Carroll?

All of thirty seconds elapsed before we had an answer: 'Yes,' a gentleman fitting that description was indeed assisting police with their enquiries and was being detained at Her Majesty's pleasure at South Kensington police station. He had been pulled over by one of their officers doing routine road checks on the Old Brompton Road. If someone could possibly come to the station with proof of the gentleman's identity and a rational explanation that might allay the officer's not unreasonable suspicions, that person might be able to bring forward his not-yet-imminent release.

'Er, could you tell me if you're holding Graham James Lloyd or Michael Patrick Carroll?' I asked embarrassingly, not wanting to turn up with Mick's passport if he wasn't Michael Carroll on that particular day.

'We think it's Michael Patrick Carroll,' said a rather disappointed officer. 'We're still doing our checks.' Irrespective of whoever the police thought they were holding, at least we had our travellers' cheques back.

Top Deck Daze

The buses rolled into the National Car Park (NCP) at the top of Warwick Road, Earls Court, at daybreak on the seventh. The sixty passengers, accompanied by assorted friends and well-wishers, waited in the chilly morning mist and gave a cheer as the buses came into sight. There was a tangible air of excitement and expectancy, more evident than on previous departures. The big six-cylinder diesels purred away in unison. Shafts of red-hued morning light cut through steam rising from the condensation on the engine cowlings, and from the breaths of the intermingling crowd.

I sought out as many of the London/Sydney passengers as I could find. I would be flying back to Sydney shortly to organise the Perth/Sydney leg, so I would be seeing them all in Oz in twenty-two weeks time, God permitting. I wished them well and a safe and exciting trip.

The three-to-four days before any trip departure were inevitably physically and mentally exhausting. You would work fifteen or more hours a day, and sometimes around the clock. There was always the possibility that something major would go wrong and then it wasn't just the prospect of more long days, but the placating of, and possible confrontation with, the irate passengers — the thought of which was often more draining than the actual event. There wasn't a single Channel crossing I did as a crewmember on which I didn't crawl into a bunk on the bus the second the ferry door closed and lapse into a torpid sleep.

This same feeling overcame me when the overland buses finally departed and the car park emptied. I told Screw I was going out to the Richmond yard to clean up after the past hectic few days but, in truth, I wanted to bludge and went to find a cosy bed on one of the buses not due out for another week, and slept soundly till early afternoon.

It was after 3:00 p.m. when I got back to Dawes Road and heard the news. Kessa Ware, who ran the office, was still visibly shaken. At eleven o'clock sharp the office had been visited by two inspectors from the Department of Transport (DOT) with the

Dodgy at Dover – London 1976

news that the just-departed overland buses were being held on the docks at Dover. The crews were being interrogated by other DOT inspectors and the police. Embarkation was being refused. Top Deck's directors, Messrs Turner, James and Graham James Lloyd were being put on notice that there were innumerable irregularities about the operation of passenger service vehicles by Top Deck, and further action by the Department was to be expected within days.

My knees quivered. A nerve at the side of my mouth started to twitch uncontrollably and my bowels started to receive 'action station' signals from the relevant lobe of my brain—a fairly dominant and active one in my case. My immediate thoughts were quite clear and simple, under the circumstances: 'Let's piss off quick,' and, 'Thank bloody hell I wasn't here at the time the inspectors called.'

What a good move it had been to go to the yard. I was hopeless in the presence of authority. Screw hadn't been at the office either but, if he had, I would have hated him for his coolness and well-chosen words.

All the horrible thoughts that had bedevilled me the previous night (when we'd misplaced Mick and the travellers' cheques) returned, but twenty-fold. This was 'Shut Up Shop', 'All Over Red Rover' and 'The Fat Lady Sings' all rolled into one. It was not possible to recover from this situation. If all the punters turned up on our office doorstep the following day to demand their refunds, well, we just didn't have the money. They would string us up by the proverbials to the nearest telegraph pole. We'd better leave tonight. If they could extradite us from Majorca, I was already preparing my defence: 'It had nothing to do with us. It was all Graham James Lloyd's fault. He was always off travelling somewhere and left us here holding the can.'

Much later, Mick and Dave Reed were able to give us a rundown of events as they occurred in Dover. No sooner had the buses pulled into the dock area than they were surrounded by three cars, two from the DOT and one from the police. What

Top Deck Daze

preplanning had gone into the raid was never determined, but the simultaneous arrival of the inspectors on the docks and at the London office suggested it did not happen by chance. We could have been dobbed-in by someone from a rival company. Perhaps we had overstepped the mark one too many times.

The six crewmembers were asked to leave their vehicles and accompany the officers into a room in the customs hall. The DOT leader, in obligatory hat and trench coat, bore an uncanny resemblance to Inspector Gadget.

'Now, gentlemen,' said Gadget, 'There are several issues at hand. Let us deal with them in order, shall we? Firstly, Road Tax?' Current Road Tax certificates were meant to be displayed in small, circular, glass-fronted discs fixed to the side of the driver's cab. A junior officer was dispatched to retrieve one from the buses.

'Thank you, officer. Hummm, what have we here?' Gadget perused the evidence.

'I see.' Pause. 'A label off a bottle of Guinness stout.' Pause. 'Of similar colour, shape and design to a Road Tax certificate, I agree, but of little assistance to the Chancellor of the Exchequer when it comes to balancing his budget.'

'Let's move on then, shall we?' continued Gadget, undeterred. 'Secondly. Registration papers?' Mick produced and unfolded a soiled and tattered piece of paper from his wallet and handed it to Gadget, who read from it: 'Make: Bristol. Year of manufacture: 1955. Colour: Green and white.' The inspector surveyed the buses through the window. 'Your bus is not green and white, Sir.'

'Well, it was yesterday morning,' replied Mick, holding up orange, paint-covered forearms.

'Wise guy, eh?' said the look on Gadget's face.

'Thirdly. Passports?' The junior officer had, in the meantime, taken possession of all the passports, identified the crew's, and now handed these to Gadget. 'Let's see now,' he said. 'The first one belongs to a New Zealander, a Mr Kevin Olliff.' He looked at the photo, and then up at Tiny. 'Good. Now, the second one belongs to … a … Mr Kevin Olliff. I see,' he said, but he didn't.

Dodgy at Dover – London 1976

'And the third one? Ah, also belongs to ... a ... Mr Kevin Olliff? How very strange.'

Multiple passports? Surely this could only mean the bearer had some felonious intent? Tiny had simply done what many experienced road crew were forced to do, that is, get two or three passports by claiming you had lost your original. Visas to the obscure countries we travelled to could take weeks, months even, to process. If you waited till your one-and-only passport did the rounds of the various embassies, you could be off the road for half the year. So you travelled with three passports and produced the correct one as and when required. It was pointless explaining all of this to Gadget.

'Fourthly. Drivers' licences, please?' Wallets were emptied and an oddly assorted pile of licences were heaped on the table in front of the inspector. For many minutes Gadget filed through them. 'Well gentleman, this is most interesting. Most interesting, indeed! We have before us an enviable array of licences.' He held one aloft. 'Here, we have an Australian articulated vehicle licence. Here,' holding up another, 'A New Zealand taxi-driver's licence. Here,' holding up another, 'A Rhodesian motor-scooter licence,' and so on, through the pile. 'But nowhere do I see anything resembling a licence to drive a British-registered double-decker bus, which, unless my eyes deceive me, is what you have just alighted from.'

The questioning went on and on, throughout the morning. The only area of the law with which the buses or drivers complied was in regard to insurance which, to our way of thinking at the time, was the only important one.

As the hours dragged on, the passengers obviously became increasingly frustrated and suspicious. Dave Reed kept returning to the buses with lame, clichéd excuses: 'A minor hiccup', 'A slight technical hitch', 'Won't be too much longer now'. The remainder of the crew were asked to stay in the interview room with no idea as to their fate.

At last, at 2:00 p.m., a burly sergeant of police who had not been involved directly in the interview process to date, came into the room. He was a Cockney with a well-lived-in face. He stood, leaning forward, resting his knuckles on the table.

'All right, lads. We've come to a decision. We're as bloody-well sick of this damn farce as you are. Here, take your duck-shootin' licences and your fishin' licences or wotever you've got,' he said, pushing the pile across the table in the direction of the crew, 'And youse can go. But just let me give you one little piece of advice before youse do.' He lowered his head and his voice. 'Git in your fancy buses and go to Timbuctoo or wherever you're damn-well headed, and take your time gettin' there.' Then he lowered his head and his voice still further. 'And one more thing: If youse ever show your bleedin' faces in this 'ere country again, and we catch youse, you won't be goin' nowhere again for a long time. Got it?'

Passengers writing 'Australian Tourists' in Farsi.

Chapter 9
BLUNDER DOWN-UNDER
(AUSTRALIA 1977)

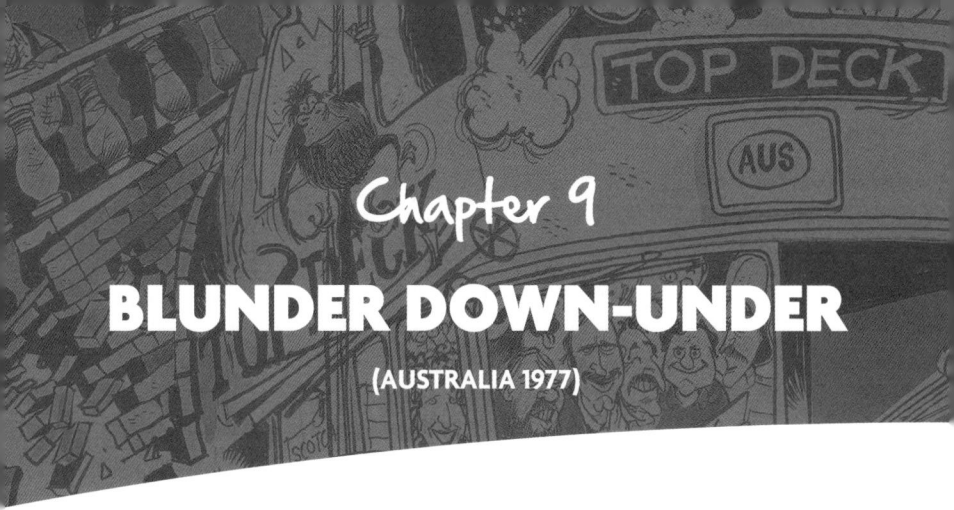

There were several reasons for me spending the bulk of 1977 in Australia. For starters, there was the immediate need to provide a bus for the Australian leg of the London/Sydney overland. Then there was the need to market our European tours, and especially our Sydney/London and Kathmandu/London overlands, through Australian travel agents. But more importantly, for our own personal reasons, Liz and I needed some time back home. While we loved London and enjoyed all our time there immensely, we now felt we needed a break from the London scene and some quiet times together. Every day in London had been spent in the office or at the workshop. Top Deck had become a big business with all its attendant hassles and stresses. It was no longer just a 'fun thing to do'. Screw seemed happy to forge ahead with the expansion but I wasn't 100 per cent sure that's what I wanted, especially if it meant spending the foreseeable future in London. For everyone in Top Deck, the company was a way of life, not just a job. There was no differentiation between work and social life. Liz and I just wanted some space and to be by ourselves for a while, so the challenges that presented themselves in Australia were too appealing to turn down. We received great support from our respective parents. A week after our return to Australia, an ex-Sydney Transport double-decker was being fitted out in my parents' small suburban backyard with my father, Charlie, as the labourer. It was difficult for Mum (who'd kept house and worked full-time to pay my school fees and had supported me through uni) to tell her friends that her son was now 'driving old double-decker buses' for a living. So much for all her hard work! But if either she or Dad was disappointed or concerned about my future, they didn't give me any indication of it. Nor did Liz's parents, Nancy and Bill. Far from expressing any concern about the dubious financial prospects of their new son-in-law, they urged me to give the new business a go in Australia.

By mid-February the new Australian decker was ready for the road. For once bureaucracy and red tape didn't hinder the new operation because the Australian Constitution guaranteed that, 'Customs, trade, commerce and intercourse among the States, whether by means of internal carriage or ocean navigation, shall be absolutely free,' and so no route licences or the like were necessary, provided you were taking passengers across State borders.

Using the Sydney Morning Herald and notices in backpacker hotels in Kings Cross, I advertised a ten-day, $100 Sydney/Perth trip. I managed to get twelve punters and as it only cost $400 to get to Perth, I made a flying start towards covering our overheads.

On 7 March 1977, at Perth Airport, I met the London/Sydney passengers that I'd farewelled in London twenty-two weeks beforehand. The London deckers had terminated in Kathmandu. It proved far too costly to ferry them from India to Malaysia. The original crews had stayed with their buses for the return trip to London and Greg 'Wombat' Ettridge had escorted the Sydney-bound passengers on a flight from Kathmandu to Rangoon, with a week in Burma, then on to Bangkok, then by public transport to Bali and by plane to Perth.

We'd met Wombat in London in 1974. We named him after 'Bruce the Wombat', a cartoon character who featured in London's Australasian Express, drawn by Bob Maher. The two Wombats shared similar statures and attitudes.

Our Wombat was a big, burly, curly-haired fellow, with a deep Aussie drawl, twinkling eyes, and a permanent, cheeky grin.

Blunder Down-under – Australia 1977

He'd been brought up on a wheat farm outside Quairading in Western Australia. We loved his National Country Party political and economic views ('Gough's stuffed the country so badly Dad can't afford to buy another Cessna [plane].'); his views on Asian weather ('There's only two seasons, hot and fucking hot.'); on Asian food ('I've only had "hot salad" to eat for two whole weeks, "Gidday, Gidday, and egg"' that is, Indonesian Gado-Gado.); on

Top Deck Daze

liberal social values ('We could fix the world if the hungry would eat the poor.'); and so on. The punters loved him, which was the main thing, and all of them were in tremendous spirits on their arrival in Australia.

Wombat had contacts everywhere and we were hosted to barbecue lunches and dinners for days on end. The highlight for our Pommie punters was two nights free-camping by the estuary of the Bunbury River. We feasted on huge mud crabs, succulent prawns we'd caught and juicy oysters we'd collected, together with fresh-cooked damper, golden syrup, and billy-boiled tea. As for the Aussies, they knew they were home.

Our final night of festivities before the main trek east was spent on Wombat's uncle's farm at Quairading where we were treated to a whole-roasted lamb, roast veggies, and all the beer the punters could drink, compliments of the local cockies. We were overwhelmed by the generosity of our hosts and conviviality of all the families that dropped by during the evening to say hello.

It was well past 1:00 a.m. when we turned off the bus lights and except for the glowing embers of the campfire, the moonless night shrouded the now-featureless station yards and sheds in a curtain of black.

One of the punters was 'Baked Bean Charlie', a small, fair-haired, goodhearted New Zealander, well known to Wombat and me. He'd done several Top Deck European tours including one where Wombat had assisted another of our drivers, 'Light Blue' Ramsey, repair a decker that had developed severe engine-timing problems. The job entailed stripping the front off the bus and lining up the timing cogs that coordinated the crankshaft, pistons, engine valves and fuel pump, none of which had the correct markings on them. It required someone to be under the bus to crank the heavy flywheel around with a screwdriver while Wombat and Blue worked on the motor. Charlie was their man. The weather had been bitterly cold and the laborious, hit-and-miss job went on for five days. Charlie, a loyal, full-fare paying passenger, spent five days on his back in the freezing conditions,

Blunder Down-under – Australia 1977

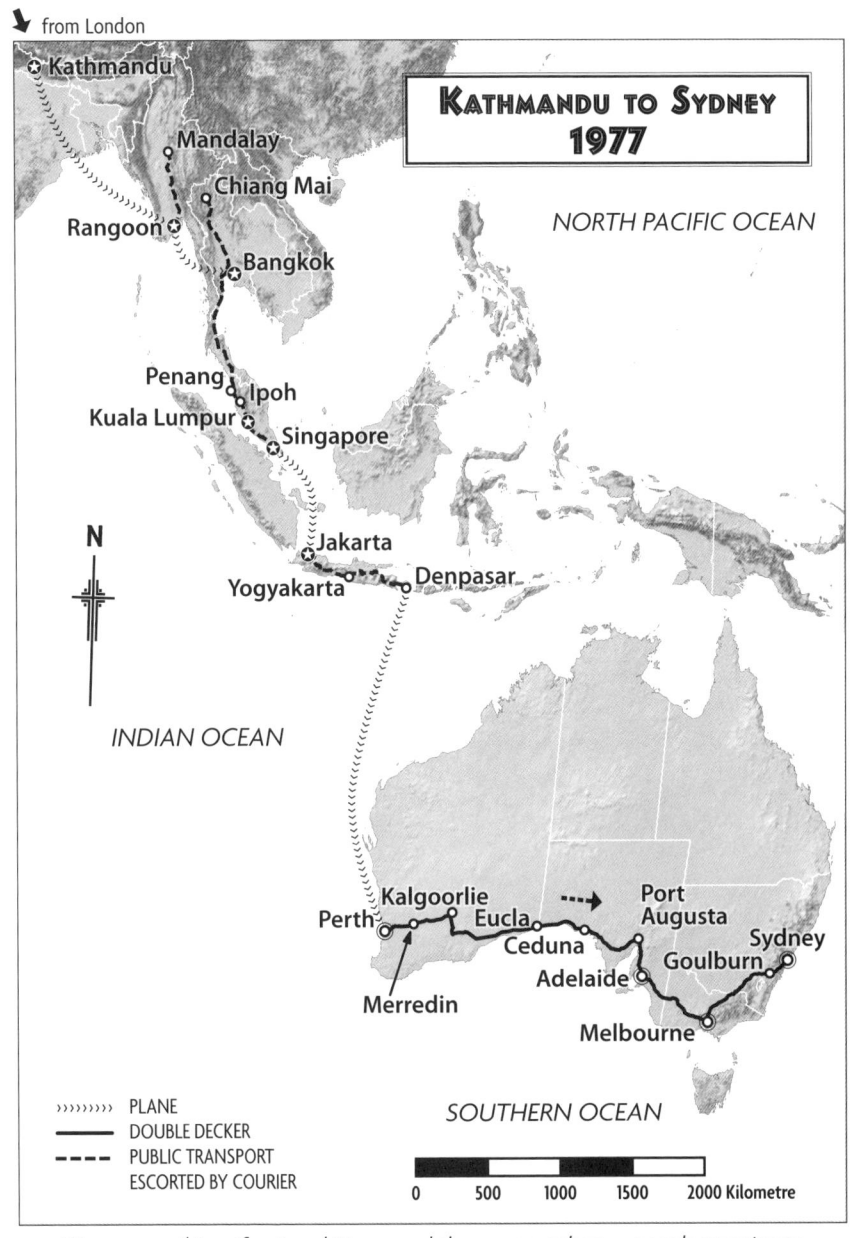

KATHMANDU TO SYDNEY 1977

from London
- Kathmandu
- Mandalay
- Chiang Mai
- Rangoon
- Bangkok
- Penang
- Ipoh
- Kuala Lumpur
- Singapore
- Jakarta
- Yogyakarta
- Denpasar
- Perth
- Kalgoorlie
- Merredin
- Eucla
- Ceduna
- Adelaide
- Port Augusta
- Melbourne
- Goulburn
- Sydney

NORTH PACIFIC OCEAN
INDIAN OCEAN
SOUTHERN OCEAN

N

>>>>>> PLANE
——— DOUBLE DECKER
- - - - PUBLIC TRANSPORT
ESCORTED BY COURIER

0 500 1000 1500 2000 Kilometre

We were nothing, if not ambitious; and there were takers—people wanting to reach Australia for family Christmases.

Top Deck Daze

screwdriver in hand. Blue wouldn't allow him to come up for lunch, so bowls of baked beans were shoved under the bus for Charlie to enjoy at his leisure. Wombat also called him 'Top Dead Centre Charlie' after this (mechanics will understand) and owed him a few favours.

Baked Bean Charlie had a bad habit of sleepwalking after a long evening on the turps, and Wombat and I learnt to sleep with half an eye open on such occasions, just like this night on the farm. Sure enough, I was just drifting off into a deep, sweet dream when Wombat shook me awake.

'Billy,' he whispered hoarsely, 'Get up, get up, he's gone. We'd better find him!' I knew immediately what Wombat was on about.

There were wells, old mineshafts, dams and sharp farm machinery ready to ambush the innocent night-wanderer. We needed to find Baked Bean and return him to his bunk before he did himself some serious damage. We armed ourselves with torches and plotted a pattern, trekking in ever-widening circles from the bus.

More than half-an-hour of fruitless searching passed. With mounting anxiety, we'd only paused for a second to ponder our predicament before we were startled by yells and screams and the flicker of internal and external lights issuing from the main station homestead.

'My God! Sounds like a murder,' I said, clutching Wombat, as we sprinted in the direction of the fracas.

We were taken aback when confronted by Wombat's uncle escorting a still half-asleep Baked Bean onto the wide homestead veranda. Somehow, Bean had managed to find his way into the eldest daughter's bedroom and curl up in bed beside her in a subconscious pursuit of a comfy night's sleep. We knew Bean was devoid of any ill intent, but it was mighty embarrassing for us to try and explain all this to our host, especially in the light of his wonderful hospitality during our brief stay.

It was time to move on. We were now beyond the reach of Wombat's generous friends. It was hard enough for punters to budget their spending money for a three-week tour of Europe, let alone now, after more than twenty-two weeks and 20 000 km on the road. Our group was stone-motherless broke. They didn't have a brass razoo to rub between them. The over-supplemented food kitty could only stretch so far. It was such a shame because the buoyant mood of the group demanded a much-more generous budget for drinking and socialising.

Wombat had done everything humanly possible to save the punters money and give them the best possible value. The seven-day tour of Burma had been a good example. The official rate of exchange at the time was seven Burmese kyat to the Australian dollar, but Wombat had managed to pick up fifty kyat to our dollar on the black market in Chiang Mai, Thailand, on the way up. Burmese beer was cheap anyway, but Wombat found an excellent garden bar in Mandalay where he could buy beers for one kyat each. That equated to fifty beers for one Australian dollar! The group was cock-a-hoop and stayed for five days, refusing to move on. The flight from Pagan to Mandalay had been just as amazingly cheap. Based on the black-market rate, it had cost exactly $1.67 for the return journey, including transfers! The Burmese planes consisted of old, clapped-out, ex-Pan-Am propeller-driven Lockheeds. They lost four planes the following year, so maybe it wasn't such great value after all.

An extraordinary solution to our lack of beer-drinking funds in Australia presented itself to us the very next evening in Merredin, an outback town on the road to the Nullarbor. We found ourselves in the town's main hotel for a strictly one-round-of-drinks-only session, compliments of the food kitty. It was a Friday night and the bar was chockers with every shearer, miner, cocky and jackaroo for miles around, in for their end-of-week drink. We got talking to a group of farmhands who still wore their sweat-soaked hats over ears big enough to swat flies with. Even the beers they were drinking had two heads.

We, too, had the motliest assortment of a group you could ever possibly imagine: Aussies, Kiwis and Poms of all shapes and sizes. Travelling on a decker parked right outside the pub, we were an obvious curiosity, but one of us in particular was an absolute standout — a small, pale-skinned, bleached-blonde, crew-cut, tattooed, ring-earred, big-booted, Liverpudlian we called 'Killer.' A gentler nor kinder soul you couldn't possibly find, but Killer was a Sex Pistols lookalike, which was hardly a common sight in downtown Merredin. Killer stood his ground at the bar for hours, cheerfully fending off taunts as he sipped away sparingly on his tiny, seven-ounce ration of beer while the thirsty farmhands threw back schooner after schooner of Swan.

After two hours of 'big girl's blouse' barbs, and 'weak Pommie bastard'-type jeers, a group of our boys fell for the bait. I trembled in trepidation as six of them, Killer, Wombat, Bean, Bongo, Mumbles and Fyfe Campbell, lined up for a 'boat race' with six of the shearers. The prize: Losers to 'shout' the winners and selected friends beers till closing.

Well, that was it — the end of the food kitty, plus some, for the rest of the trip! It would be a ration of bread and water from here on in and an express run to Sydney. What a sad way to end such a great trip.

The opposing teams lined up in traditional boat racing formation, each team facing the bar, in line, abreast. The barman filled a schooner of beer and placed it in front of each contestant. The publican was called on to adjudicate. He pushed back the assembled onlookers to ensure that he had a clear view of the teams. Customers from the saloon bar and lounge crowded the public bar, and the snooker competition was suspended for the duration.

'Gentlemen, face your glasses,' proclaimed the publican. The crowd hushed. 'On the count of three: One, Two, Three,' and the teams were away. The first contestant of each team had to scull his beer and upturn the emptied glass on top of his head as a signal for the number two to go, and so on, down the line. Our team was a whisker in front after our bow and numbers two, three and four had sculled — they were just plain thirsty — but, when it came to number five, Fyfe, and stroke, Wombat, it was 'no contest'. We won by an easy five seconds. Fyfe and Wombat had that extraordinary ability to open their gullets and simply empty the contents down their throats. No need for swallowing. The fact that the shearers had been 'practising' for three hours hadn't help their form.

An almighty roar echoed around the bar, but nothing to match the whooping and dancing of our mob. Free drinks for the whole night! They couldn't believe it. We had discovered a brilliant means of overcoming our grog rationing that would see us through the remainder of the trip. The boat-race team perfected their pre-contest charade, acting out the weak Pommie bastard role, in the mining towns of Coolgardie, Boulder, Kalgoorlie and Norseman—so much so that the locals simply couldn't resist when the challenge was issued. Our team won us four consecutive nights of free grog so by the time we were ready to tackle the 800 km of Nullarbor dust masquerading as the Eyre Highway, a water-only ration for three days was quite a relief.

Drinkers at the local pub in Ceduna at the eastern end of the Great Australian Bight heralded our navigation of the Nullarbor sand-sea with a generous round 'on the house'. We settled into the lounge bar in front of the television that was beaming the famous Centenary Cricket Test between Australia

Top Deck Daze

From the west we enter the Nullarbor Plain, Australia.

and England, live from the Melbourne Cricket Ground. Heaven! This was too good to rush. Somehow we must find an excuse to delay our embarkation for a few days while devising a method of victualling our sturdy vessel and her salty crew with all the beverages they might require.

The local Aussie Rules footy team was due to meet in town for pre-season training that afternoon and would be holding a fundraising dance and bush cabaret in the evening. A 'bush cabaret'? The possibilities that such an event might present seemed too fortuitous not to explore. There'd be a big roll-up from all the stations near and far, and we were welcome to attend, so we were told. Under the circumstances, we simply couldn't refuse such a kind offer.

Dusk settled and in the hot, muggy hall, multicoloured lights began to flicker around the lonely dance floor. The bushband was setting up on stage while a growing but-still-circumspect crowd of 'Bachelors & Spinsters' filtered into the hall.

Our group of nineteen occupied the tables and chairs commanding immediate access to the dance floor.

Most people are familiar with such evenings. They invariably follow a similar pattern. Quiet and reserved for the first hour or two, no one willing to make the first move to get the place moving, with lots of milling around just in and outside doorways, waiting for the alcohol to lower inhibitions and loosen repressed desires.

The MC knew this routine only too well. He'd had to coax the crowd countless times before. Ambling unsuspectingly to the microphone, he announced, 'There's a prize of three bottles of wine for each of the first couples on the dance floor …' He'd only uttered the first few syllables when the hall erupted with the crash, bang and wallop of up-ended tables, chairs and glasses, as all nineteen Top Deckers lunged at the dance floor like an All Black rugby pack at kick-off. Killer waltzed with Bongo, Fyfe tangoed with Wombat, boy with boy, girl with girl—whoever was closest. Bean, the odd number nineteen, embraced a chair as he jived and rumbaed his way around the room. Eureka! Three bottles of wine per couple! All I had to do was ensure the boat-race team paced itself for the inevitable 10:00 p.m. scull.

Many of the footballers worked on the fishing boats at the tiny port of Thevenard, only a stone's throw away, and two of them rowed Wombat and me to their boats at 2:00 a.m. to make a selection for tomorrow's lunch and dinner. Bream, whiting and snapper swam live in the saltwater holds and we fished out our choice with nets.

We had good cause for a further delay. Bean 'went walkabout' again that night. The upstairs front of the decker had seats and tables that folded into a big triple bed. The Aussie buses had large sliding windows, on the side, upstairs. One of our passengers 'Midge' Tuena, who occupied the front bed, said she was still awake as Bean stumbled down the aisle towards her.

'He's going to look out the window,' she thought. 'No, he must want to pee out the window.' Then, 'My God, he's walked out the window!' By the time Midge checked, Bean, who'd fallen the four metres head first, had curled up in a downstairs bunk, still sound asleep.

Top Deck Daze

En route to Sydney.

When we surfaced for breakfast the next morning, poor Bean's badly broken forearm was swollen like a balloon. As we rushed him to the district hospital in the back of the footy captain's ute, he still had no recollection of how it had happened.

Screw was in Sydney when our decker arrived on 19 March 1977. In early 1976, in London, Screw had run across a girl he'd known at uni, Jude Stent. Screw recognised her immediately. She had made a lasting impression on him with her good looks and unaffected personality. Screw had asked Jude for a date as soon as they'd met in Brisbane. Wisely, Jude had declined. Any self-respecting girl knew that the undergraduates of Emmanuel College were, with good cause, known as the Animals. Why risk one's reputation by lowering oneself to

Screw and Jude were married in Brisbane in 1976.

168

Blunder Down-under – Australia 1977

Dingo, Neil Armstrong, Spike Cawthorne, Blue Ramsey, Dennis Brown-Kenyon, Jude and Screw.

that level? Thanks, but no thanks. Quite by coincidence, Jude had walked into the Dawes Road office in 1976 to book a Moroccan trip.

Screw wasn't scheduled to be the courier, but how things change. Surprise, surprise, the original courier was inexplicably summoned to London two weeks into Jude's trip, to take out another tour, and who should turn up as his replacement? Correct! The rest, as they say, is history. Screw and Jude decided to marry in Brisbane in late 1976. It was a small, casual, family affair so, in typical fashion, Screw was using every other available moment to further the interests of Top Deck during his brief stay before returning to London.

The first-ever Sydney-to-London trip was due to depart on 24 March 1977. It cost $1200 plus $180 food kitty for the twenty-week tour. We hired Rob Frazier, a passenger on the just-completed London/Sydney overland, to be the Sydney/Perth driver. Wombat would escort the trip though South-East Asia and link up with the London-based buses in Kathmandu.

Next, Screw and I had to find a general sales agent (GSA) who would represent Top Deck in Australia. The GSA acted as the travel agents' agent, marketing the product and processing the bookings. One possibility was Trailfinders. Their head office was in London at the top of Earls Court Road. In the late 1980s and 1990s they became the single biggest travel agency in the world. In 1977 they were still camping-tour and overland specialists and just about the only agent that would deign to sell Top Deck in London.

Alan Collingwood had set up Trailfinders in Australia in 1973 but when I went to say 'Hello' I discovered that the Sydney manager was none other than our old ex-Siafu friend Peter Baily from whom we had taken over the lease at Dawes Road, our first office in London. Peter suggested I check out Trailfinders' Melbourne office so I met with the manager there, Sally Keogh. Sally explained the set-up and introduced me to a lovely Irish lady who had been their second employee in Melbourne in 1975. Her name was Maureen Wheeler. She and her husband, Tony, had travelled the overland and we chatted about our respective adventures.

'Tony,' she said, 'has just written a book based on our experiences.' 'What was it?' I enquired.

'South-East Asia on a Shoe String,' she replied. Little did I know (nor did Tony and Maureen, for that matter) that the book would become a raging bestseller and spawn the Lonely Planet publications that are now the most widely-read travel books in Australia.

Another possibility we explored was Treasure Tours, run by a Kiwi of Dutch extraction, Art Van Sarloos. Treasure Tours specialised in Australia/London tours via the Trans-Siberian Railway which were very popular at the time. We'd heard Art was gaining something of a reputation as a 'resurrection specialist'—that is, buying companies that were on their way out financially, such as Hughes Overland and Intertrek, and turning them around. I thought he might come in handy some day.

In the end, we chose to go with a company called Travelscene. It was run by Bob Steel (who subsequently sold the business for squillons to the Stella group) and Paul Glynn (later CEO of Ocean Blue Resorts). Other senior managers were Bill Hollow

Blunder Down-under – Australia 1977

and Dave Woods. Another young staff member was a vivacious, red-haired young lady by the name of Marg Mulholland. Later, Marg joined Flight Centre and progressed to become one of the company's most senior executives and a director of the board after its public float in 1995.

There was no commercial logic for Travelscene to become the GSA for Top Deck in Australia, as it would cost them a lot of money to promote our product, with no guaranteed return. I'm sure Bob Steel just took pity on us.

Travelscene was booming, carrying young passengers by the planeload to their main destination, Bali. Virtually every travel agent in Australia was a Travelscene supporter. Bali was the 'in' place to go and the one-week packages were cheap and hassle-free to sell. We thought Top Deck might gain some credibility by associating itself with such a successful company.

Much of my time was taken up with repping agents and presenting weekly slidenights. The overlands proved very popular, even if we didn't have much early success with selling European tours.

I was in awe of Bob Steel and his success. Travelscene had their offices in Campbell Parade, Bondi Beach, and it didn't take long for them to outgrow those. They relocated to bigger, better offices at Bondi Junction and I was invited to their opening party. Doing my best to drain the promotional budget by quaffing the Chateau Gratis, I joined a group that included Travelscene's Bill Hollow and another guest, a senior manager from Qantas. The Qantas executive asked Bill if Travelscene wanted to change the timings and frequencies of the new 747 jumbos they had just introduced to the Bali route! I swooned. The national carrier was prepared to alter its flight scheduling just to fit the whims of a local wholesaler? Now that was power and success on a scale yet to be imagined.

During the year I acquired another decker to operate Australian tours. Before fit-out, I was approached by a big Sydney advertising agency to participate in some of their future

Top Deck Daze

PASSENGERS ALIGHT AFTER A SIX-MONTH BUS TOUR

Warrnambool became a major stopover on the itinerary of a unique London to Sydney bus tour at the weekend and the 20 passengers will long remember the hospitality extended to them.

The tour is unique because the passengers, and there were 23 of them for most of the trip, live on board a double decker bus for the six months that it takes to visit 22 countries.

Another unique aspect, which according to 'Top Deck Travel' tour courier, Greg Ettridge, has caused many Australian tour companies some embarrassment, is that the tour price including three meals a day, is $1008. This is $6 a day.

The reason Warrnambool became a major stop on such a long journey and the reason for the degree of hospitality extended, is that three Warrnambool girls were on board, at least from London to Adelaide.

The girls, Margaret and Alice Guyett and Marilyn Green, flew ahead to see their families and to prepare a welcome for their fellow passengers.

They rejoined the bus at Port Fairy on Saturday afternoon and soon after, the brightly painted double decker bus arrived in the yard at Mr Jack Guyett's home in Timor street.

WELCOME

A rousing Warrnambool welcome included a barbecue attended by about 100 people.

Festivities, centred around a barrel of beer provided by Mr Guyett, continued late into the evening.

Afterwards, the eight British, four New Zealand and eight Australian passengers unfolded the assortment of bunks ingeniously placed on the two levels of the bus, and took advantage of their quiet parking place in the Guyetts' yard.

In spite of the warm hospitality, the tour members who leave Warrnambool today were disappointed to be leaving "three live-wires" behind.

They have another 10 days of travel before the end of the tour in Sydney.

Alice, Margaret and Marilyn left Australia for Italy by ship in April 1975. They then travelled to London where they bought a van which was to be their home for the next four months.

They obtained jobs as buffet assistants at London's Heathrow Airport before heading for Munich for the 1975 October 'Bierfest'.

On their return to London, they moved into a house near the airport and obtained jobs in the area.

DISCOVERED

It was then that they discovered 'Top Deck Travel' as an economical means of travelling Europe with other young people. The company has a suggested age range for its passengers of between 18 and 30.

They went on a 6½-week tour of central Europe, another tour which took in France, Spain, Portugal and Morocco and included the famous bullfight in Pamplona, and made a return visit to the Munich 'Bierfest' all with Top Deck Travel.

Alice then went on a tour of Russia, Scandanavia, Poland and West Berlin with a friend she had met with Top Deck.

The three left London on October 7 on the first overland to Australia to be tried by the company.

Pictured after the bus arrived in Warrnambool on Saturday are from left, Marilyn Green, 23, Alice Guyett, 24, tour driver and courier, Greg Ettridge, 26, of Western Australia, and Margaret Guyett, 22. The courier's job is to organise the tour's finance, provisions, visas and bookings.

Countries visited after the bus moved through Europe included Turkey, Syria, Israel, Iraq, Iran, Afghanistan, Pakistan, India and Nepal before a month's stop-over at Katmandu.

During the break, the girls climbed the foothills of the Himalayas while some of the more adventurous members of the party set their sights on higher slopes.

The party left Katmandu on January 10 after leaving the bus, and headed to Calcutta in India. They then went to Burma for a week and then on to Bangkok, Malaysia and Thailand, travelling by ferry and public transport.

The group travelled by train to Penang and after several days in that area, travelled on by train to Malacca and then by bus to Singapore.

They then flew to Indonesia where they spent six days before flying on to Sydney where they boarded 'Top Deck's' Australian double decker bus, which is fitted out like the bus they started the journey on, with washing, cooking and sleeping facilities.

BEGINNING

Top Deck Travel was started when two Australians in London, a teacher and a veterinary surgeon, fitted out a double decker bus to drive back to Australia.

After advertising for passengers for a trial run to Morocco, the bus set off with 18 on board. On their return, more people asked to go and from that, the company grew and now has 13 buses.

This includes two coaches for conventional camping trips to Russia and Scandinavia. The only reason that coaches are used is that the company's double decker buses cannot fit under the bridges in Scandinavia.

The London/Sydney overland created tremendous interest and gave us some helpful publicity.

Blunder Down-under – Australia 1977

campaigns. The money was too good to refuse. The first one was for draught Guinness. The agency painted the bus in the appropriate livery and my job was to drive around Sydney in the vicinity of a pub soon to 'come on line'. Guinness gave me hundreds of vouchers, representing free middies, to give away as promotional incentives whenever I stopped the bus. Of course I always kept a third of them for me and my friends for the following Friday evening. Inevitably, I acquired a lifelong taste for Guinness.

Another contract was for the launch of a new brand of peanuts called 'Havesome'. The same deal applied and I had enough peanuts to keep the Taronga Park Zoo chimps well fed for a decade. One variant, though, was that I was required to don an enormous plastic peanut outfit while giving away my samples. God knows what Mum was telling her friends now. Free enterprise was one thing, but this was getting ridiculous!

Peanuts *visits the PM.*

Chapter 10

BOOM OR DOOM

(LONDON 1977–78)

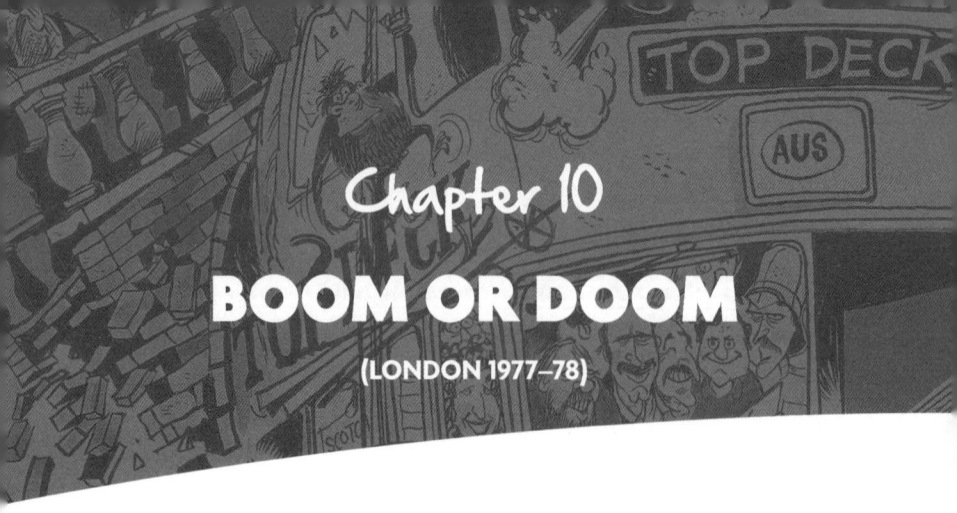

Liz and I returned to London for the northern winter from December 1977 to March 1978. Screw wanted some time in the Australian summer with Jude and to take the opportunity to do some marketing while things were quiet in London. Jude and her brother, Mike Stent, had produced an excellent twenty-page brochure, our first in full-colour, for the 1978 season—a great improvement on the twelve-page 1977 brochure which had been no more than a reprint of the 1976 version with new dates and prices. Screw had great plans for Top Deck's expansion in the year ahead. Top Deck now had more than fifteen double-deckers on the road and the business was entering its most expansionary phase. There were more than fifty European tour departures, eight Russia/Scandinavia coach-camping departures, and the festival tours as well as the overlands.

Before Screw left for Australia we had a long talk about our respective futures. I was still fairly committed to reside in Sydney for the foreseeable future. Among other things, Liz had gone back to uni to do a Masters degree and it was unreasonable for her not to have the opportunity to complete it. There was far too much work for one senior manager to handle in London and so, after much deliberation, I decided to sell half my shareholding in Top Deck London to Mick Carroll for A$15 000. That made it fifty per cent for Screw and twenty-five per cent each for Mick and me. I thought I'd done well—a big return on my initial investment of £600, anyway.

Boom or Doom – London 1977-78

Screw welcomed Mick as a new partner. Hopefully the shareholding would prove enough of an incentive for Mick to hang around for a long while. Energetic, personable and with a comprehensive knowledge of all aspects of the business, Mick was more than an equal replacement for me.

Screw and Mick knew that it was, in many ways, a big step for me to be no longer working full-time in London as a director. The job carried with it a degree of status and you were certainly at the centre of all the work and social action. In order that there was some continuity of management style, they decided to appoint, as my replacement, a new London-based director. He was a likable-enough chap, but had a rather complex personality. He'd obviously had a difficult childhood and spent some time in a 'home' for wayward youth at Battersea. By coincidence, he was also named Bill, but he had four legs, not two.

Bill the Dog settled in immediately to the rigours of his new position. The regime of the Battersea Dogs' Home was obviously quite similar to that of Top Deck's head office.

I settled in for my three-month stint in the London office. One of my first management dictates was to improve the phone-answering techniques of all the office staff, especially those in sales. I felt their manner was rather slack and I didn't think it created a very good impression with customers. Therefore, I sent around a memo stating that, 'The phone must be answered as follows: "Good morning, this is Top Deck Travel. Bill speaking. How may I help you?"' Within an hour of the memo's dissemination, I received a series of at

Bill Barking and Mick.

Top Deck Daze

64 Kenway Road, Earls Court, our main office from 1977 to 1985 — definitely on the way up, located in with the competition.

least ten phone calls. All the callers had strange, foreign accents, and followed the same routine: 'Ello? This is Mr Singh calling. Is that Mr Bill Speaking?' the suspect Indian would ask. 'Yes,' I would reply, 'How may I help you?' 'Oh, I am wanting to speak to the other Bill, Mr Bill Barking, is he a-wailable?' From that day onwards I was referred to as Bill Speaking, to differentiate me from the dog that everyone now called Bill Barking.

We had a new shop and rear offices in London as well: 64 Kenway Road, Earls Court. Significantly, this was just down the road from the pub where Barry Humphries and Bazza Crocker had filmed the movie The Adventures of Barry McKenzie. We still kept the premises at Dawes Road, as they were invaluable as a hostel, but Screw quite rightly felt that Dawes Road was a bit out of the way. Kenway Road wasn't quite Earls Court Road but it was much closer to the heart of the action. The office move had been done in haste and it hadn't been possible to inform all the crew, many of whom were on the road for months at a time.

Greg 'Five Eights' Lloyd, one of our drivers, had his Mum come to visit him from Australia. I happened to be in the front office at Kenway Road, during the first week after my return, when Mrs Lloyd came in.

'I'm looking for Greg Lloyd,' she asked of Kessa Ware who was working behind one of the desks. No one had ever known Greg's real name. He'd always been known to us as simply Five Eights. Most of our crew had nicknames and it was quite common not to know them by any other name.

'Greg Lloyd? Oh, we don't have a *Greg* Lloyd working for us,' Kessa said. 'You must mean Graham James Lloyd. I'm terribly sorry, madam, but he's in ah, ah, Morocco this week.' Kessa had just had her regular weekly visit from the local constabulary, in the form of Police Constable Davies, with his fifty summonses for G. J. Lloyd. PC Davies had been visiting Top Deck for so long he was on first-name terms with all the staff, and had developed a crush on Kessa and had even asked her for a date.

'No, no. Not Graham Lloyd. Gregory Lloyd,' insisted Five Eights' Mum. 'He's my own son. He definitely works for you. He's been writing to me for over a year now.' Kessa called out to Dave Reed, the new operations manager, in the back office, 'Dave, do we have a Greg Lloyd working for us?'

'Never heard of him,' yelled Dave. 'They must mean Graham James Lloyd, but he's in Kathmandu this week …'

Mrs Lloyd was in tears now, 'He, he …' she sobbed, 'He said he'd be here to meet me.' I comforted the poor distressed mother as best I could and then helped her to find accommodation in a nearby hotel. I assured her I would keep in touch and pass on any relevant news.

The following day, Five Eights came into the Kenway Road office.

'Where the hell have you been, Five Eights?' queried Dave, the operations manager. 'You were due back here from your trip three days ago.'

'I did get back three days ago,' said the peeved Five Eights. 'I've been at Dawes Road, waiting for my mother. It's taken me

Top Deck Daze

Enterprise Hotel.

three days to find out what's going on! Nobody bothered to tell me we'd moved offices.'

'Hang on. Hang on. Did you say, "Waiting for your mother?"' asked a surprised Dave. 'What the hell is your real name, Five Eights?'

Top Deck was shocked to discover it did have a real G. Lloyd on its payroll after all. Mother was finally reunited with son (Greg) in tearful hugs and kisses. Where might this trail lead? After all these years on the run, perhaps the illusive Graham James Lloyd might yet reveal himself to us one day in the flesh? It was a chilling thought.

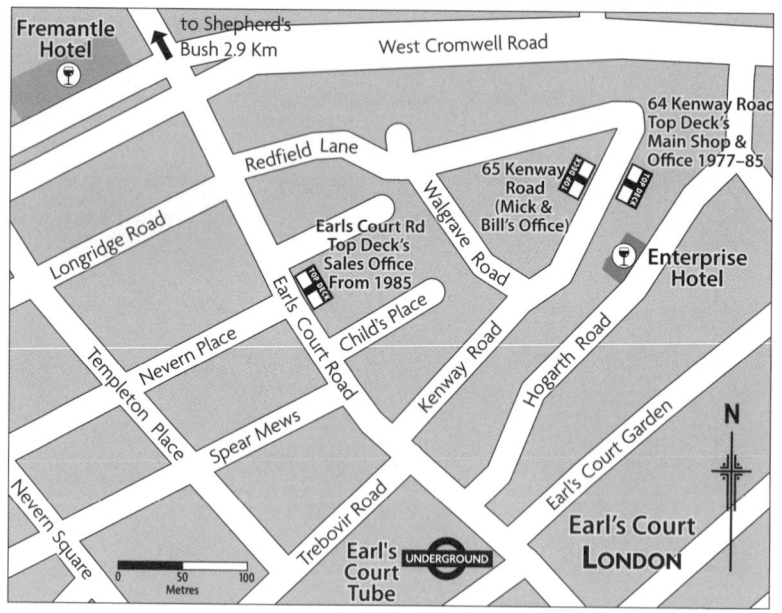

Top Deck expanded so that three offices opened between 1975 and 1985, and there was still need for further expansion.

Boom or Doom – London 1977-78

As well as the new offices, Top Deck had also acquired a new bus yard during the year. In early 1976, when Screw had bought the 'job lot' of four new buses to take our total to seven, we outgrew our first little yard at Chelsea. We managed to rent some open space at a yard at Richmond from the lessee, Continental Pioneer. Their sixty coaches were principally engaged in school runs and local charters.

The arrangement was good for us in one way because it was so cheap; we only ever paid for three bus spaces, even though our fleet had grown beyond fifteen. As was the case with so many things in Britain, the conditions were bearable only in summer. Best of all were our lunches, taken al fresco on the top deck of *Tuft*. The old girl (our third bus) was now retired with half her roof rolled back like a sardine can. Rex Julian was the first of many of our crew to have an altercation with a low-flying bridge, this one in Amsterdam. No injuries, thank God.

Kerry, Kirsty and Ros – three of our key personnel.

Top Deck Daze

On the flip side, the working conditions at the Richmond yard were, on the whole, atrocious. There was only one power lead stretching over the open ground for ninety metres. It would be severed in a shower of sparks several times a day, whenever it was run over by a Continental bus. We had one tiny garden shed, the size of an outhouse, in which our tools were stored. You'd have to lie on the bare, muddy earth to do any work on the underside of a bus. It might have been tolerable in the short summer months but in the cold, wet and ice of the other nine, it was bloody miserable. In addition we had to cope with the bossy manager of Continental Pioneer from whom we rented our parking spaces—a vertically/follicularly challenged Pommie coot called Arthur. He compensated for his lack of self-confidence by throwing his weight around and wielding his management power like a miniature Napoleon.

It was interesting for us Aussies to witness the different ethics of people in the businesses we dealt with. Those in British management positions invariably acted in an autocratic, authoritarian manner. Conversely the members of staff (in the case of Continental Pioneer, the drivers and mechanics) were obsequious, calling the manager 'Sir' and physically cowering in his presence. We found it was automatic for British staff to think their managers were 'the enemy'. Rarely were they proved to be wrong.

The opposite was the case with Aussies and Kiwis. They might treat their managers with caution, but would wait until the person proved themselves, one way or the other, before forming an opinion. They would then grant the manager the respect, or otherwise, they believed he or she deserved. Consequently our crew either ignored Arthur or laughed and ridiculed him on the odd occasions he came over and abused us for some misdemeanour, real or imagined.

'Which one of you Orstralian bastards has been taking tools from our workshop?' he'd roar.

'Geezez, Arthur, have you got the rags on today?' would come the reply, and from another, 'Check your pantyhose, Arthur.

They look as if they're a bit tight under the armpits,' and from another, 'Yeah, and remember, don't fart while you've got them on, Arthur, or you'll blow your boots off,' and so on, until Arthur disappeared, swearing and cursing and threatening to throw us out the minute he saw Screw. Fortunately, his business was so busy he either never got around to it or, most likely, used us as a means of letting off his ample supply of steam. So we tolerated Arthur's yard and Arthur tolerated us—to a point, that is.

No planning whatsoever went into the acquisition of new buses. If a particular departure date for a trip sold well and looked like having an excess of punters, Screw demanded the sales staff keep taking the bookings. Then he simply sent someone up to 'Norths' in Leeds with £400 and, hey, presto, a new bus would appear in the yard the following day. Amid much mayhem, a new, impossible record time for a fit-out would be set. Work would continue twenty-four hours a day in all sorts of weather.

Up until this time we had hand-painted the buses. Mick was painting away one day in the pouring rain because the newly converted bus was due out the next morning and great streaks of orange paint dribbled down the side panels onto the ground. Arthur pulled up in his Jaguar and surveying the ridiculous scene, rolled down the window and yelled, 'You can't paint in the rain, son.' Mick just smiled as he kept working away.

'Waterproof paint,' he called out in reply, without looking up. Poor Arthur just shrugged his shoulders, shook his head in disbelief, and drove off.

In the search for better quality and use of time, Screw decided that we ought to hire a spray-painting machine and give the four buses in the yard at that particular time a once over to tart them up. Good idea. The buses were driven out into the open and lined up, end-to-end, while trestles were set up and all the preparations of taping-up bus windows, etc. were completed.

Screw would invariably turn up at the yard having already been to the office, or out selling, dressed in reasonably good slacks, shoes, collared shirt (and bag of fruit and tie, if he'd been

Top Deck Daze

to the bank) but he would never change into work clothes or overalls before launching himself into the manual labour. He'd finish the day covered in grease and mud from head to toe. He was true to form on this particular day as he barked orders while he mixed the paint, his good clothes already half-orange and black before the spray-painting machine was even turned on.

Screw put on a wonderful performance, tie flapping in the breeze as he scampered up, down and along the trestles, jumping from one bus roof to another, till they'd all been given a thorough going-over. We stood, looking up, nodding our encouragement and we were rewarded by the occasional wave. After half-an-hour of furious activity the Rembrandt of Richmond climbed down from his artist's lair and we all stood back to admire his handiwork.

Much self-congratulation was going on until, from immediately behind us, there was a furious outburst of rage.

'You stupid, reproducing, female body parts!' (or words to that effect) Arthur screamed at the top of his lungs. 'Look what you've gone and bloody well done to my Jag!' Arthur's month old, latest version, biggest model, XJ6 Jaguar was completely covered in a none-too-fine orange spray. And not only Arthur's! Twelve cars in all, belonging to the Continental Pioneer staff, were covered in a bright orange overspray as a result of Screw's artisanship. The cars were in the lee of a rather stiff breeze that we hadn't really accounted for, distracted as we were by Screw's zealous activity.

After twenty minutes of a running, jumping tirade of uninterrupted, slanderous invective from Arthur, we were left with the unmistakeable impression that we were no longer welcome in his yard. As we cleaned up the buses, Screw stood calmly, arms folded, watching Arthur's ballistics. When Arthur was finally able to get some comprehensible words through his frothing mouth, he made it understood that Screw would be paying for the cars to be 'buffed' before we were sued by every lawyer who'd ever taken silk.

As a result of all this, I was keen to have a look at the new workshops we'd rented at Shepherds Bush, not far from the Latimer Road tube station. There were some industrial units under the built-up section of the M4 motorway. Ours was an old factory, built with the typically sawtooth-shaped roof. The lease was held by a company called Omnibus Promotions that did the same type of advertising work with double-deckers that I'd been doing in Australia. They only needed a small section of the factory. Fortunately the street was a dead-end, so we used it for overflow parking.

Shepherds Bush was a great improvement on the Richmond yard, especially as it was only ten minutes from our new Kenway

Top Deck Daze

Road, Earls Court, shop and offices. We were lucky to have anything at all, given such accommodation was at a premium in the crowded metropolis. On the downside, even though we had a roof, of sorts, most of the glass skylights were broken, exposing buses and workers to the dreaded elements. Grime, muck and grease covered the floors and walls. We could have cleaned it up, but bus preparations always seemed to be our first priority.

We had a new sales manager in London too, Bob 'Bob-a-Job' Sanderson. Bob-a-Job started off by handing out brochures at Aussie House and running promotional slide evenings at the Fremantle Hotel where we booked passengers wanting pre-or post-tour accommodation. Bob-a-Job's role gradually increased in importance, often because he was the only person in the back office at the time a decision had to be made, everybody else being either at the workshop or attending to other crises.

Above all, Bob-a-Job was loyal, to the company and especially, to Screw. Typical of many of our staff, he was devoted to Top Deck. All his waking hours were taken up with work or social commitments involving the company. Top Deck became a family; a way of life for the majority of our crew. We were away from family and familiar friends and somehow the unique experiences we shared on the road and in our London sojourns developed a bond between us that extended beyond normal friendship. It was a kind of brotherhood spirit that bound us for life. There was also something about the old deckers themselves. They seemed to have a character all their own. They toiled away in heat waves and blizzards, in places they

'Bob-a-Job' Sanderson, Top Deck's first sales manager.

Boom or Doom – London 1977-78

were never meant to go, like devoted, uncomplaining friends, and many of the crew developed an affection for them that was hard to describe.

It was Bob-a-Job who offered to take me to the Shepherds Bush workshop for the first time. Bob-a-Job had just taken possession of a snazzy little white MG convertible. It was second-hand, but in top condition, and great for impressing the girls. It had a black, canvas hood that could be folded back in good weather—but this was December, and the hood was well and truly up and the heater on full bore as we made our way up the narrow streets to the workshop.

The working conditions may not have been as crude as Richmond, but it was still bitterly cold in the workshop when the icy westerlies blew, as they did this day, from the North Atlantic. To afford some protection from the cold, the boys would fill a big, forty-four gallon drum with timber offcuts and get a good fire raging.

It was lunchtime when we arrived. About a dozen of the crew stood around the drum, tea mugs in hand, when Lew Pulbrook,

Annie Bulmer was our first specialist airfare consultant. 'Dillon' O'Sullivan was Top Deck's Operation's Manager.

Top Deck Daze

a driver who'd just returned from an overland, lobbed a Delhi bunger into the middle of the fire from the mezzanine level of the workshop.

Anyone who hasn't been on an overland might fail to appreciate the role fireworks play in the lives of those on the subcontinent. During my first few days in Pakistan, I was in a chai-house when I heard this extraordinary succession of explosions that I thought was either the outbreak of civil war or an escalation of the border hostilities with India. On investigation, it turned out to be merely a wedding procession through the streets. Births, deaths, marriages, ceremonies of any description, were an excuse for fireworks. You could buy monsters that dwarfed the two-penny bungers we bought as kids which used to blast tin cans twice as high as telegraph poles.

It was one of these brutes that Lew lobbed into the fire just as Bob-a-Job and I pulled up at the entrance to the workshops in Bob's MG. The boys standing around the fire had seen Lew's act of sabotage, and all Bob-a-Job and I caught sight of was a dozen figures darting to the farthest corners of the workshop. Bob had

At the India Pakistan Border—all buses carried a plentiful supply of Indian fireworks.

just pulled on the handbrake when there was an almighty 'Kaar-booooooooom'. A tongue of flame and cinders shot metres into the air. Huge chunks of burning timber hurtled end-on-end through great arcs, with one flaming six-by-four landing smack on the top of Bob's roof. We flung ourselves out of the car doors. I ran to find a blanket as poor Bob-a-Job looked on, gaping mouth frozen in shock as he gazed at the smouldering canvas hood, now crumpled on the floor of his once snazzy little car.

I changed into overalls and started working on the buses; nothing too technical, just general maintenance work and cleaning. The workshop manager was a fantastic guy by the name of Milton Hornhardt. He set me to work replacing the rear wheels on one of the deckers parked in the street. Another driver spied my singled-handed struggle and walked over and introduced himself. 'Dillon O'Sullivan,' he said, extending his hand with a big, friendly smile. 'Having a bit of trouble there, digger?' combining a touch of Anzac mateship with a subtle inference that I was making heavy weather of a relatively simple task. The wheels were obviously well ahead on points at this juncture. 'I'll give you a hand, mate.'

I stood up and introduced myself. We worked away happily for some time, claiming victory over the wheels, then moved on from job to job. Dillon was a Kiwi of medium height and trim stature, but looked strong and shook hands with a firm, sure grip. He had dark, curly hair, a thick but neatly clipped moustache, and walked with a confident, almost cocky, swagger. He hadn't been working for the company long, but his competence appeared to match his confidence and he dished out orders to me at regular intervals and inspected my work from time to time, apparently not rating it that highly compared to his exacting standards. 'New driver are you, mate?' he asked after some time, obviously intending to give someone a quiet word about my limited potential. I explained my history and position in the company with some embarrassment. 'Shit. What do you know? I thought you were a trainee or something.' We both found the incident equally amusing and agreed to meet for a drink in the pub after work. We became great mates and a year or so later, Dillon moved into operations.

With a new director (Bill Barking), new office (Kenway Road), new workshop (Shepherds Bush), new operations manager (Dave Reed) and new sales manager (Bob-a-Job), I felt proud that Top Deck was obviously moving to new levels of professionalism. It was great to have someone like Dave Reed in operations to take the pressure off us directors. He was filling me in on his new role when the phone rang in his office. I was to get a 'live' demonstration of how he operated.

To avoid run-ins with the Department of Transport, the procedure was now for couriers to meet their passengers at Victoria Station and catch a train to Dover where they would meet their buses which would have travelled empty from our London yard. These were the days before the European Economic Community brought in common transport policies so, if we avoided problems in England, continental authorities seemed happy to ignore us. The phone call that Dave Reed received was from a driver departing on

Top Deck Daze

an overland, en route to Dover to meet his passengers and courier. He'd only made it to Farthings Corner Services, halfway to Dover, when the bus had broken down. It was serious, a big end bearing by the sound of it, and he was calling Dave for instructions. Dave decided he'd have to take a replacement bus out to the driver and so asked me to accompany him. We could talk on the way.

'This guy's obviously pretty experienced,' I quizzed Dave about the overland driver.

'Not really, but he was on the training trip we organised earlier in the season.' *Training Trip?* That sounded impressive. I'd never heard of us doing one of those before. Top Deck really was moving ahead then. 'Unfortunately, he failed,' Dave added, putting things in better perspective. 'We're a bit short of crew.'

Up until this season, all trainees went on the scheduled trips, taking any free seats that were available. This was okay but there was no real means of 'quality control'. Few, if any, of our existing crew had been given any formal training themselves. So, while we had some outstanding crew, standards were, understandably, not that high.

Screw, Dave explained, had decided that a training trip would be the solution. We could weed out the underperformers. Rex Julian would be the courier. He was the obvious choice, given his experience and popularity. Fifteen trainees were assembled for a three-week European. At the last minute, Rex was called on to do a Russia/Scandi—there was always a chronic shortage of crew. Next day, the trainees worked with the driver, Alan Rowe, preparing the bus for their trip, but with no trainer-courier in sight.

'Hell, Dave, there's got to be someone here who can take the trip?' Screw demanded.

'The only one in town is Tom the Pom, and he's a driver.'

'Well, he'll do, damn it. Find him, wherever he is.'

Of course Steve 'Tom the Pom' Parkhill was at the Cock, the crew's favourite pub at the time, drinking his meagre bonus from the trip he'd just completed, and looking forward to a well-earned rest. Screw and Dave decided to ensure the trip got under way okay, and so joined the decker, with the trainees on board, at Earls Court before it trundled·down North End Road and pulled up outside the Cock. Tom the Pom was paralytic by this stage. Dave and the driver, Alan Rowe, were summonsed by Screw to drag Tom to the gents, douse him with cold water in a vain attempt to sober him up, and carry him, rugby-hooker style, onto the bus. Alan and Dave put the still semiconscious Tom to bed upstairs while Screw lectured the trainees on the high standards the company expected of its future crew and what would, and would not, be tolerated in terms of their behaviour, over the next three weeks. Screw made a special point about how the company frowned upon the excessive consumption of alcohol.

Dave explained all this while we fetched a replacement bus. Finally we reached Farthings Corner where we located the broken-down bus. I introduced myself to the unfortunate driver.

'Gidday,' he replied, 'Timmy Oliver's the name. Pleased to meet you.' While I chatted to Tim (he became known to everyone as 'Mrs Oliver', or 'Mrs Oliver's Little Boy'), Dave inspected Tim's bus. It would take us more than an hour to transfer the gear.

'What's all this, Oliver?' Dave said accusingly to Tim. Stowed under the stairwell and seat lockers was every conceivable spare part a decker could possible need. Virtually the entire yard's supply was there. Not only that, but every tool that wasn't nailed to the wall had been taken as well, including the workshop's prized possession—its one-and-only torque wrench.

'Bloody hell, Oliver,' yelled Dave, picking up the torque wrench with great care, then cradling it with reverence, as if it were the Holy Grail. 'Did you leave anything behind?'

'Geezs, you never know with these old buses,' stammered Tim defensively, as we surveyed his haul. Well, Dave could hardly argue with that. 'And, besides, 30 000 km is a long way for a bloke to drive. Nothing like being prepared,' concluded Tim defiantly.

Dave was fuming and his temper wasn't abated by the sweaty job of transferring all the supplies and changing over all the mattress covers and curtains, etc. Dave saw to it that not one single spare, nor one single tool, went onto Tim's replacement bus. I could see the longing look on Tim's face, but he daren't challenge the authority of the new operations manager. Finally the job was done, and with great ceremony, Tim climbed into the driver's cab for a second go at his long haul to Kathmandu. Dave and I stood beside the open door to say goodbye.

'Oh, one more thing,' said Tim to Dave. 'I was told on the training trip that all drivers were to be provided with comprehensive trip notes, guidebooks, and maps for their tours. There's not a skerrick of anything like that on either of these buses.' Dave stared at Tim and said nothing. Notes? Maps? Guidebooks? What would the crew be asking for next? Presumably such a stupid, inane request wasn't worthy of a reply.

'Well, what are the directions to Kathmandu, then?' Tim asked to break the embarrassed silence. There was another long, deliberate pause before Dave condescended to reply. 'You take the ferry from Dover to Calais, okay?' he said in an exaggeratedly tolerant manner.

'Yeah,' said Tim, concentrating hard as he committed it all to memory.

'Then you get to the docks on the other side, okay?'

'Yeaaah,' said Tim nodding slowly, still fully focused.

'You drive to the end of the docks and there's a big set of gates, okay?'

'Yeaaah.'

'Then you turn right,' said Dave, as he slammed the driver's door shut and stormed off.

Chapter 11

FARE'S FAIR

(AUSTRALIA 1978)

I finished my three-month stint in London in March 1978 and returned to Australia but, before I did, Screw sat me down to explain how he saw the future development of the company in the Antipodes. He announced that we were to become, among other things, travel agents, concentrating on selling airfares.

This was not entirely foreign to me because we had always sold airfares out of our London offices. Rod McEwin (husband of Di, who had thought up the name 'Top Deck'), a vet mate of Screw's on a working holiday in the UK, was the first employee to do this on a regular basis way back in 1974–75. If Rod couldn't sell someone a Top Deck trip on the front steps of Aussie House (where he worked as a commission salesman), he would ask them if they needed a flight to somewhere. He'd take their phone number and guarantee to beat any quote they could get. It didn't take him long to find a string of wholesalers or 'bucket-shops' (cheap, non-licensed travel agents) where he could acquire a better wholesale fare, making margins of £10 or more—good money at the time. From then on, selling airfares from the front office at Dawes Road and, subsequently, Kenway Road was a regular occurrence.

When we were at Dawes Road in 1976, we were introduced to, and became good friends with, Peter Hicks, the manager of the London office of the Australian Union of Students Travel (AUS). It had a tremendous worldwide network of cheap student airfares, having negotiated deals with all the major airlines.

Top Deck Daze

The agency was even permitted by the International Air Transport Authority (IATA, the regulatory body governing all airlines) to print its own 'brown cover' tickets (as distinct from IATA's blue ones). No other agency group worldwide, to our knowledge, had permission to do this.

Peter Hicks allowed Top Deck London to on-sell AUS's 'brown' tickets at a modest commission. You had to be a genuine student to buy one of those tickets and, as proof of identity, you needed an official student ID card. The AUS agency was a legitimate, student-owned organisation and, as such, had access to the officially printed cards. It wasn't permitted to extend this favour to Top Deck. Needless to say, this was no barrier to Screw. He got the printer who was doing our brochures to whip up some student cards in no time.

Top Deck was soon making more money from selling its student cards than it was from airfares. The cards were in great demand as they entitled the bearer to all sorts of discounts in Europe, from entrance fees at places of interest to buses, trains, and the like. It brought potential customers through our door at Kenway Road as well.

The AUS's financial management was, if anything, worse than Top Deck's. Consequently, it wasn't long before they went broke in a big way. From the ashes rose Student Travel Australia (STA), a far more commercially oriented animal, no longer owned by the Students' Union. However, the London manager of STA, Dick Porter, still kept up the old arrangements with Top Deck for the supply of 'brown' tickets. He often had cause to rap us over the knuckles (and temporarily withdraw supply) when airlines complained that seventy-five-year-old grandmothers were turning up to their flights with brown tickets bought with their new student ID cards from Top Deck.

Back in Australia in 1978, while Travelscene had served us well as a general sales agent (GSA), Screw felt that the future of Top Deck, and our own personal interests, would be best served if we took responsibility for the marketing of Top Deck into

Fare's Fair – Australia 1978

our own hands. During a brief visit to Brisbane in 1977, Screw opened up our very first shop in Australia, at 333 Queen Street. He installed Greg 'Wombat' Ettridge as the manager, who took over the responsibility for marketing Top Deck in Queensland. In 1978, I rented a small, first-floor office in Berry Street, North Sydney, installing Ros Diprose as manager, to represent Top Deck in New South Wales. Ros and her sister Liz had worked with us in London, and I knew Ros had all the talents necessary to run New South Wales autonomously.

From the beginning, the shops doubled as retail travel agencies and so, in this way, the seeds of what was to become 'Flight Centre' were sown.

I organised for Ray Smith to help open and then manage our first office in Melbourne. Ray was an ex-Geelong, ex-Atrek, ex-Top-Deck courier with a round, short-sighted, bespectacled face. After a stint abroad, Ray was keen to settle back into a more sedate Melbourne lifestyle and we felt lucky that he was keen to join the Australian team. A genuine super-salesperson, he always had me in fits of laughter, sometimes intentionally because he was a paid-up comedian but, at other times, because of his 'absentminded-professor' manner.

We selected a site opposite the trendy IXL 'Jam Factory' shopping centre in Chapel Street, South Yarra, as the first Victorian Top Deck travel agency. It was a stinking hot day when we were putting the finishing touches to the fit-out of the shop. I ducked up to the local pub to get us half-a-dozen bottles of Vic Bitter as a reward for our sweaty endeavours. I filled up some plastic cups with the cold amber fluid. Ray was painting some brochure racks and he was also using some small plastic cups to hold his paint.

'Take a break, Ray. You've earned it,' I urged him. Ray stood up, relaxed against the counter and stood back to admire his work. He reached over and picked up a cup and, with an initial look of great satisfaction, downed half-a-pint of green paint.

When Screw next visited Australia, he wasn't at all happy with the obscure location of the North Sydney office I had chosen.

Top Deck Daze

He had the vision (as always) to see that if we intended to make a success of retailing travel, the location of the shops would be critical. I was a nervous wreck when he relocated us to a very prominent shop at 83 Mount Street, North Sydney, committing us to a three-year lease at the exorbitant rent of $12 000 per annum. I tossed and turned at night wondering how we were ever going to make ends meet.

There was no discounting of airfares in Australia at all at this time, and never had been. The airline regulator, IATA, was one of the most successful cartels in the post-1945 western world. There was no such thing as a Trade Practices Act to ensure competition. In fact, difficult to believe though it may be, given today's cutthroat retailing, travel agents were threatened with fines from the Department of Transport if they were caught selling airfares below the published levels set by IATA. Consequently, all the agents made a cosy living on their set commissions, until Top Deck came along, that is.

We had seen the situation in London where the discount 'bucket-shop' travel agents sold both charter and scheduled airlines at a fraction of the IATA prices. Sure, the odd one went broke, and some people lost their money, but if the consumer was sensible when selecting an agent he or she could save heaps of money.

One of the best airfare deals we had in London was with Philippine Airlines on the return route between London, Sydney and Melbourne. Of course, the arrangement wasn't available to us in Australia, but we advertised the fares here nevertheless (that is the Sydney/London sector) without specifying the carrier, at forty per cent below the normal selling price, and booked the flights by telex with our London office, paying by telegraphic transfer. The fares were much cheaper if bought in the UK and the exchange rate was in our favour as well. This was called 'cross-border' ticketing and was an absolute 'no-no' as far as IATA was concerned. It was so audacious that no one could figure out what we were doing, nor how we were doing it, including Philippine Airlines itself, in Australia.

Fare's Fair - Australia 1978

Sales boomed for four months before the scam was discovered and Philippine Airlines pulled the deal in London, but we made as much profit in those four months as we would have normally made in fourteen. More importantly, we defied IATA and the Department of Transport and got away with it, and established our image in Australia as a discounter where a genuine bargain airfare might be had for the very first time.

We capitalised on this with other simple, but very effective, marketing ideas. Ray Smith painted his Melbourne shop window with 'Discount, Bali' and the price, in big, bold 'butcher-shop window' style, iridescent green and orange paint. Most travel agents had dark, dingy, boring shopfronts and hated the very thought of any form of discounting, so this type of display stood out like the proverbial dog's behind and sales went through the roof. We copied this idea in Sydney and Brisbane.

Ray (in Melbourne) and Wombat (in Brisbane) were always exchanging crazy, innovative ways to market and passing their ideas onto me (in Sydney). Neither had been travel agents before starting with Top Deck and so weren't shackled by old ideas. When I went to visit Wombat for the first time in his new Brisbane shop, I passed a big-footed abominable snowman figure handing out ski brochures on the city footpath.

'Gidday, Bill,' said the snowman as he thrust a brochure at me, 'Friggin hot, ain't it?' It was Wombat's unmistakeable voice.

Gradually, by wholesaling Top Deck through other travel agents and by direct sales using our own promotional ideas, Australia continued to grow as a source of substantial bookings for the London-based tour operations. We became particularly successful at filling the overland buses doing the return legs from Kathmandu to London. Additionally, our retailing of airfares and other tour products was becoming more and more successful and was adding significantly to the profits of the Australian shops.

Chapter 12
PISSED ON THE PISTE
(ANDORRA 1978)

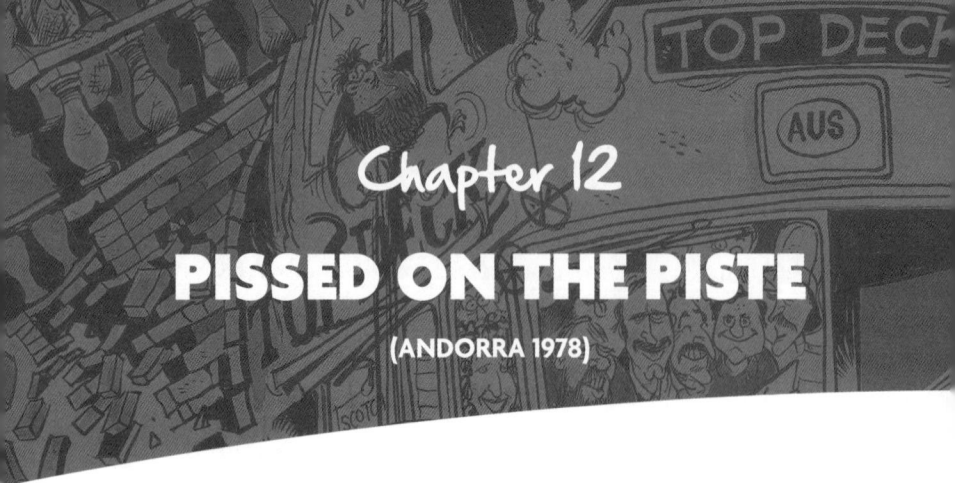

In absolute terms, 1978 was Top Deck's greatest year of expansion. The fleet grew from fifteen to twenty-six buses. There were over seventy decker European tours of three weeks duration or longer, as well as overlands, festival trips and coach-camping tours to Russia.

The Beerfest in October signalled the end of the season as far as bus touring on the Continent was concerned. Winter was high season for our overlands but, with the exception of the Moroccan tours, most of the other Top Deck buses were off the road until the new season began in March/April of the following year. Most of the bigger camping-tour operators had European ski operations over winter, and so it was only a matter of time before Top Deck did the same thing.

When a small company called Panther Tours, run by a Kiwi, Dave 'Worm' Silk, got into difficulties in 1976, Screw helped out financially. In a joint venture, we ran ski tours in a Panther minibus to a small village in Austria. Even one of the deckers, *Tuft* (our third bus) did a trip down there, but no serious attempt was made to establish an ongoing ski operation until the winter of 1978–79.

It was Screw's idea that Top Deck's ski venue should be Andorra. Almost everyone's reaction was the same: 'Where's Andorra?' and, 'Are there any mountains there?' and, 'Do they get snow in winter?' With all the ritzy, instantly recognisable resorts that he could have chosen in the Alps, an obscure,

Pissed on the Piste – Andorra 1978

unheard of principality tucked away in the Pyrenees Mountains between France and Spain seemed like a crazy, typically oddball, Screw decision. It was. But, like the majority of Screw's oddball decisions, in the end, it turned out to be a master stroke. I say 'in the end' because, as with most of Top Deck's operations, turning theory into practice was a process fraught with potential disasters.

I had been to Andorra for the first time in the summer of 1974, so at least I knew the answer to the question, 'Where is it?' but the first I heard of the intended ski operation was on my first night back in London from Australia in December 1978. Again, I was to spend four months in London over the northern winter. While drinking with Screw and Mick at the Fremantle Hotel bar after work, one of our couriers, Graham Sewell, came in.

'Ah, I see you've made it, Graham,' said Screw. 'It's your birthday too, isn't it? Have a beer,' and, with that, and no further

Camel *passing through Lauterbrunnen in the winter of 1988.*

small talk, Screw proceeded to lecture Graham on the intricacies of running a ski operation in Andorra. I assumed Graham was to be the resident courier for Top Deck. Unlike our double-decker tours, Screw explained we would accommodate the punters in a low cost, but good value, hotel (warning lights were already flashing in my mind). Transfers from London to Andorra would be by coach, a twenty-four-hour trip, one way, if everything went according to plan (the operative word being 'if'), departing on a Friday night and returning on the following Saturday.

Pissed on the Piste – Andorra 1978

Graham just looked at Screw with a vacant stare through most of the verbal barrage. 'Got that?' said Screw. Graham nodded vaguely. 'How much money have you got on you?' Screw asked. 'Two hundred pounds,' replied Graham wearily.

'Look, cash flow isn't the best right at the moment,' Screw frowned, trying his best to look worried. 'We know you blokes make money on the black market. That'll be enough cash to get you going. Give us a "Hoy" when you run short and we'll send you a bit more.' Again Graham nodded absently and then, after a suitably polite pause in the conversation, asked to be excused so as to have an early night now that he knew he would be up at first light to drive to Andorra by car the following morning.

I was really concerned about Graham. He just didn't seem with it. Physically, he stood about the same height as Screw and had similar, sandy-coloured hair. He was not quite as solid, however. Graham loved the outdoor life though, and sailed and skied at every opportunity, so normally he looked fit, suntanned and brimming with good health. I'd known him as a bright, cheerful guy, always ready for a beer, a laugh and a funny story to relate in his lively, crisp New Zealand accent—but not on this occasion. Here he was, taking himself off to bed while the night was still a pup. He seemed pale and drawn, almost a shell of his former self.

'Is Graham all right?' I asked Screw with genuine concern, as Graham left the bar. 'He looks absolutely shattered.'

'Graham? Shattered?' Screw looked at me quizzically. It was obvious he had no idea what I was on about 'Naaa. Course not. He's all right. Nothing a few hours kip won't fix. Just the drive here, that's all.'

'The drive? Where from? Shepherds Bush?' I thought he'd just come in from the bus yard, only a suburb or two away.

'Shepherds Bush? No, stupid. Teheran, of course.'

'Teheran? Iran? My God! When did he leave there?'

'Five days ago,' said Screw, nonchalantly.

'Five days ago! That's impossible! Who was his driver?' I asked, knowing that Teheran to London in five days would have

Top Deck Daze

been a superhuman feat for just two crew—and in a Top Deck bus, for heaven's sake!

'Driver? He didn't have a driver. Well, he did have one before then—Robbie Goodall, but he's rooted. We call him Robbie Good-For-Fuck-All now. The bugger's got typhoid. Picked it up from the curry-munchers, I suppose. He had to fly back from Iran. They've got him in "Infectious Diseases" at Fulham Hospital.'

Screw was completely oblivious of Graham's physical state and couldn't understand my concern and, as far as he was concerned, that was the end of the conversation. He turned to Mick and launched into a dissertation on the best ways of marketing a ski resort that no one had ever heard of.

Before we left the bar later that evening, I suggested to Screw that, as it was more than a week before he and Mick left for their breaks in Australia, I may as well accompany Graham to Andorra. They agreed as there wasn't much for me to do in London in the meantime. Thirty-six passengers had booked on the first ski departure. On the following Friday, they would leave London on one of the two coaches (*Gonor* and *Rhea*) we used for the Russia/Scandis, with Rex Julian as the courier. Graham and I would leave a day earlier so as to be in Andorra to meet the coach on its arrival on the Saturday.

It was early on 10 December 1978 when Graham Sewell and I departed London, en route to Andorra, in one of the company cars, a ten-year-old Fiat 124 with suspect tyres and an even more suspect motor. 'Flat out' meant fifty kilometres per hour. It was fortunate that the most direct route to Andorra was south of Paris via Toulouse on the secondary N20. Had we driven on a motorway we'd have been rammed up the backside by a speeding truck, for sure.

Poor Graham was like a zombie for most of the trip, but he drove well enough in that trance-like state that comes from countless hours behind the wheel. All the overlanders experienced it. There were times when you drove from memory, as if everything was stored in the subconscious mind. When you

Pissed on the Piste – Andorra 1978

finally pulled up, hours later, you couldn't recall a single metre, nor a single moment, of the entire journey.

At other times Graham was quite lucid and recounted experiences from his just-completed overland. He had been in Kathmandu, at the Hotel Withies, with Robbie Goodall, Russell 'Dial' Facer, Lew Pulbrook, Mrs Oliver's Little Boy Timmy, and Dillon O'Sullivan, when he received a phone call from Screw. It was the first they'd heard from, or of, London, since leaving three months before. 'Don't call us, we'll call you,' was Screw's usual farewell to the overlanders and, on this occasion, he'd been true to his word.

'That you, Graham?' came Screw's crackling voice down the London/Kathmandu phone line.

'Yes, Screw. What can I do for you?'

'You ski don't you?'

'Yes.'

Kathmandu 1977, (left to right) Russell Facer, Tim Oliver, Dillon O'Sullivan, Robbie Goodall, Mrs Uncle, Lew Pulbrook, Mick, Graham Sewell and (in front) Uncle Arnu.

Top Deck Daze

'Good. You're the new courier for the ski program we're starting next month. Get yourself back here as soon as you can.' Click. End of conversation.

At least one of the seven deckers in Kathmandu at the time had to do an empty 'flyer' back to London because there still weren't enough bookings out of Australia to fill all the return trips.

Robbie chose to go as Graham's driver. To say Robbie wasn't fond of the subcontinent and its inhabitants was an understatement. The sooner he got out of there the better.

Graham and Robbie tried to pick up paying passengers en route, mainly out of Delhi, as all the 'flyers' did. This was a dangerous business as you encountered the oddest assortment of hippie backpacker types, and Graham got more than his fair share. One drug-crazed Italian tried to slit Graham's throat in Iran when he caught the Italian trying to bring hash on board the bus.

Hippies leaving Kathmandu.

Pissed on the Piste — Andorra 1978

When Robbie did less and less of the driving, Graham thought he was just slacking, until it was obvious that there was something seriously wrong with Robbie's health. By the time they reached Teheran, Robbie was almost unconscious, totally dehydrated and urinating blood. The only western doctors were on a US air force base which was now blockaded because of the pending revolution which deposed the Shah of Iran in the January of 1979.

Graham and Robbie bribed an Iranian driver to smuggle them in under a pile of firewood on the back of a truck that was supplying the base. The US doctors loaded Robbie with a concoction of drugs—enough, at least, to have him accepted on a commercial flight back to London. Graham then faced the long journey back to London as the lone driver with the remaining crazy backpackers.

It was nine o'clock on a Friday night when we made our way over the Pas de la Casa on the French/Andorran border, high in the Pyrenees Mountains. The driving sleet we'd encountered on the Haute-Garonne, south of Toulouse had, at this altitude, turned into sheets of snow. Drifts, two metres deep, lined the Port d'Envalira, the highest pass on the mountain, before the road swung down into the valley of the Valira d'Orient, past the little ski village of Soldeu, and on to Encamp where we were to find our hotel.

For the first one thousand years AD, Europe consisted of countless different fiefdoms ruled by an array of feudal lords of various persuasions. Over the centuries these tiny, independent principalities combined to form empires which, in turn, evolved into the countries that we recognise as the Europe of today. Some of the original principalities remain, such as Monaco, San Marino and Liechtenstein. Likewise, Andorra is a hangover from these feudal times.

Geographically isolated until the 1930s, when the first roads were built, Andorra has been ruled for 700 years by successive bishops from Urgel, Spain, in conjunction with the presidents of France. These 'princes of Andorra,' as they are known, made few laws to fetter the lives of the good citizens of the principality. Best of all there was little income tax and no sales tax, so goods of all description were to be had duty-free.

We arrived in Andorra three weeks before the season started. The map shows Encamp, where hurried arrangements were made to house thirty-six Top Deckers due the following day.

Pissed on the Piste – Andorra 1978

Andorra's delights were still a well-kept secret at the time Screw chose it as our ski resort.

The village of Encamp was in total darkness when Graham and I drove through the sleepy little backwater at ten-thirty that night. We made our way to the Hotel Encamp, at the far end of the main road through the town. The ski season didn't officially start for another three weeks—that is, the first week of January 1979—so most of the bars and restaurants were still boarded up. Roller-shutters secured all the shopfronts. The sombre buildings, dimly lit streets, and freezing conditions failed to conjure an air of holiday romance.

Our flagging spirits were hardly uplifted on arrival at the hotel itself. No hot toddy, no burning log, no light, however dim, greeted the weary travellers. The red carpet had been rolled away and the welcoming committee ignored our hammerings on the doors and windows. There was nothing for us to do but make as much noise as possible for as long as we could. Eventually, a sleepy-eyed, shawled woman unbolted the door.

'What is the matter?' she said crossly in broken English.

'We're from Top Deck, the English ski company. Aren't you expecting us?'

'What is this?' she replied uncomprehendingly. No amount of explanation on our part enlightened her.

'Well, can we have a bed for the night then?' said Graham. 'We've come all the way from London. We have nowhere to sleep?' he pleaded. Even I felt sorry for him.

'No. We are closed. We have no staff. No linen. No food. Come back in January when we are open.'

'But, but, where can we sleep? Nothing else is open.'

'You have a car, no?' she said accusingly, as if offering us a luxury upgrade.

The car it was (our Fiat 124). Next morning, frozen, sleepless and hungry, we were at least able to put our case to both the woman and her husband. Carmen and David Savarlas listened politely but sceptically. Yes, they could remember some

Top Deck Daze

Australians (Bob-a-Job Sanderson and Mick Carroll, and before them, Ray Smith and Shelley McBride) visiting some months earlier but, if any contract in the name of Top Deck was sent for signing, they had no knowledge of it now. All sorts of people came here and promised so much. Few, if any, delivered.

'But look, Mr and Mrs Savarlas, we have thirty-six people arriving tonight by coach—the same each week, every week, and many more as the season progresses.' To build up our case, Graham and I started to lay it on a bit thick. We represented Australia's 'largest youth operator'. We were 'London's student travel specialists', and so on. At this rate, the Savarlases would need a second hotel by Christmas.

Unfortunately, the presentation of our case was slightly weakened by the fact that Graham's sartorial and physical demeanour failed to match the eloquence of his words. The rigours of the last three months on the overland had obviously taken their toll. A week of unshaven stubble covered his rather sallow jowls. Unwashed hair stood on end. Crumpled shirt and jacket hung loose. A splash of colour topped off the whole outfit. The crotch of his jeans had split exposing a, hopefully, well-washed section of red jocks, from which Carmen had great difficulty averting her gaze.

Whether by force of personality or due to the effects of the Sambucas over lunch, the Savarlases' finally accepted his word. The season was to start three weeks early for the Hotel Encamp. Paco the chef was summoned from a nearby bar. Maria the maid was located at her aunty's. Cleaners were put to work on the first-floor rooms, boilers were stoked and, most importantly, food was brought in, and preparations made for a hearty, Catalan meal for the thirty-six Top Deckers due in at 6:00 p.m.

At ten-to-six, the exhausted hotel workers joined Carmen, David, Graham and me at the bar, all except for Paco the chef who still slaved feverishly in the kitchen over his gourmet meal. Six o'clock came and went, with no sign of *Gonor* the bus, Rex Julian the courier, nor any of the punters. More drinks

Pissed on the Piste – Andorra 1978

The proprietors of Hotel Encamp, Carmen and David Savarlas.

were ordered. Seven o'clock came and went. No *Gonor*. More drinks. Eight, nine, ten o'clock. No *Gonor*. No phone call. No explanation. No nothing, just more drinks to cover our acute embarrassment.

At seven the following morning, *Gonor* pulled into the vacant lot beside the hotel. I didn't need to know the story; I'd heard it too many times before. *Gonor* was a single-decker Bristol coach, one of two we had acquired in 1976 and 1977 to run the first six-week, coach-camping, Russia/Scandinavia tours. As well as mechanical problems, the heating system had packed it in. Icicles hung from the interior roof. Ice-covered clothing crackled as the frozen punters attempted to move numbed limbs.

But hey! It was ski holiday time, and Graham and I moved up and down the coach with forced jocularity, welcoming everyone to their fun destination. Arm-in-arm we escorted them in circles

Top Deck Daze

around the car park to get the circulation flowing through their congealed veins and rigid joints. Two slackers stayed on the coach, unwilling to move. We beckoned them to join us for our brisk morning drills. All they did was grimace and make odd pointing gestures to their heads.

We ignored this curious behaviour for several minutes before we realised that perhaps something was wrong with them. I hopped on board.

'Come on, boys and girls! Wake up! Time to rise and shine!' Still more grimaces and much pointing to heads. I couldn't hear what they were mumbling, so I moved further down the coach. 'What's wrong, guys?' I entreated. 'Time to move!'

'We can't move you stupid, fucking bastard. Our hair's frozen to the fucking window.'

'Oh,' I replied constructively. 'Er, hang on there a minute,' as if they had a choice.

Graham and I ran to the outside of the bus and rubbed vigorously on the window at the point of contact with the palms of our hands, trying to generate some heat. Maria arrived at last with hot water in a kettle from the kitchen and we were finally able to escort the unglued remainder of our merry group into the bar for a sumptuous continental breakfast of yesterday's stale bread and coffee.

Fortunately, spirits rose as bodies thawed. Rex Julian and Graham were irrepressible characters and with Kessa Ware (who'd accompanied Rex on the coach) assisting, it wasn't long before everyone actually began to enjoy themselves. The skiing at Soldeu was great. The beginners' slopes were on a gentle plateau at the top of the mountain, avoiding the usual sludge encountered at base stations. As the vast majority of our punters were beginners, and only stayed for a week, it mattered little that the more difficult blue and black runs were rather limited.

Special functions were organised for each weeknight. Monday, we dined on the best steaks in Europe at Bill and Nancy's Shangri-la Restaurant. Next evening we ate in, at the Encamp Hotel. It had

Pissed on the Piste – Andorra 1978

been Tuesday afternoon before Paco the chef could be enticed back to the kitchen, his Spanish pride still smarting from the perceived snubbing of his Saturday night meal. Wednesday night was at 'Snails and Quails', up the mountain at the Soldeu village. The restaurant was run by a strange, one-eyed Catalan who always carried a silver pistol in his belt. A hometown peasant-boy-made-good, it was rumoured he'd made his money during World War II, escorting refugees over the mountains, and shooting the odd few along the way for the gold in their teeth. Thursday was Disco night. Friday was fancy dress night and a 'Red Faces' talent quest back in the bar of the hotel. The first week established a routine that was to be followed for many years to come.

Several doors down from the hotel, there was a shop, slightly set back from the street and enclosed by a makeshift fence behind which prowled a fierce Alsatian watchdog. Inevitably the poor dog was teased by inebriated punters on their way to and from the hotel and he barked, growled and hissed at every would-be intruder.

On the Friday evening, the last before departure, the whole group decided to walk down to the Shangri-la for a few drinks before returning for the 'Red Faces' quest. This time, the poor dog was in such a state of excitement that he managed to leap the barricade and make a beeline for Kessa Ware's backside. Fortunately the thick, knee-length jacket she was wearing blunted what might otherwise have been a vicious mauling, not to mention the possibility of tetanus or rabies.

Poor Kessa was in a state of shock. All the spirit drinks in Andorra were 'free pours'. Like Spain, alcohol was so cheap,

Top Deck Daze

no one bothered with 'measures', so it only took a couple of gin and tonics to settle Kessa's shattered nerves.

The dog attack consumed much of the evening's conversation back at the hotel and was still very much on everyone's mind when, on the stroke of midnight, Kessa came stumbling into the bar, ranting, raving and frothing at the mouth in a wild, rabid fit. With shrieks of horror the bar emptied in seconds. Half-an-hour passed before Kessa, after washing the toothpaste out of her mouth, could coax anyone to rejoin her in the bar for a nightcap.

Andorra became one of Top Deck's great successes. The name of the resort didn't matter to our passengers who were either Aussies, Kiwis or, surprisingly, British uni students. Andorra became the 'in' place to go as far as the UK uni students were concerned and sales through campus agencies boomed. What did matter was the low-cost tour price and the extraordinary good value of the food and drink. The skiing wasn't Kitzbühel, and the nightlife hardly St Moritz, but it was more than adequate for our needs and comfortably unpretentious. On my only previous visit to a ski resort, it was *de rigueur* to be seen in the right imported gear, looking as much like a rainbow lorikeet as possible, but in Andorra you felt comfortable in daggy jumpers and jeans. The high altitude ensured reliable snow. The ski school was run by an Englishman, Mike Archer, and all his teachers could speak English (even the Americans) and they were encouraging and patient with all our beginners. Mike referred to me as 'Jafa' (Just Another Fucking Australian), but he was a good bloke and could take as much lip as he gave.

One of the Top Deck couriers to take up residence in Andorra with Graham and Rex was Ray Robinson, another of Mick's Leeton mates. Ray's dad had been an Aussie digger in the forces occupying Japan at the end of World War II who befriended, and subsequently married, a Japanese lady and brought her back to Leeton after his discharge. One can only imagine the awful prejudices the family must have endured in that small country

Pissed on the Piste – Andorra 1978

town, given the animosity that existed towards Japan at the time. Ray must have copped heaps at school but by the time he and the other Leeton guys reached London they constituted a tight-knit group of genuine friends. One of these mates was Mick 'Slippers' Smith who drove for Top Deck. He had given Ray the nickname of 'King Prawn Cutlet'. Wrong country, but presumably all Orientals looked alike to Slippers. This name was subsequently abbreviated to 'KPC' or simply 'Prawn'.

By the time Prawn arrived on the scene, passenger numbers had

Ray 'Prawn' Robinson and Mick Carroll—scores of boys from the small town of Leeton worked for Top Deck.

grown to the point where the Savarlases did indeed require an additional hotel for the overflow of guests from the Encamp. Numbers in the resort regularly topped the two hundred mark. The party atmosphere was simply fantastic, but the overcrowding in the hotel caused dramatic problems.

It was Prawn who alerted us to the seriousness of the problem in one of the sarcastic letters that I was privileged to receive from him from time to time. This one read, in part:

Dear Bill Speaking, ... I am so proud to work for a company that, though limited in resources and operating on the tightest of budgets, could have the foresight to pioneer such an experiment in social engineering as we are privileged to witness here in Andorra. We have people who don't know one another, people who love one another, people who hate one another, all united in one, common bond: their excruciatingly small hotel room. They lie together, cheek by jowl, shoulder by shoulder, crutch by crutch. The social and interpersonal relationships that develop as a result of being thrust together in such circumstances are a revelation to behold ....

I was the brunt of many a Prawn joke. One Saturday morning during a break from Andorra, he came into the crowded front office at Kenway Road.

'Is Bill Speaking here?' Prawn yelled at the top of his voice. 'Bill, Bill. Come here. Quickly!' Thinking that there must have been a disaster of some sort, I rushed into the front office. 'Turn around. Turn around,' he ordered me. I turned around. There was nothing there, just a blank wall. After several seconds, giggles rippled throughout the office. As I turned back to face Prawn, he was putting away his hair comb. He'd been using the bald spot on the back of my head as a mirror. On other occasions he'd tell someone he had on his 'Bill James pants' that day.

'What do you mean, your 'Bill James pants?'' they would ask.

'Because I put them on reeeeeal sloooowly,' he'd explain.

The resident couriers who served in Andorra (Graham Sewell, 'Sexy Rexy' Julian, Andy 'Randy Organ' Morgan, Pat Cantwell and Prawn, among others) did plenty of their own form of 'social engineering' with the guests. The ski season at Encamp was one, long, non-stop party. Hundreds of young guys and girls would all be out for a great time. If you were looking for a partner and missed out in Andorra, well, it was time to join a monastery. It was an example of crude Darwinism at work—you were certain to find one of your own species if you looked long enough and hard enough. At times it was all too much for the devoutly Catholic Carmen Savarlas.

'They behave like dogs on heat,' she once remarked to me in disgust as we stood back and watched the comings and goings in the bar.

Unfortunately for me, the subsequent visits I made to Andorra were not always that much fun. I had to renegotiate the contracts for the following season with the managers of the hotels, the

Pissed on the Piste - Andorra 1978

ski school, the ski lifts, the ski hire, and the local bus transfer company, leaving little time for skiing or socialising. Bargaining with these seasoned campaigners was out of my league and I found it unenjoyably stressful.

From 1981, instead of using the Top Deck coaches, we chartered buses from a British company, Trathens, which made the transfers quicker, warmer, and more reliable. However, we considered many of their drivers to be cowboys who drove too fast and who ignored our appeals, and those of their own management, to drive more slowly and safely. Eventually we were forced to charter from a variety of other companies.

In the second season, the winter of 1979–80, Top Deck was able to offer seats on other companies' charter flights via Toulouse or Barcelona, with a local coach transfer to Andorra, which further added

Robbie — before he became Good-for-Fuckall.

to the program's popularity. Chartering a plane in Europe was as simple as hiring a coach in Australia, so when Chris Greive and Andy Morgan took over operational control of Ski in 1983, they organised Top Deck's own charter flights, usually eighty-nine seaters out of Stansted or Gatwick. Excess seats were sold via brokers through what was called the 'Baltic Exchange'.

By any measure, Ski Andorra was one of Top Deck's more memorable successes.

Chapter 13

RANDY IN SCANDI

(SCANDINAVIA 1979)

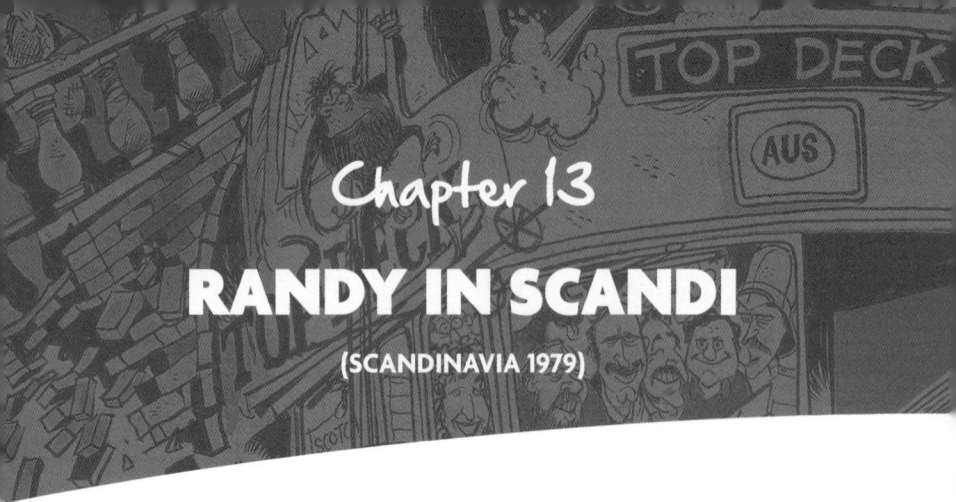

I remained in London until the end of our first ski season in Andorra, April 1979, awaiting the return of Mick and Screw from their visits to Australia. Bookings for Top Deck tours were looking good for the months ahead, especially for some of the newer, more innovative itineraries that Screw had dreamt up and included in the latest brochure. One of these was a three-week mini-Scandinavian trip to be undertaken in a double-decker. Given the unexpectedly busy start to the season, we were short of a driver, as usual, so I decided to take the first of these mini-Scandinavians myself. It departed on 7 April and was due back on the twenty eighth, just in time for my return flight to Australia.

I only met my courier, James Kemsley, a week before departure. I regarded James as a 'brush with fame'. I recognised him as 'Skeeter the Paperboy', host of Channel Nine's Cartoon Corner children's television program that was popular in Australia in the early 1970s—which, I suppose, said something about my taste in television (or lack of it). James was an extroverted ball of energy, small in stature with a Beatles' mop of hair and bright, expressive eyes. He could talk underwater with marbles in his mouth and it was exhausting just listening to him. His bright, yellow T-shirts and willingness to chat away to no one in particular earned him the nickname of 'Budgie'. I quickly learnt his passions were cricket and movies. I have since discovered there is no truth to the rumour that Budgie was the product of a brief dalliance

Randy in Scandi - Scandinavia 1979

"FROGIN' 'ROUND EUROPE"

Throughout the pages of our brochure you'll notice "Daffy" and "Freckle", two of the characters from the London comic strip "Frogin".

"Frogin" is derived from the verb "to frog", based on rhyming slang for "Frog and Toad" meaning "to hit the road".

This is your opportunity to join the "Boys" and the fun Frogin' 'round Europe with TOP DECK.

© Kemsley 1983.

James Kemsley became a renowned cartoonist. His early strip 'Frogin' appeared in Top Deck brochures and London magazines. Back in Australia he drew the iconic 'Ginger Meggs' strip for twenty three years before his untimely death in 2007.

Top Deck Daze

between Sir Donald Bradman and Lauren Bacall—I've seen him bat and act!

I was amused when Budgie told me the story of his arrival in London and how he landed a job with Top Deck, especially as it was probably typical of many of our crew. While he'd been very successful in domestic television, like most young Australian talents of the time, the lights of London beckoned. Budgie managed to find a job on a cruise ship bound for the UK, teaching people, of all things, how to draw comic cartoons. (He wasn't bluffing. After his return to Australia, James drew the immensely popular 'Ginger Meggs' comic strip for over twenty-three years before his untimely death from motor neurone disease in 2007.) After being knocked back by the BBC, he found a job packing Christmas hampers in the basement of Harrods, seven days a week and, consequently, never saw the light of day for a whole month. He then took two jobs to make ends meet, at a bakery by day and at a pub by night.

Dispirited and exhausted, Budgie contemplated returning home. He happened to be invited to a party where, for the first time in London, he encountered some other Australians. One of the guests he got talking to was named Ron, a rough ocker from Queensland who made Sir Les Patterson sound like Renaissance Man. Ron was treating his lovely American girlfriend coarsely.

'Get us a beer, ya moll,' he'd say.

'Sure, Ron. Any crackers or nuts, Ron?' Nancy drawled lovingly.

'What's the matter with you and your girl?' Budgie asked after Nancy moved away.

'Ah, she's not me girl. She's just me daffy duck for the week. I'm goin' away again termorra and I'm tryin' to give 'er the flick.'

'You're kidding?' said Budgie with mounting interest. On quizzing Ron further, it turned out he was a driver with Autotours and, together with his courier who was also at the party, was about to take out a six-weeker.

'There's always forty chicks on board. A bloke doesn't need any complications,' complained Ron.

Randy in Scandi – Scandinavia 1979

Up until now the only 'couriers' Budgie had ever heard of were people who flew from London to New York carrying satchels handcuffed to their arms.

'No, no, no, Budgie. The driver drives,' clarified Ron, displaying a unique mastery of linguistics, 'And the courier's the bloke who runs the whole show and looks after all the sheilas. Know what I mean, eh?' creasing up at his own wit.

'Yeah, yeah, Ron. A wink's as good as a nod to a blind man.'

'The pay's not much but with kickbacks, the black market and whatnot, we clear about a hundred quid a week, each,' Ron explained further. Budgie had reasonably assumed that Ron and the courier's job would be like working at an American Summer Camp, where you were provided with food and lodging but the actual work was so sought-after, it was unpaid.

Budgie could hardly believe what he was hearing. 'Now just hang on a second here,' he said. 'Have I got this straight? You and the courier go away on bus trips for six weeks at a time with forty girls just like this Nancy you've got here, and you get

Leylandi *at La Place de la Concorde, Paris. The new FLF-model Bristols, with the stairwell positioned behind the driver's cab, were fine, sturdy, reliable vehicles.*

Top Deck Daze

paid for it? A hundred quid a week?' Budgie was aghast. His two jobs of eighty-hours-a-week cleared him just over £50. By the time he left the party, Budgie had scribbled on the back of an envelope the name of every coach-camping company that had ever operated a tour, and the thought of busloads of Nancies left him salivating at the mouth and weak at the knees.

Being February, Top Deck was the only company to give him an interview so early in the season and, better still, promised him a start on the mini-Scandinavian. Budgie and I were to meet our double-decker, one of the newer FLF-model Bristols, in Calais as it was doing a 'turnaround' there, having just completed an earlier trip. The 'F' series Bristol was first manufactured in 1959. The 'L' stood for 'Long' and the 'F' for 'Front' because the stairway was positioned behind the driver's cab, as opposed to in the rear as in the earlier LD models. These were fine, sturdy, reliable vehicles with good, clean lines and quite a deal of internal room.

We were to meet our passengers at Victoria Station and catch the boat-train to Dover. As we travelled together on the underground from Earls Court, twenty minutes late, Budgie was just about beside himself with excitement at the prospect of his first busload of girls. The way he spoke, he obviously considered himself a ladies' man, but the poor lad hadn't had anything to do with something in a skirt since leaving the cruise ship. I tried to tell him not to get his hopes up too high. Sure, there were going to be plenty of girls on board but, as we would constitute an average group of Aussies, it was highly unlikely he'd be fending off twenty Miss Americas. The usual spot for meeting the punters at Victoria Station was under a big clock with a Nat West Bank sign above it. As you came up the ramp from the tube, your eyes were at ground level and you could get an excellent view of your group well before they saw you. One look at this group standing under the clock just about gave me heart seizure. What sort of God did this Budgie guy have on his side? There, huddled together, bags packed and ready to go, was the most drop-dead gorgeous group of young things you could ever

Randy in Scandi – Scandinavia 1979

possibly imagine. What unbelievable luck! It was like heaven on a stick. Budgie stopped in his tracks. He took in a deep breath, settling himself from the rush and excitement. A wide, lurid grin besmirched his face. It was the smile of a carpet snake in a fowl house. He licked his lips and rubbed his hands together as if to say, 'Now wheeeere do I start?'

Pulling in his stomach, raising himself to his full height of five-foot nothing, and lowering his voice to the best of James Bond pitches, he sauntered over to the young things.

'Hi, girls. My name's James. James Kemsley. I'm going to be escorting you on your trip to Europe,' he informed them.

'Oh, hello, James. Hi, James,' chorused the giggling young things, flashing eyelids and flicking back hair as they buzzed around their very own 007.

Gallons of endorphins were surging through Budgie's bloodstream when his mental orgasm was rudely interrupted by the booming, fog-horned voice of a middle-aged, tartan-skirted matron, directed at him from forty paces away.

'Just what do you think you're up to young man? Unless you have business with our finishing school in Switzerland, I suggest you move right on along,' she thundered as she came bounding towards us. 'Now hurry along girls or we'll be late for our train.'

'Bye, James. Lovely to meet you, James. Sorry you can't join us, James,' twittered the waving, smirking, departing, young things, leaving Bond and me alone under the clock.

Just then, another voice accosted us, but this time it had the unmistakeable twang of an Aussie.

'Hey, youse blokes. Are youse the Top Deck crew? Bit late, aren't chya?' The girl introduced herself as a friend of one of our punters, who'd come to see off the group. 'They'll be back in a minute. They've just gone to the shops,' she reassured us. She carried an 'Aussie Passport' as well—that is, she was six axe handles across the acre.

The poor London diet, lack of exercise, and absence of the need to struggle into summer cossies meant too many of us

Top Deck Daze

carried excess kilograms on our behinds. We could see some Aussie backpackers stuffing themselves with doughnuts, muffins and biscuits at the nearby snack bar. The food was consumed with such gusto one could only assume they expected continental Europe to be ravished by a famine of catastrophic proportions at some stage over the next three weeks.

Budgie ignored my nudge in the ribs and comment about what a good sort the girl was.

'Pity she's not coming with us, eh, Budgie? More cushion for the pushin'.' He completely ignored me.

A despondent Budgie contemplated future employment in finishing schools in Switzerland before beginning the task of checking off the names of the punters as they came drifting back to our meeting point.

'Now we're just missing three,' he called out to the group after several minutes, 'Campbell, Lewis and Hopkins. Anyone here by that name?' No one owned up. It was now only minutes till the train left for Dover and we were just moving off towards our platform when we spied three fellows shuffling towards us. Wearing dark glasses, they were in Indian file, number three with his arm on number two, and number two with his arm on number one, who was leading the way with a white stick.

'Yoo-hoo. Top Deck? We're looking for the Top Deck group?' called Number One.

'Over here. This way,' Budgie directed them. 'Er, not Campbell, Lewis and Hopkins, surely?' Budgie asked incredulously.

'Yes, that's us.'

'But, but, you're, you're …?'

'Yes,' said Number One with great confidence, 'But I can see shapes quite distinctly. We don't run into things, much. We get by very well actually.'

And so they did. Three more fabulous guys you couldn't wish to meet. Number One, Raymond, was more outgoing than Tom and Nick, but their extraordinary good natures, happy disposition, fierce independence, and self-deprecating humour made them the focal point of our attentions. The girls fussed over them incessantly and included them in all the action. Budgie was a bit nonplussed at first. On city tour commentaries, like our first stop at Cologne, he'd say, 'Now, on your left you can see the cathedral with its magnificent ..., well, ... *some* of you can see the cathedral with its magnificent stained glass windows—for the others, well, they're big and they have lots of different colours ...'

Our third and fourth nights were spent in Berlin, Germany's capital and one of Europe's great cultural, political and economic centres. In the final, dark days of Germany's capitulation at the end of World War II, the Soviet armies invaded from the east while the Allies closed in from the west and when they met, Berlin was more than 100 kilometres inside the Soviet zone of occupation. Berlin itself was divided with the eastern sector becoming the capital of Communist East Germany.

In 1979 you still had to enter West Berlin along a 100 kilometre corridor of motorway through barricaded East German territory. The Berlin Wall, built in 1961, was still the predominant feature of the city. On previous visits we had encountered no problem gaining entry as tourists, on foot, into East Berlin via Checkpoint Charlie, one of the few gateways in the Wall but, on this visit, a greater surprise awaited us. Budgie discovered from the East German border authorities that we would be granted permission to enter East Berlin and then East Germany itself, in the bus, and exit the country to the north-west. This was amazing news to us because we had never heard of anyone being allowed to do this previously. It was a new adventure for us so we decided to take the opportunity. It was our third day in Berlin when we crossed through the Wall and headed in the direction of Rostock on the Baltic coast.

We knew East Germany was a backwater but nothing prepared us for the economic and environmental wasteland that we experienced. For the 300 kilometres we travelled to the West German border at Lübeck, there was not one sign of anything available to a consumer. Those shops that were open seemed devoid of produce and, worse still, we were running desperately short of fuel but there were simply no service stations, or at least none that were functioning, where we could fill up.

When I reached the border, it was after 2:00 a.m. and everyone on board was fast asleep. The novelty of the excursion had long since worn off and they hastily returned to their bunks once the East and West German border guards concluded their cursory inspections.

By now, I was running on empty but I had no option other than to continue in the hope that I would soon find some services now that we had returned to civilisation. A kilometre further on, the inevitable happened—I was out of fuel and I coasted to a halt by the side of a feeder road that led to a major autobahn. I swore and cursed to myself. The weather had turned foul, I was tired and cold and just wanted to curl up in bed, but I either made the effort and found fuel now or waited a few hours till dawn when I would be just as tired and probably more irritable.

I took out the two empty jerry cans that I had used some hours before and leaving everyone on board sound asleep, set off to either walk or hitch a ride to the nearest services. I had on a duffle coat and beanie pulled down over my head as protection against the biting wind. At last, a car came into view. The driver saw me and slowed down. As he drew level, our eyes met through the misted window. There was a moment's hesitation before the car sped off with a screech of burning rubber. I must have been a suspicious-looking character walking down the road at that time of night.

The same thing happened to me twice more before I finally struggled on foot to a set of services, filled the cans, and asked a reluctant truckie to give me a lift back to the bus.

I had just bled the fuel lines, a laborious task if you run a diesel motor out of fuel, and was just about to fire up the engine, when there was a wail of police sirens that seemed to be converging on the area from all directions. A grey, murky dawn was just breaking and the first of the punters were stirring, the sirens alerting everyone to potential trouble. Budgie offered to drive to the services so we could breakfast and use the washrooms and I was just settling into a bunk when we pulled in there, too tired to bother explaining about my exhausting walk to get the fuel.

What seemed like the entire German police force and half the army, all heavily armed with submachine guns and other assorted weapons, were setting up roadblocks everywhere, while helicopters hovered overhead. Despite the commotion, I couldn't keep my eyes open and was lapsing into sleep when Budgie came back on board with great excitement.

'What's all the fuss about?' I inquired.

'It's the Baader-Meinhof gang,' said Budgie. This gang consisted of the most notorious, ruthless anarchists the West had known since the Spanish Civil War. Anarchism dated back to the nineteenth century. Its followers sought the destruction of government by violence and terror, believing any form of regulation was immoral and that all means of production should be held in common ownership. It influenced many radical groups in the 1960s, like the Students for a Democratic Society (SDS), and the Baader-Meinhof gang was a German spin-off of this, founded in the 1970s. They headed Germany's 'most wanted' list and many were still at large, terrorising various parts of the country.

'Good God!' I said, sitting bolt upright in the bunk, about to explain to Budgie my adventures of the early morning.

'Yeah,' said Budgie. 'Apparently they have been active in this area and some motorists saw one of them walking along the road just near here at 4:00 a.m. this morning. They set up an ambush for him but he must have slipped through the net. Geez, I hope they catch him while we're here.'

I thrust myself back into the sleeping-bag and zipped the cover over my head. Sleep was impossible as hot and cold shivers wracked my body. I could think of several ways to die but being shot as a German terrorist was not one of them.

Top Deck Daze

From Copenhagen, the itinerary followed what looked like two sides of an inverted, equilateral triangle, up to Stockholm at one apex, and across to Kinsarvik at the other. It then called for us to backtrack on a similar path. Budgie reckoned this was a bit boring. If we could catch a ferry across the short distance from Kristiansand in southern Norway to Denmark (as the ferry office in Stockholm assured us we could), we would complete the third side of the triangle. What we'd spend on the ferry, we could save in fuel.

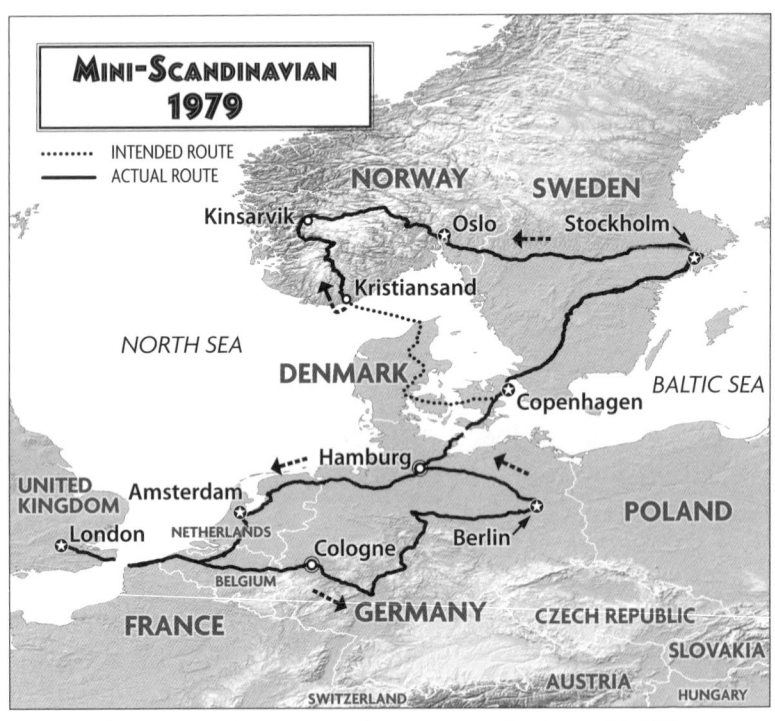

The route of the mini-Scandinavian tours that started in 1979.

'But maybe the itinerary has been designed that way because we can't get through the roads for some reason?' Budgie suggested.

'Look, mate,' I explained to Budgie, 'Screw dreams up these itineraries while he's sitting on the can. If there's a reason we can't get through, I can assure you, Screw didn't know about it when he printed the brochure.' That settled the issue.

After a week in Denmark and Sweden, we spent several leisurely days exploring the mountains, glaciers and fjords of Norway. The highlight of our stay in Kinsarvik was managing to run the bus batteries flat in the campsite. Normally you could clutch start a decker with ease. It was amazing how little movement you needed to kick the motor over, but any movement forward or back in the soft, boggy ground of the campsite proved impossible. This presented us with a real dilemma as there were no other heavy vehicles that could either give us a tow or give us a jumpstart on our twenty-four volt system. What to do? Several of the local lads and half the campsite gathered around to watch us extricate ourselves from the problem.

I remembered a story that one of our drivers, Denis Quinn, had recounted to me from one of his overlands. The idea was to jack up the rear axle of the bus till the wheels spun freely out of gear. You wound a long coil of rope around one of the rear tyres and then several guys pulled the rope as if you were starting an old Victa lawnmower. Meanwhile, the driver in the cab depressed the clutch, put the gear lever into fifth and, on a yell from the rope-pullers, let the clutch out with a bang, to kick the motor over. We decided to give it a go and, after several aborted attempts where we all fell in a heap as the rope came loose, on the third try, we got it right. The engine roared into life to much applause from the bemused spectators, all of whom, by this stage, had thought we had gone quite balmy. We disengaged the gears, lowered the rear axle, engaged first gear, and then smugly waved goodbye as we made our way out onto the road.

The southern coast of Norway is spectacular with archipelagos of water-torn rocks hugging the shore. The gigantic fjords eventually forced us onto a densely wooded inland road on which we made our way southwards towards the ferry at Kristiansand. Within a couple of kilometres of our goal, we just managed to scrape through a very low road tunnel, inching our

Top Deck Daze

way along and bringing down a shower of ice-encrusted dirt from the tunnel roof as we did so.

We were actually within sight of the ferry terminal at Kristiansand when we saw the railway line hugging the coast. It was the branch line linking Oslo with Stavanger. We couldn't believe it. We had come over 400 kilometres from Kinsarvik and were within 500 metres of the ferry terminal when the railway bridge barred our way. It was too low, by a good one-and-a-half metres. There was no way around. 'Damn!' and 'Blast!' We'd have to backtrack almost the whole way to Kinsarvik to pick up the road to Oslo. Had Screw known we couldn't make it? I doubted it very much. He'd have just picked it on instinct.

We were already way behind schedule, and this would add another two days to the trip unless we did some seriously long spells behind the wheel. Budgie and I agreed to take it in six-hour shifts. We asked a local how far it was to the nearest service station. 'Twelve miles,' we were told. It came into view 120 kilometres later. By this stage I was coasting down the hills, running on empty again, and thoughts of being shot as one of the Baader-Meinhof gang came flooding back. I was furious at being misled as to the distance until the attendant at the service station explained to us that, in this part of the world, a 'mile' is measured as ten kilometres and has no relationship to the English measurement at all. You live and learn.

I was still feeling fresh and so decided I would continue the driving for another four or five hours. As it turned out, I drove for another six and it was the middle of the night when I pulled into another small village to fill up with fuel again. I woke Budgie up and he willingly took over the driving. Like the rest of the passengers, I'd slept soundly for the whole six hours of Budgie's shift and only awoke at dawn when he pulled in for another fuel stop.

We all climbed out, used the washrooms and stretched our legs, pausing a moment to take in the beautiful Norwegian scenery being unveiled under the lifting morning mist. A sense of deja vu came over me.

'Budgie. Doesn't this place look familiar? I mean, I know we came down this road a few days ago, but isn't this the place where we stopped for fuel the first time last evening?' He took a long look around.

'Naa. They're all the same these places. Anyway, we've been driving for twelve hours since then.'

'I know. I know. That's what's bothering me.'

I rummaged through my pockets for the receipt from our first fuel stop. There was no mistake. We were back within 120 kilometres of Kristiansand! Somehow Budgie had been disoriented at our previous stop. The bus had been parked at right angles to the road and instead of continuing north he had turned in the wrong direction and had just spent six hours travelling south, retracing my previous stint behind the wheel. Twelve hours driving to cover zero kilometres—that had to be some sort of a Top Deck record. Just the thought of it exhausted me. It was as much my fault as Budgie's and we agreed to say nothing to the punters and to carry on as if nothing had happened, and no one, except my aching back and eyes, was any the wiser.

Our last three nights were spent in Amsterdam, that most schizophrenic of cities—an extraordinary mixture of the world's best museums, galleries, monuments and historical sights standing side-by-side with quirky, hash-reeking cafes frequented by a hotchpotch of pushers, pimps, prostitutes, and tourists, all rubbing shoulders with the occasional 'normal' resident. Negotiating the decker through the narrow streets and then duelling on the broader boulevards with the trams that appeared from nowhere was enough to give even the most experienced driver palpitations.

In addition to the essential sights of the Magna Plaza, the Rijks and Van Gogh museums, Rembrandt's and Anne Frank's house, and so on, no visit would be complete without a night visit to the red light district. No other European city has anything to quite compare. The area is innocuous by day but, at night, it's like paddling down the sewer in a glass-bottom boat. Dealers,

Top Deck Daze

bars, porn shops, live sex theatres and streetwalkers do a brisk trade. You can just whet your appetite, if you wish, by doing a bit of window-shopping beforehand. Most of the brothels, bordered by red neon lights, have large glass windows behind which the ladies of the night display their wares to the passers-by, hawking their forks in a variety of poses and apparel.

Top Deck had a tradition whereby any tour that had its last night in Amsterdam organised a 'daffy duck raffle'. Anyone could enter. The courier would price a visit to a brothel and the raffle participants would all pay their share for a ticket. Over drinks in a bar, a lucky person's name would be drawn from a hat. The winner was duly escorted to the house of ill repute and made to stay there for an hour, minimum. Of course, the raffle was often rigged by the courier. We'd pick the shyest, most reserved, most easily embarrassed male. Even if he hadn't bought a ticket, we'd guarantee his name was the one that was pulled out, claiming someone else must have bought a ticket for him and entered him in the draw.

On this trip, Budgie ensured the winner was Blind Man Number One, Raymond. His reaction when he heard his name read out had to be seen to be believed. I laughed so much I could hardly talk. Poor Ray had never been alone with a woman before in his entire life. Except for his blindness, he was in every way a normal guy ... well, abnormal in that he wore his heart on his sleeve. He

Negotiating the decker through Amsterdam's streets, then duelling with the trams was enough to give a driver palpitations.

Randy in Scandi – Scandinavia 1979

was torn by the full gamut of his emotions at the prospect of the visit to the brothel—one moment sheer terror, another total embarrassment, another unbridled passion, one moment hiding under the table, the next straining at the bit to go.

At last none of us could contain ourselves any longer and Ray was led to his destiny at a relatively discreet location just off Warmoesstraat. Budgie and I chose his consort and we kept vigil for him for well over an hour. At last Ray emerged with the look of a man who, when called upon to do his duty, had stood upright and been counted.

'It's a dirty job,' I reassured him, 'but someone's got to do it.'

Back at the bar, no amount of probing or cajoling could coax Ray to give us a rundown on events, so we finally left him alone at a corner table, drink in hand, head bowed and eyes closed, with the touch of a smile, deep in peace with his thoughts. The bar was emptying when we decided, at last, to call it a night and Budgie and I eased a none-too-sober Ray to his feet. I was on one side of him and Budgie was on the other, as the wobbly Ray draped his extended arms over our shoulders and around our necks for support, and we escorted him down to Dam Square to catch a cab back to the campsite. We'd walked several hundred metres in silence, willing Ray to relive the night's experience over and over in his mind. All of a sudden he stopped. He pulled both our heads close to his in a tight huddle.

'Bill, Budgie, tell me something, will you?' he whispered earnestly, 'Be honest. Was she good looking?'

Top Deck Daze

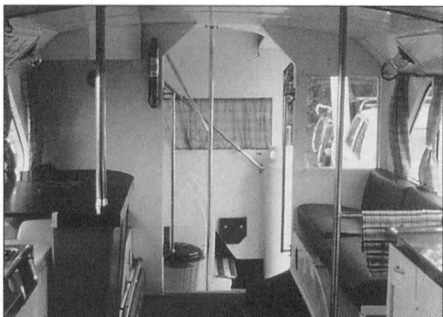

The yard at Shepherds Bush.

232

NARVIK
2420 KM FRA NORDPOLEN

293 BODØ	HARSTAD 129
919 TRONDHEIM	TROMSØ 266
1479 OSLO	HAMMERFEST 655
1697 STOCKHOLM	NORDKAPP 672
2072 KØBENHAVN	KARASJOK 774
2386 HAMBURG	KIRKENES 1039
3257 PARIS	BORIS GLEB 1051
1586 LENINGRAD	WARSZAWA 3170
4538 BEOGRAD	KIRUNA 167.2 km. / 592.
3525 WIEN	ROVANIEMI 734
4168 ROMA	HELSINKI 1518

Tim Oliver and Buddy Asif.

Dave Reed, Narvik Norway 1977.

Withies Hotel Kathmandu ca 1979 L to R: Dillon O'Sullivan, Tim Oliver, Mrs Uncle, Mick Carroll, Uncle Arnu (Withies Hotel proprietor), Robbie Goodall holding child, Graham Sewell, Russell Facer.

A Typical Bus Conversion

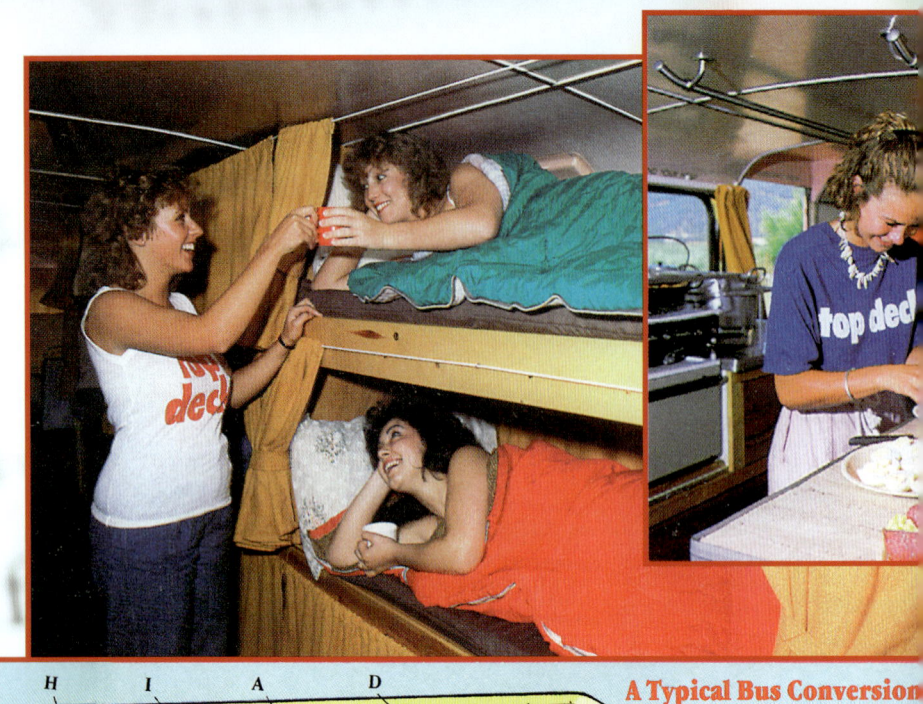

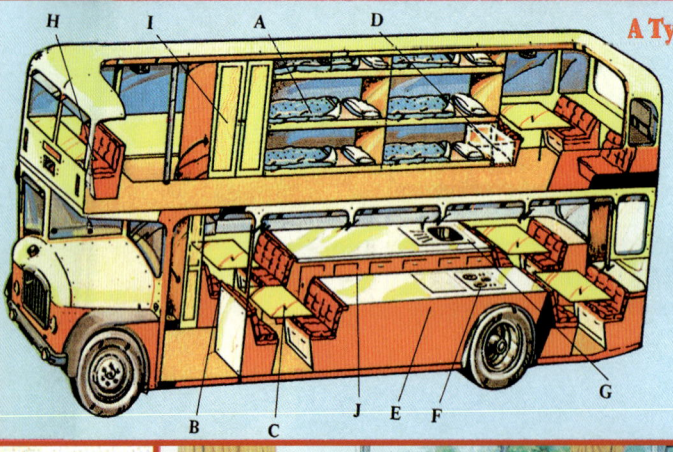

Passenger capacity 22
- **A.** Comfortable sleeping facilities.
- **B.** Ample seating.
- **C.** Dining tables – also for writing letters or playing games.
- **D.** Water tank – 40 gallons.
- **E.** Oven – great for roasts and cakes.
- **F.** Hot plates – cater for the entire group.
- **G.** Sink and running water.
- **H.** Sightseeing Deck – for unparalleled views.
- **I.** Personal storage cupboards.
- **J.** Food and storage cupboards.

Brochure Europe 1986.

London 1977 L to R: Unknown, Kerry Overland, Ken 'Black Dog' Stewart, Joe 'Jag' Coelli, Jude Turner.

London 1977 Robert 'Two Sheds' Dickinson.

Spike Cawthorn & Kerry Ware 1978.

London 1978 Kerry 'KO' Robinson. Yet to become Benn Robinson's mum!

London 1977. Screw (getting emotional) and Jude.

1978 Dennis Brown Kenyon – a courier.

Peter & Rhonda Cawthorn.

Kyber Pass 1976.

Belch at Roman Ruins side on Turkish coast. Ca 1977.

Mark, Steve, Pam, Jane, Bill, Monte Carlo 1976.

Dawes Road, Fulham 1976 L to R: Rex Julian & Mick 'Slippers' Smith.

Dawes Road, Fulham 1976 Dave Reed & Janno Wiese.

Bryan 'Light Blue' Ramsey.

Dawes Road, Fulham 1976 L to R: Jackie, Carlo, Dinga, Jen Fen.

Dawes Road, Fulham 1976 Marg & Grant (Dog) Doherty

Promo Shot for Brochure early 1980s.

Grunt in Yugoslavia, winter 1976–77. First 'Christmas in Bethlehem' trip.

Turkey winter 1976–77. First 'Christmas in Bethlehem' trip.

Knackers boiling over Kyber Pass 1976. Dave Reed knocking off radiator cap with a broom.

The original steel arch Maslenica Bridge across Novsko Zdrilo Inlet at Maslenica village, Posedarje, Croatia. This bridge was destroyed on 21 November 1991 during the civil war, and rebuilt in 2005.

Near Aqra, India 1977. *Belch* outside Akbar's Tomb.

Overlooking Wadi Rum, Jordan 1978. This was where they filmed Lawrence of Arabia.

After voting in Australia's 1975 Federal Election, Graham, Bill, Liz, Grilly, Steve, Screw and Terry gathered outside the Australian Embassy in Delhi, India, December 1975.

Screw in the camp ground wash room, Damascus, Syria, 1975.

Being a journalist, Grilly rarely played with a straight bat. Delhi Tourist Camp, India 1976.

Rawalpindi 1977. *Belch* surrounded by a typical curious crowd that gathered around the bus whenever you stopped anywhere in India.

Knackers, crewed by Blue Ramsey and Dave Reed in Calcutta Jan 1977. Only bus to ever get there.

Monte Carlo 1976. *Grunt* crossing the Monte Carlo finish line. Impossible to do in later years due to tighter security.

Afghanistan 1978. Passing a camel train.

Local servo, Pakistan 1977. *Belch* at a fuel stop.

Ishak Pasha Palace, located near the town of Dogubeyazit.

(Back row, left to right) Graham (new Tee shirt style), Duncan, Dinga, Terry, Jacqui, Bill, Steve (old Tee shirt style). (Front, left to right), Jacqui, Lesley, Kerrie, Steve, Liz. Delhi Tourist camp, India, 1976.

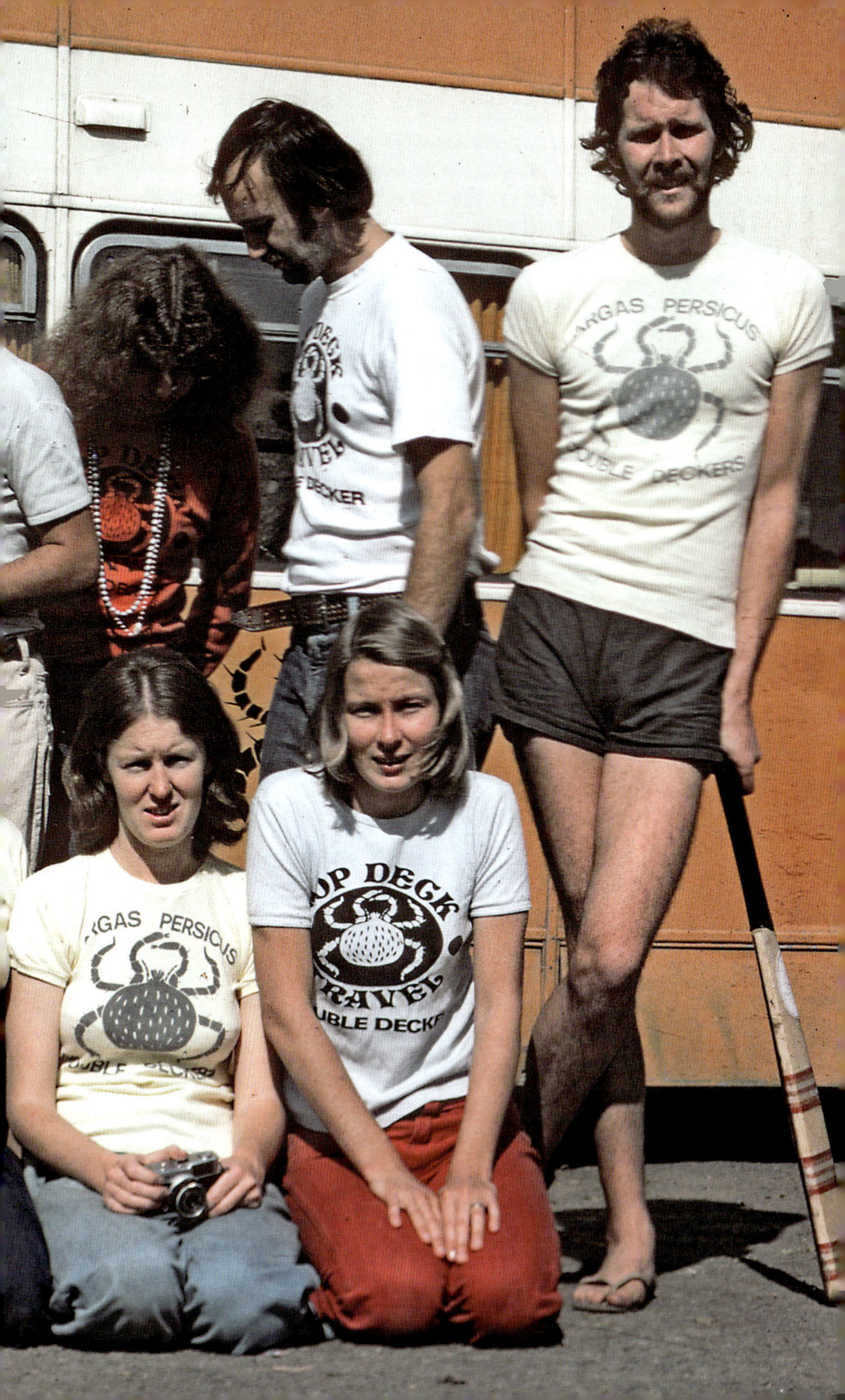
ARGAS PERSICUS
OUBLE DECKERS
OP DECK
RAVEL
UBLE DECKE

Bill and the first Australian bus 'Peanuts', 14 Sailors Bay Road, Northbridge, NSW 1977.

Screw fine tuning the business, Northbridge, 1977.

Screw, Charlie and Bill, Northbridge, 1977.

Jane, Bill and Liz in the backyard of 9 Mablethorpe Road, Fulham, June 1976.

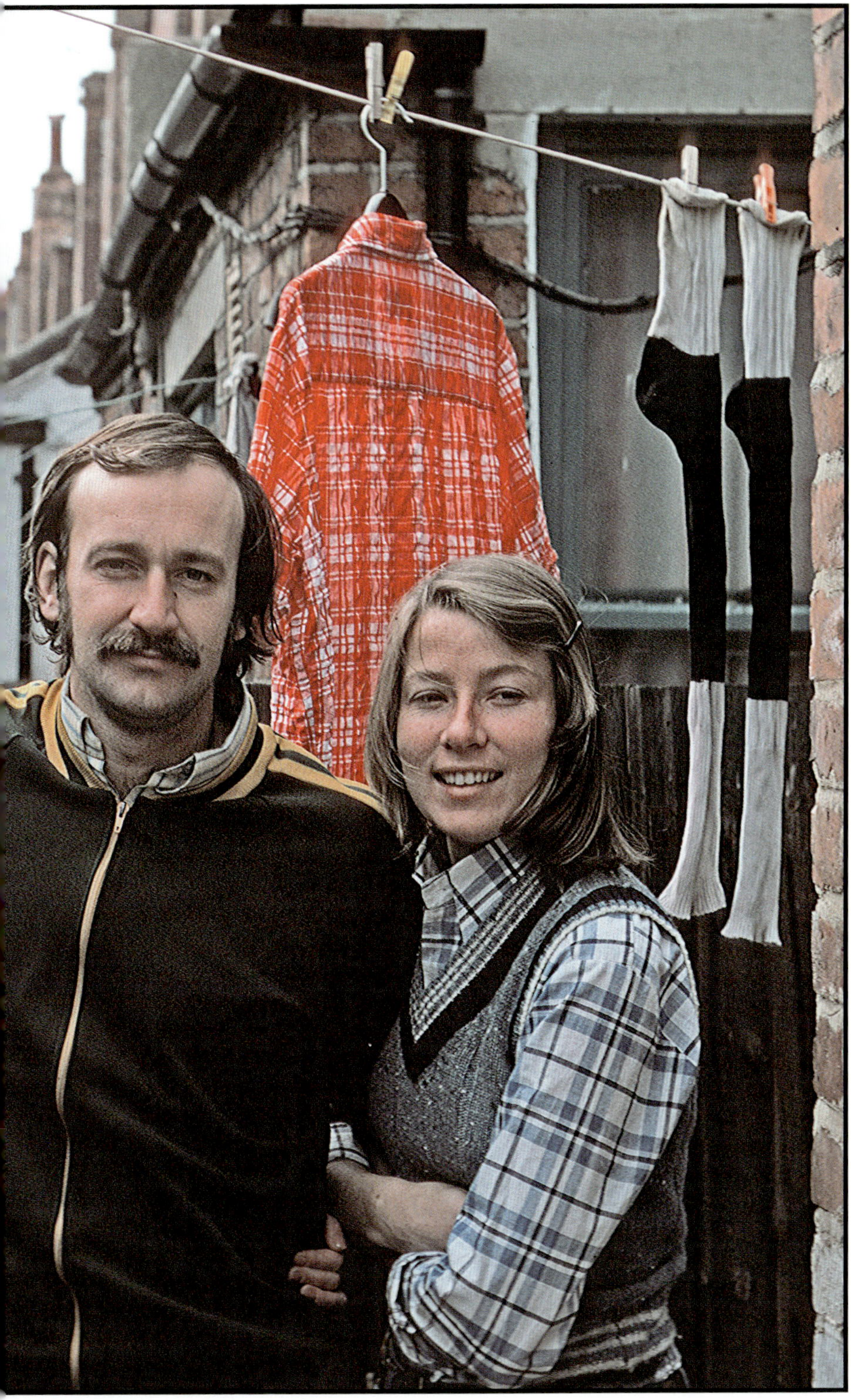

Belch Afghanistan 1977.

Belch in Pokhara, Nepal 1977. In the background: the new Green Lake Hotel and the Himalayas.

Belch at Durbar Square Kathmandu 1976 (parking here in now long prohibited)

Grunt at the Nordic Museum, Stockholm 1978.

Knackers in Rome 1976.

Pont Du Gard 1975.

Knackers in Afghanistan 1976.

Morocco 1976.

Bollocks at the Khyber Pass 1978.

Khyber Pass.

PART 3
Getting Too Big

Chapter 14

WORRY WARTS

(LONDON 1980)

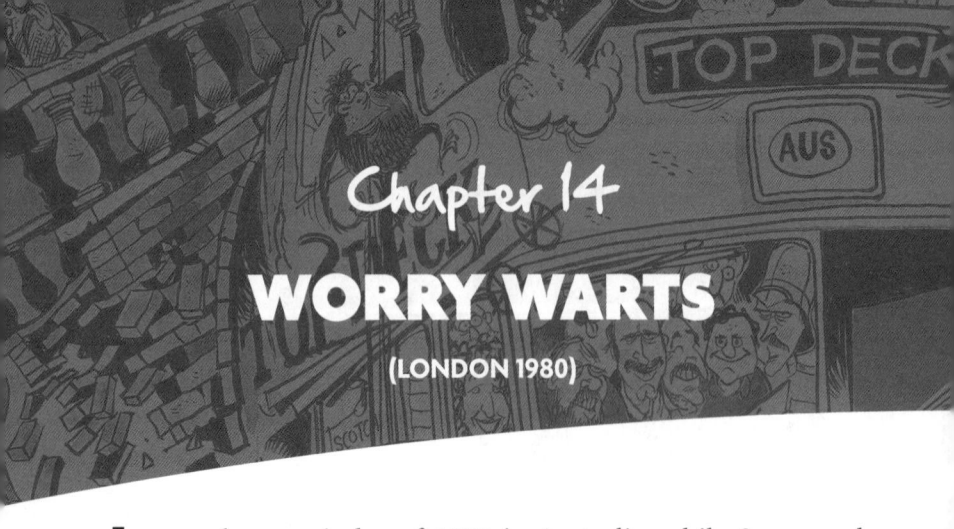

I spent the remainder of 1979 in Australia, while Screw and Mick continued to expand Top Deck in London. During December 1979 and January 1980, I received a series of phone calls from Screw asking me to return to London on a permanent basis. It was pretty clear that Screw and Jude were at the stage that Liz and I had reached in 1977. It was time for them to take a break from the London scene but, for Screw and Jude, it was to be for good as they were never to live and work full-time in London again. The lives we led in London inevitably put a strain on any relationship. It was a hectic whirl of travelling, working, and socialising. We lived in shared accommodation with a constant stream of visitors. The company had grown so much in the late 1970s it was now a very sizeable operation. The infrastructure had not kept pace with the growth and this placed enormous strains on management. To Screw and Jude's credit, they valued their relationship enough to realise it was time to pull back a little and experience a change of scene.

The idea of returning to the UK full-time was a difficult decision for Liz and me to make but Screw, quite rightly, pointed out that if I wanted to retain a share in Top Deck and realise some return from my investment, it was time I put in some more of the 'hard yards' in London. So, we packed our bags, bade farewell to 'Godzone', and headed off for another stint in the Old Dart.

Worry Warts - London 1980

These changes in our personal lives seemed to be reflected in the seemingly tumultuous events evolving on the world stage: Revolution in Iran; Russia's invasion of Afghanistan; India's squabbles with Pakistan; ferment in Iraq; and the ongoing troubles between Israel and its neighbours, all impacting directly on Top Deck's overland operations.

I spent three weeks with Screw in London, catching up on events, before he was due to leave. Mick was going back to Oz for holidays as well, so I needed to reacquaint myself with all the recent developments. I must admit I was pretty daunted by what I saw. Top Deck now had seventy buses, more than 250 staff and crew, two offices in Kenway Road, Earls Court, a three-bedroom house in Ealing, five Renault cars, and a farm in Woking, Surrey, about an hour's drive from the office, which was now used as a workshop and base for the buses, replacing the yard at Shepherds Bush.

In theory, the idea of a farm as a workshop and base for all the deckers and their spare parts made sense. Given the space available, it was unlikely it would be outgrown like all the previous premises. Also, the farm was bought freehold rather than rented, so it would be an asset that would appreciate over time. The only problem was that the farm's location, Horsell Common at Woking, was an environmentally pristine bushland setting, interspersed with the odd sixteen-acre hobby farm like the one we'd purchased, and the area was greatly valued by the locals. The sight of convoys of Bristol double-deckers, spewing diesel fumes and trailing oil leaks though the quiet, nearby villages as they took up residence at the farm, understandably sent the genteel, conservation-minded community into a state of apoplexy. Coincidentally, Horsell Common had been the landing place for the Martians in H. G. Wells' *War of the Worlds*. I'm sure the Martians would have received a far more cordial welcome than the one we experienced. The fact that a bus depot operating on a farm contravened every planning law ever drawn up in the UK since King John signed the Magna Carta simply never

Top Deck Daze

Top Deck directors bought Young Stroat Farm in Woking, Surrey, as an investment but locals never welcomed us or appreciated our using the farm as a bus depot.

entered Screw's head or, if it did, never bothered him in the slightest. Legal battlelines were drawn up between Top Deck and the local council on day one of our occupation.

While the size of the fleet and the acquisition of all these assets looked great on the surface, it was starting to place enormous physical and financial strains on the company and its management. The buses, the farm (at £76 000) and the Ealing house (£36 000) had all been paid for in cash, as the bank wouldn't lend us any more money over and above our overdraft.

In addition, we'd made one of our first major strategic mistakes. With the intention of expanding more quickly, we had bought an ailing company called Atrek from its New Zealand founder, Merv Hannah. The initial cost had been small and the idea had been that Merv would stay on and run Atrek, but the working capital required to keep the thing going just kept adding up. In the end, we had no option but to shut Atrek down and

Worry Warts – London 1980

we were genuinely shocked to realise that the whole exercise had cost us more than £40 000. We had nothing to show for our investment other than a bigger overdraft.

Had we learnt our lesson it would have been worth it, but we made the same mistake time and time again. It took us another fifteen years until the message finally sank in—if you're going to expand by acquisition, beware! One can be lucky with this strategy—when the business acquired is an absolute, deadset, winner, and at a bargain price. But, from our experience (with the odd exception), we usually ended up buying someone else's problems. Our belief now is that, if one must expand, and that is the best thing for any business, one should try and do so organically—that is, by using one's own resources and own culture.*

Above and beyond all this, we were still absolute novices with regard to management and leadership issues. If we were able to fill an extra trip, we'd simply buy another bus to run it, so Top Deck had grown exponentially from 1976. Proper management systems were either poor or nonexistent. We still ran the company the same way with seventy buses as we had done with seven. There were no management accounts, for example. A 'balance sheet' and 'profit and loss' account would be drawn up every year for statutory purposes but, by the time it hit our desk, it was eighteen months old and of no use whatsoever for management purposes.

It was to be a steep learning curve and the seeds of potential financial disaster had been well and truly sown. On a personal financial level it didn't affect us greatly. We drew modest salaries but lived well, always socialising, eating out, and travelling extensively.

Big lunches, especially on Fridays, were the norm. I was still on my reorientation program with Mick and Screw when we all went out to lunch with our printers, Dave Walker, John Glenn

---

* I spoke too soon when I wrote this paragraph in 1999 for the first edition. In 2008 Flight Centre made a disastrous acquisition, buying the US-based company 'Liberty Travel'. Total losses on this deal exceeded $250 million.

Top Deck Daze

and Nick Philp from a company called MGS Ltd. Top Deck was now producing a full-colour, twenty-page European brochure as well as the Asian overland and ski brochures, not just for the UK but for overseas agents as well, and the printing bill ran to more than £30 000.

We took the printers to our favourite restaurant, Bistro Benito's, and plied them with as much wine as they could drink. We left it till 4:00 p.m. for Screw to announce, 'Well, Dave, we've got some good news and some bad news. The good news is: We've bought our seventieth bus, our fifth car, a farm at Woking and a house at Ealing. The bad news is: We don't have any money left to pay our printing bill.' We expected Dave to stand up, walk out, and declare the friendship over.

'Ah, that's all right, Screw,' said Dave in his wonderful Liverpudlian accent. 'Just order some more wine then and let's get on with it.'

It was a good lesson for us. All Dave, John and Nick wanted was a commitment from us to pay the account in the next six to twelve months. Bad payers were obviously a regular occurrence for MGS, but most of their other creditors would try and avoid them at all costs. We, at least, promised to pay our bill at some time in the future, *and* get them drunk regularly while they were waiting which, as far as Dave, John and Nick were concerned, was a pretty good deal. It was fortunate we'd struck some drinkers with a level of addiction on a par with our own.

Screw and Jude finally returned home and Mick left at the same time for two months holiday so, early on a Monday morning in February 1980, I turned up at the Kenway Road offices to take over as a managing director again. I'd been caught in a downpour of sleet and snow on the walk to the office and the atrocious weather seemed like an ill omen. It was so cold I even saw our bank manager walking down Earls Court Road with his hands in his own pockets.

I felt inadequate. It was like coming from the Juniors straight into the First Division. I was out of my league. I hardly knew any

Worry Warts – London 1980

of the crew any more, nor they me, and the business had grown and changed so much, I doubted my ability to make any sound commercial decisions.

I sat there, staring at the empty desk, wondering how the day would unfold. The phone rang. It was one of our drivers, Five Eights, calling from Istanbul. He was on an overland en route from Kathmandu to London.

'G'day, Five Eights. How's it going, mate?' I greeted him enthusiastically. At least I knew Five Eights.

'Shithouse,' was the descriptive reply.

'We were in Kabul (Afghanistan) last week when the Ruskies finally overran the place.' [The Russian invasion, of Christmas 1979, was less than two months old.] 'The war was going on all around us. Guns, tanks, artillery. We were lucky to get out alive. We had to leave the three deckers there.' [Three buses had been travelling in convoy.] 'We've flown to Istanbul. Get some replacement buses down here as soon as you can. More money too! It's costing us a fortune. I'll ring you again tonight to see what you've organised.'

It was still midwinter. We had no spare crew and no spare buses fit to go anywhere without a week's work. The farm and the workshop were almost deserted. How could I afford to extricate fifty punters and six crew members from Turkey?

The overlands were becoming a continual source of almost insurmountable operational problems. For example, during that year, there was a spate of motors blowing up in the most obscure of locations; Mrs Oliver's Little Boy Tim, Trevor 'Tricky' Carroll and Terry Pride were stuck in Iran in the middle of the revolution, and were lucky to get out; Nick Duce had to be flown back from Pakistan with a virus that nearly killed him; and Dillon O'Sullivan was jailed in Iran after defending the honour of one of his female passengers, putting the offending campsite manager in hospital with a broken jaw and two broken ribs. Dillon was jailed for his troubles and it cost US$1200 in fines (or bribes—we could never tell the difference) to get him out. Add border closures, wars, invasions and revolutions, and you had a tour operator's nightmare.

In addition to Five Eights' dilemma, there was already a rescue underway. Murray 'Tyres' Dunlop and Chris 'Prong' Gilbert-Wilson (or Chris 'Dribbling-Nonsense' as Screw would rib him after he'd had a few beers) had stacked one of the buses in Turkey on a Holy Land tour, and they were stranded for fourteen days until we could get Chris Jones down to retrieve them.

The phone rang again. It was the Engineers' Department at Woking Town Council. It was to inform me that, because we didn't have planning permission to use the farm as a workshop, the council and residents' committee would be seeking a court order to throw us out of there within days if we didn't relocate the buses immediately.

Again the phone rang. It was the ski school in Andorra. They hadn't been paid for two months. When were they going to see their money? What sort of operation were we running there anyway? Another call: Trans Atlas, our agents in Paris. Three students had been booked on our coach to Andorra but hadn't been picked up as arranged. What was I going to do about it?

I soon realised that this was a typical day at the office. Somehow I made it through the week. Liz and I went away for the weekend on what was to become a regular jaunt, staying in old manor houses or country hotels. I experienced my first decent night's sleep for a week. I came to work on the Monday determined that nothing would frazzle me—and my positive frame of mind lasted until at least ten o'clock.

A phone call conveyed news of an incident so serious it almost resulted in the severing of Italian/Australian diplomatic relations. It was the Australian High Commission in London informing me that one of our drivers, Mrs Oliver's Little Boy Tim, was now under arrest in an Italian jail and could I arrange conditions for bail. It took several more days to get some idea of what had happened and it wasn't until I spoke with Tim in person, back in London, that I got the full story.

Worry Warts – London 1980

It had been a cold, wet Sunday evening in Sorrento and Tim and the courier, Jess Skepper, were disappointed to find the campsite hadn't yet opened after the winter recess. The boys were on the very first central European tour of the season and the Continent had not yet geared itself up for the annual tourist invasion. They decided to make their way down to the waterfront and free-camp for the night before catching the ferry the next day to the Isle of Capri. Tim wound his way down the narrow Sorrento streets, built more for donkeys than double-decker buses. He was unfamiliar with the directions. It was dark and the traffic was heavy and he crawled along at fifteen miles an hour, copping the usual horn-blasts from irate Itie drivers.

'You're okay ... keep going ... she's right ... no worries,' Jess directed Tim as they rounded a tight corner. A grinding, crunching noise, setting the decker back on its haunches, alerted them to other possibilities. The decker was jammed tightly under a bridge. That was bad enough but the bridge turned out to be a 430-year-old historic treasure. It connected two houses on either side of the road, one of which was a family-owned-and-run hotel. The bridge looked decidedly unstable and a huge crack appeared down the wall of the building. Pandemonium broke loose and the Italian family was distraught with grief. The grandmother was

Mrs Oliver's Little Boy Tim's altercation with an historic bridge in Italy led to the roof of the decker being completely rolled back.

241

Top Deck Daze

the most abusive and gave Tim a good clip around the ears and a conk on the bugle for good measure.

The police cordoned off the area. Jess led the passengers away to the safety of a pension for the night, while Tim waited for hours by the bus until a gigantic, mobile crane was seconded from the naval dockyards at Naples and driven to the scene. A

Worry Warts – London 1980

great sling was strung around the bridge and, after the front tyres were let down, Tim was finally able to back the bus out. For several seconds the bridge seemed to pivot slightly on the sling and then, with an almighty 'Cruuuuunch', it came crashing and crumbling to the ground in a great cloud of masonry dust. After a hefty fine, a spell in jail, and many diplomatic appeals for leniency, Mrs Oliver's Little Boy was eventually allowed to return to the UK. Years later, on a motoring holiday in Italy, I located the scene of the crime. Liz knew enough Italian to translate the plaque on the wall. What had read, 'Here is situated …' had recently been changed to, 'Here was situated the ancient bridge of …'

Nine-out-of-ten Top Deck trips were simply fantastic. Everyone would come back having had the time of their lives with memories and friendships to last a lifetime. Sometimes the crew were not that good, usually because of inexperience or lack of training, but the punters were great and so everyone had a wonderful time. At other times, the punters were hard to get on with but our experienced crew won them over. However, every now and then, a bad crew would combine with bad punters, culminating in disaster. Because the buses were away for such extended periods (up to six weeks in Europe and six months on an overland) problems went unresolved and so, by the time the trip returned, it was too late to do anything about it.

One of the hardest tasks imaginable was to confront a group of angry punters keen on revenge. It would have been so much easier if we could have just thrown money at the problem, but we couldn't. The more money we gave away in refunds, the fewer resources we had to run good trips in the future, so we just had to wear the flack as best we could.

It was essential for future bookings that the company appeared to be financially sound, so we couldn't confide in our staff that we were chronically short of cash. Extensive questionnaires were handed out to punters at the end of every trip and crews' bonuses were based on the results. Unfortunately, many hardworking crew members had their bonuses whittled away as we tried to save money, and they resented us, and especially the operations managers, for our hardnosed attitudes.

Fortunately, from 1980 onwards, more and more good people took up management positions. Christine Dunn ran the Kenway Road office. Chris had on-the-road experience as well as all the qualities necessary to fulfil the role of general manager of the whole company, and I put this proposition to her on many occasions. Unfortunately, like many of the Aussies passing through London, Chris did not see Top Deck as a long-term career. Nevertheless, Chris was a tremendous asset during her tenure, and was of particular support to me during Mick's absences. Annie Bulmer joined the front office from Trailfinders and, being an airfares expert, Annie greatly added to the professionalism of the sales team. In succession, Dave Reed, Mick 'Mario' Bowman, Brian 'Dillon' O'Sullivan, Timmy Oliver, Johnno O'Donnell and Mick Wiles ran operations. Five Eights and then 'Diesel' Dave Morse ran the workshop at the farm. Chris Greive followed Dave Farrell and Bob-a-Job Sanderson as marketing manager and then ran the ski tours with Andy Morgan. Graham Sewell followed Chris into marketing. Murgha Mack developed the charter division, which became an increasingly important part of the company.

'Diesel' Dave Morse managed the workshops and later bought into the company.

Chapter 15
SALES TALES
(LONDON 1980)

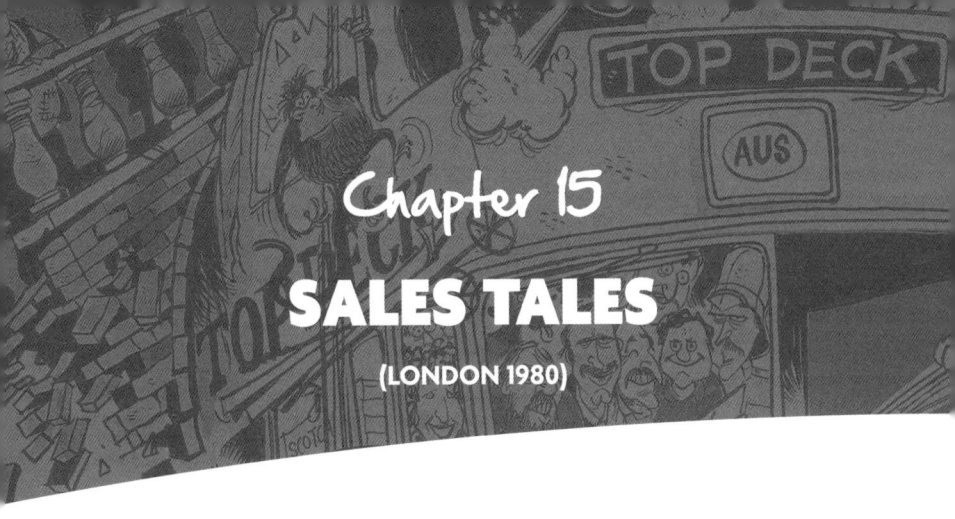

Not long after he took over as marketing manager, Dave Farrell noted that we weren't getting many sales from travel agents in London and he set himself the task of researching ways to improve the situation. I agreed, as the only agency that was supporting us in the UK at the time was Trailfinders. Trailfinders was an interesting case. By 1999 it was to be recognised as the biggest, single retail travel agency in the world with more than 350 consultants in its main office in Kensington, London. Its owner, Mike Gooley, was included in *Who's Who* as one of Britain's wealthiest men, with a personal net worth of more than £50 million.

Had you met Mike Gooley in the early 1970s, as we did, it would be hard to imagine it would lead to all that. He set up shop in 1970 in small premises at 46–48 Earls Court Road. Initially, eighty per cent of his business was acting as an agent for overland operators such as us. In the mid-1970s, Mike developed what he called 'Connecting Flights,' buying punters air tickets to and from their tours. Within four to five years, selling airfares became ninety per cent of the business, and he never looked back from there.

Trailfinders' formula for success did not go unnoticed by us. Selling tours on commission was obviously easier money than operating them. Selling airfares seemed easier still.

When Trailfinders first started selling Top Deck trips we had to sign an agreement, drawn up by Mike Gooley, containing the infamous 'Clause 19'. This clause allowed Trailfinders to hold onto the punters' money until well after their trip departed. It supposedly provided security to the punters should the trip fail to eventuate or the operator go belly-up—a reasonably frequent occurrence in those days. But all the Trailfinders staff we drank with at the Hansom Cab told us that Trailfinders had more money troubles than we did, and Mike Gooley simply held onto the money as working capital for himself. Screw had many a blue with Mike over this 'Clause 19', but all to no avail.

It was well known that Mike's wealthy wife, Hillary, was putting in money to keep Trailfinders afloat. Hillary said as much herself, quite openly at times. It appeared that the driving force behind Mike's ambitions to succeed was to pay off his wife's loans. Such is the secret of some people's success.

It irked us that we were so beholden to Trailfinders for these extra Top Deck sales, especially as Mike held onto our money for so long, and it was this that drove Dave Farrell (the marketing manager) and me to broaden our search for more support among other London agents. Dave hit upon a brilliantly simple, cost-effective way to introduce these agents to our tours.

It was the done thing for Londoners, if they had the opportunity, to make a

Dave Farrell was Top Deck's marketing manager.

Sales Tales – London 1980

day-trip to the Continent to do some duty-free shopping. For starters, you could buy lots of things on the Channel ferries themselves and a half-day in, say, Calais, Dunkirk, Ostend or Zeebrugge could provide you with a wide variety of quality, inexpensive foodstuffs, gifts, and the like.

A new ferry service, Sally Lines, had just begun operations and was keen for our business. Dave Farrell approached them with a deal: Would they give us a free ticket for one of our buses so we could fill it with London travel agents and take them to Dunkirk for a shopping trip? We'd use our new Bristol, rear-engine, VR transfer bus. This was a fully-licensed and taxed decker we had just bought to run our passengers between London and Dover as an alternative to the train and our other untaxed buses. We'd go halves with Sally Lines in a cocktail party for the agents on the ferry on the way home and we'd all be winners. The agents would get to learn about Top Deck (without having to undertake a 'real' trip—a possible bonus) and Sally Lines could promote their new service. Sally Lines agreed and the deal was done. Dave had no trouble rounding up thirty enthusiastic agents.

Fresh from the farm with its new Top Deck livery, the VR collected Dave and the agents from their meeting point at the Fremantle Hotel and they set off excitedly for their jaunt. All went well until they reached Dunkirk—then the troubles began. The temperamental VR refused all attempts to start. It had been the first vehicle onto the ferry and so was the first to come off, and the entire unloading was held up for thirty minutes while a tractor was located, hitched to the bus, and it was towed onto the docks.

An excruciatingly embarrassed Dave enlisted the assistance of the ferry's purser to hire a local coach to take the agents into the town centre for their shopping, leaving the frustrated driver to wrestle with the VR's engine in the hope of coaxing it to life in time for the afternoon's return sailing.

The VR model turned out to be a dog. It was a much more modern-looking bus than our old LDs, and a step up from the

'FLF' models but, for whatever reason, the rear engine design and weird transmission proved too unreliable and we never incorporated them into the fleet.

To Dave's horror, the beast of a bus was still as dead as a dodo when he arrived back at the docks with the agents. But worse was in store. Two other Top Deck buses had just happened to arrive on the docks at the same time. These were no ordinary trips either — they were two overlanders, all the way from Kathmandu. Again, for anyone who hasn't done the 'Big Trip', the sense of achievement at the conclusion of the expedition is hard to convey. The two groups of punters had been through so much together in the three months, wild celebrations were in order, and to hell with what anyone else might think.

The ribald, hedonistic rejoicing that began on the docks spilled over to the duty-free bars on the ferry and, by the time the punters and the now-thoroughly-disgusted London agents were forced to share the same transfer coaches back to London,

The rear-engine VR model Bristol turned out to be a 'dog'.

the overlanders' behaviour was simply out of control. It reached its zenith when one of the couriers, let's call him ... Richard Hewitt ... because that was his name, fell into the missionary position on top of a more-than-willing female punter in the middle of the transfer coach's aisle, urged on by raucous shouts from the other punters, and any chance of salvaging something positive from the day dissolved with the copulating couple.

Needless to say, we couldn't recall ever getting a booking from a regular London agent again. It was only when Top Deck Ski started to boom among the university agents that the odd booking trickled in from some London agent still ignorant of our tarnished reputation. As a consequence of all this, we redoubled our efforts to get more sales from overseas.

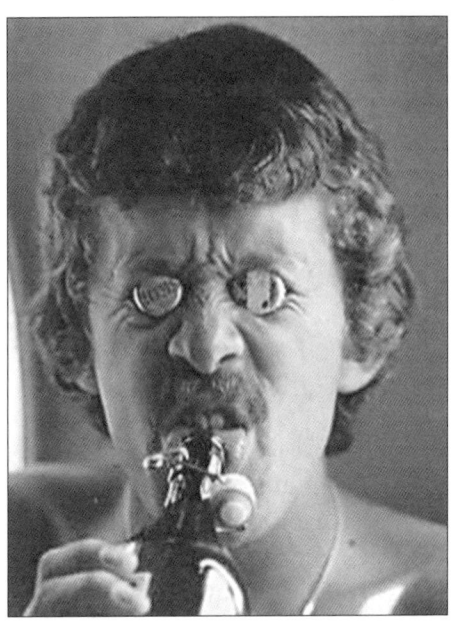

Richard 'The Unmentionable' Hewitt.

Our first agent in South Africa, Thompson Holidays, was only moderately successful to say the least, and so we had no hesitation, when the opportunity arose, in replacing them with a company called Destinations, run by a Gavin Simpson. Based in Johannesburg, Destinations was a very successful wholesaler, primarily selling package holidays to Mauritius and the Seychelles, and was very well supported by South African travel agents. Destinations also made its money by acting as the general sales agents (GSA) for a range of overseas tour operators and Gavin approached us in London to see if he could represent Top Deck in South Africa.

Top Deck Daze

A year after Destinations was appointed our GSA, by which time Gavin and I had become good friends, I spent a week in South Africa with him on a sales and promotion tour. Over dinner at his home, with his wife and friends, Gavin sent us all into uproar as he recounted his version of our first meeting in London.

His primary purpose in visiting the UK had been to meet with the owner of the Venice-Simplon-Orient Express. This was the luxury train that ran between London and Venice. It emulated the five-star service of rail, experienced during its glory days earlier in the twentieth century, when the original train ran all the way from London to Istanbul, linking the European and Asian continents. No expense was spared on pampering its fortunate customers and the service was a reflection of the man who ran the whole show. He was a multibillionaire on the Packer scale, having made his fortune in shipping with a company called Sea-Containers. The owner's office was on the top floor of Sea-Containers House in Park Lane, Mayfair, London, the most expensive real estate in the world.

Gavin arrived there at the appointed hour. Gavin was a wealthy man himself but even he was taken aback by the sheer opulence of the owner's suite of offices. The floors were covered in plush, white, pure-wool carpet. Original artworks by European Masters bedecked the walls. Chatting to the receptionist, with soothing, piped music humming in the background, Gavin couldn't help but ask her about the extraordinary desk she occupied. It was handcrafted, she said, at a cost of £12 000—and that was just in the foyer! The meeting was positive and the appointment of Destinations as the GSA in South Africa for the Orient Express tours was a major coup for Gavin.

Gavin knew little about Top Deck but, flushed with his success at Sea-Containers House, he had nothing to lose by following up his lead and so made his way by cab to the more downmarket locale of Earls Court. Mick and I occupied an office at the rear of 65 Kenway Road, opposite our main shop at number 64. The contrast with Sea-Containers House could not have been

Sales Tales – London 1980

more stark. Instead of the beautiful receptionist and secretary, Gavin was greeted by one of our greasy, overalled mechanics, in town buying spares, and it was he who showed Gavin through to our office. We made him some coffee (instant) and proffered him a seat on a low, padded lounge chair which had a tendency to do a 180° backflip if you sat in it too quickly—as Gavin unfortunately did.

Being a smooth-talking salesman, Gavin was unperturbed by this minor setback and was well into his spiel on what Destinations could do for Top Deck sales in South Africa when his presentation was rudely interrupted by Bill Barking. Bill was never more than a metre away from Mick's side. It was early summer and one of Bill's pet hates was flies. They drove him absolutely bananas.

The flies were probably in greater numbers than usual, feasting on the barker's eggs Bill had laid on the backyard lawn. A big, blue buzzing one flew into the room and Bill went berserk, barking and yelping, and taking great flying leaps into the air as he tried to catch the blowfly in his teeth. Bill landed on the low, glass coffee-table in front of Gavin, sending his coffee mug spiralling into the air.

'Diesel' Dave Morse, the workshop manager, must have called by in the Transit van to pick up the mechanic and the spare parts, just at this time and Diesel's dog, Ben, heard the ruckus and came flying in to join Bill Barking in the fly hunt. Ben was a big, black, woolly-headed hound, covered in his usual coating of mud and grease from the farm. Most normal dogs would want a bone or a big stick as a 'comfort toy' but, for some psychotic reason, Ben had chosen a pimply, flesh-pink coloured dildo he'd found at the farm, and he never went anywhere without the ugly thing protruding from his mouth. As he joined the hunt, Ben dropped the saliva-clad device on the coffee-table next to the plate of biscuits Gavin had been offered, providing a most appetising sight.

Bill and Ben never met without bunging on a blue, and today was no exception. The last glimpse Gavin caught of Mick was of him and Diesel performing a crocodile roll with their two animals, down the hallway, as they attempted to prise their fighting dogs apart.

I continued the meeting with Gavin against a background of barks, snarls, yelps and yells of, 'Oweee ... the bastard bit me!' Still unperturbed, Gavin seemed genuinely interested in the buses and when I explained that one of the deckers was parked at the NCP car park, only five minutes away, he readily accepted my offer to drive him up there to check it out. We walked out into Kenway Road and located the Renault that Mick and I shared. I unlocked and opened the front passenger door for Gavin and he was just about to climb in when suddenly Bill Barking appeared from nowhere. Obviously having vanquished Ben (and Mick), and never one to miss any of the action, Bill squeezed himself between Gavin and the car door in a flash and propped himself into a sitting position on the front seat, tongue

Gavin Simpson, far left on a visit to London, with me, Chris Jacobs, Chris Greive, John O'Donnell and Murgha Mack.

Sales Tales - London 1980

out, panting heavily and dribbling everywhere—looking at me with a look of, 'Well, get going. What are you waiting for?'

As Gavin attempted to push Bill into the back of the car, Bill turned on him with a snarl, meaning, 'Piss off, Jappie, this is my seat,' and I sheepishly explained to Gavin that Mick always allowed Bill to ride in the front seat and unless Gavin wanted Bill on his lap for the entire trip, perhaps he would be more comfortable on the backseat himself.

Gavin left for South Africa secure in the knowledge that he had both the upper and lower ends of the European tour market covered. Any other GSA business he acquired was certain to fall somewhere in between.

L to R: Driver Barry Innes and Courier Dark Blue Coubrough entertaining passengers.

Chapter 16

MARTYRS ON CHARTERS

(EUROPE 1980)

As is often the case in marketing, the places where you invest most of your resources often prove to be the most fruitless, and support often comes from the most unlikely quarters. So it proved with Top Deck when a surprising number of sales began to flow in from Asia. Anthony Chan from Chan Brothers in Singapore, and Asian Overland Services in Malaysia, sent an increasing number of passengers, primarily uni students who couldn't afford other forms of travel. So, too, did Ronald Chew from the Hong Kong Student Travel Bureau.

However, our best sales came from another student operator in Singapore, James Soh. In fact, sales increased to the point where James inquired about the possibility of chartering deckers specifically for his own groups. We responded positively. We saw James Soh and other potential sources of charters as an entirely new growth area for the company, and Murgha Mack, an Aussie from Deniliquin who had been a driver with us for some time, took over the marketing and operational responsibility for the separate charter division.

James Soh's first charter group was due into Rome where it would be met by a decker and after two weeks touring, would fly out from Amsterdam. Mick and I decided to take one of the company cars, a Renault, to Rome for two reasons. First, we could meet up with Budgie Kemsley and Mrs Oliver's Little Boy Tim who were crewing the decker, to ensure that all was in order. James Soh was coming on the first trip himself and we decided

Martyrs on Charters – Europe 1980

that as an additional PR exercise, I would travel with James Soh on the decker to Amsterdam as well.

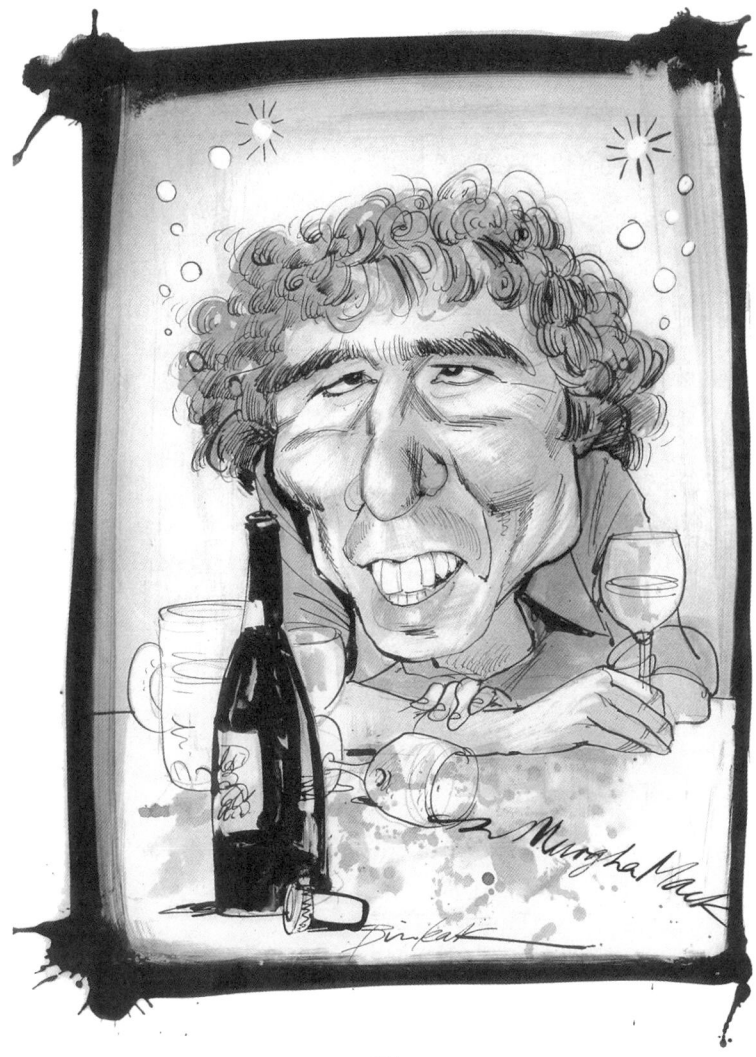

Another reason for Mick and me to visit Europe was to make PR calls on all the restaurants that supplied the national meals for our trips, as well as all the bars and shops that our tours frequented. Not only had the owners of these businesses become good friends, they were always willing to help any of our crew if ever they found themselves in trouble, and we were indebted to them on more than one occasion. More importantly, they paid our crew commission on any of the purchases that our punters made at their various establishments. These commissions substantially augmented the modest wages paid to the crew and went a long way towards mitigating any demands they might otherwise have made for an increase.

Mick insisted that our first port of call be the photo shop in the beautiful Dutch fishing village of Volendam, where all the punters dressed up in Dutch clothing to have their photos taken. The shop was run by two sisters, Carola and Miranda, and every driver and courier we'd ever employed had creamed their clogs over the two girls whenever they'd met them. Other principal establishments were Willy's Showboat, Van Moppes' Diamonds and the Last Watering Hole in Amsterdam, Codorníu Champagne Caves and the Mont Taber Leather shop in Barcelona, Marco's Murano Glass factory in Venice and, of course, in Florence, Paolo Fortini's Leather Works, Walter's Silverware, the Space Electronics Disco, and the Red Garter Bar.

Walter Gelli at his silverware shop, Florence.

Mick and I also wanted to visit the six major campsites in Europe to try and negotiate better rates and to reserve good areas

Martyrs on Charters – Europe 1980

within the camps for the deckers. Contiki, our major camping tour competitor, had stolen a march on us in this respect, as they had done in most operational areas. Somehow they had been able to afford new Mercedes coaches. While these were actually very modest by European standards, the name Mercedes was a major selling point in Australasia. Top Deck seemed to cover half the globe, while Contiki, very sensibly, concentrated wholly on central Europe. This enabled Contiki to establish some villa accommodation and permanent campsites in the major cities, all with 'supercooks' and on-site reps, meaning that, unlike Top Deck, they ran a very tight, well-controlled operation, and could nip any problems that might occur in the bud.

Despite all of this, we still felt that, on the whole, it was much more fun on top—on a Top Deck tour, that is. Somehow Contiki seemed too organised, too stilted, too sterile. Possibly it had something to do with the fact that they always carried too many girls in proportion to guys. Perhaps it was also because many of their passengers would fly in and out, just for their European tour, and so were a bit 'green' and naïve. Top Deckers, on the other hand, were more seasoned campaigners coming, as they did, from the ranks of the working holidaymakers residing in the UK—and boy, did they know how to party!

Talking about 'more fun on top', the difference between a typical Contiki and Top Deck trip was brought home to Mick and me when we visited Florence. There had been a major complaint lodged by Contiki against Top Deck for a recent incident in the campsite, and Mick and I felt obliged to visit Camping Michelangelo and apologise to their management and to assure them that the behaviour displayed on that particular trip was not condoned, nor tolerated, by our company. In reality, we couldn't do a thing about it.

The magnificent city of Florence was always a highlight for any tour. You could marvel at Fra Angelico's frescoes in the Duomo Cathedral, muse over Botticelli's masterpieces in the Uffizi Gallery, and then wonder at what, to my humble mind,

Top Deck Daze

was the most exquisite piece of artwork in the entire universe, Michelangelo's David, at the Accademia. After the best shopping in Europe, you could spend your evenings at the lively discos and bars that lined the many piazzas.

No Top Deck tour ever left Florence without spending its last night in the Red Garter Bar. Not only was it the liveliest bar in town, it was the most liberal in its supply of free grog to the buses' crews, so the punters were rarely given an alternative even had they desired one. On the night before the Camping Michelangelo incident, which led to the Contiki complaint, the Top Deck group had been in the Red Garter Bar until three in the morning, before returning to the campsite.

Camping Michelangelo had the best location of any campsite in Europe. Its stepped, terraced banks provided campers on any level with wonderful panoramic views of the city, just a stone's throw away across the River Arno. The Top Deck bus had been parked on one level, and a Contiki group camped on the level immediately below. This was one campsite where Contiki didn't have the luxury of a permanent site, and the punters had been put to bed early by their courier in preparation for an early morning rise to break camp, breakfast, and be on the road by seven.

No such thoughts had entered the heads of the Top Deckers. They would leave when they were well and truly ready, hangovers permitting, and a party raged on board till sun-up. Top Deck had been joined by a group from Vikings, a camping-tour company with a culture similar to our own, and the party was still in full swing when the Contiki group rose, laid out their folding tables and chairs, and all sat down to breakfast.

No sooner had they begun to eat when, glancing up pensively to the raucous laughter and music blasting from the decker above, they saw a naked girl stumbling from the doorway of the bus. She fell to her knees, clutching the chain wire fence on the terrace immediately above them, and was violently ill. If that wasn't enough to put the campers off their cornflakes, what followed certainly did. Sam, the Vikings driver, equally starkers and equally inebriated, stumbled after the girl and the unspeakable happened, in full view of the nauseated voyeurs below. The Contiki punters must have spent the day writing thank-you cards and sending flowers to their travel agents back home for booking them with the right tour company. Then again, were they missing out on some occasionally hilarious times? ... well, perhaps not on this occasion.

It would be a mistake, however, to think that the passengers on Contiki, or any other tour company for that matter, held the high moral ground. Debauched behaviour was common on most tours, it was just that the majority of those who engaged in such activity were a little more discreet in choosing their time and place. There was ample evidence of this, for example, at Camping Seven Hills in Rome where Mick and I next stopped.

The owners of Camping Seven Hills, the brothers Tony and Piero Alpocelli, were as well known and as popular as any in Europe, on a par with Chris and Henry at Lauterbrunnen and Renato at Fusina, Venice. The campsite, on the Via Cassia, was also one of the best equipped. It had bungalows (for quiet nights alone, of course), a supermarket, pool, pizzeria, barbecue, restaurant, bar and disco.

Mick and I met up with Budgie and Mrs Oliver's Little Boy Tim, who were already in Rome with a decker, awaiting the arrival of the James Soh charter. The four of us had just ordered drinks in the campsite bar when Piero came down with an urgent message. Rocky, the operations manager from one of our rival camping-tour companies,

Chris and Henry from Lauterbrunnen Campsite enjoy a glass of wine with Mick's friend, Jane McLean.

Sundowners, had just phoned. One of their longest-serving drivers, Leo, had just had a heart attack at the wheel of his coach near Sorrento.

Fortunately it had occurred while they were at traffic lights and the bus and everyone else on board was okay, except they were now stranded because neither the cook nor the courier could drive. Rocky requested assistance from any other tour operators in Rome at the time.

Budgie and Tim had no hesitation. They took our Renault and were off to Sorrento within minutes. It was an unfortunate time in Sundowners' history. With the exception of Contiki and Top Deck, just about every other major European camping-tour operator went belly-up at some stage, often in messy circumstances, and it was no different with Sundowners. It wasn't long after this particular incident that telexes were sent to all their crews on the road: 'Sorry, guys and girls. No mon. No fun. We're going down the gurgler. You're on your own. Do what you can to get the trips back to London.' Mick and I had come to know their managing director, Kevin 'KD' Dunning, quite well, and it was a traumatic time for him and his staff.

It was late the following evening when Mick and I met up again with Budgie and Tim in the bar. They had effected their rescue mission and brought the Sundowners coach up to Rome. A replacement driver was on his way and the punters would have no trouble sightseeing in Rome using the Vatican shuttle, a sightseeing bus that called by the campsite every day. Budgie and Tim, however, were in the middle of a roaring argument when we joined them in the bar.

'It's four nil, I tell you, four nil,' Tim was yelling.

'It's not four nil, you cur. You couldn't possibly count that one, you rat. It's still three nil and that's final,' Budgie countered.

'Of course it counts. The poor girl was suffering. I was only trying to take her mind off things.'

Unfortunately for all concerned, Leo's heart attack had proved fatal and he'd passed away just before Budgie and Tim had arrived at Sorrento. The supercook had been Leo's girlfriend, and poor Leo was still warm in the Sorrento morgue when Tim and the girlfriend had formed a liaison. 'Disgusting, bloody disgusting, I tell you. He's got the morals of an alley cat, the cad,' Budgie continued. Even the barman was drawn into the discussion on the morality or otherwise of the affair. The barman was a South African guy on a working holiday who lived-in at the campsite and doubled as the lifeguard at the pool during the day. He was tall, blonde and bronzed, and built

Piero and Di Alpocelli, from Camping Seven Hills, Rome.

like a Greek Adonis. His popularity with the girls was almost an embarrassment to all concerned. What made us guys even madder was that he was actually a hell of a nice guy as well.

The argument dragged on into the wee small hours, by which time the overwhelming consensus was that Tim was indeed a bounder of monstrous proportions and nothing short of castration was warranted. It was so late that Adonis was forced to close the bar, but kindly invited us back to his tiny flatette for a nightcap. We accepted with much appreciation.

Sitting around the room finishing our drinks, Tim caught sight of a large poster pinned to the back of the flat's door. He walked over and checked it out. There, listed in date sequence, were the names of over 220 girls. 'What's this?' asked Tim incredulously, not really wanting to know the answer.

'Oh, that's last season,' said Adonis.

'And this? This is this season?' asked Tim, wide-eyed, pointing to the poster adjacent to the first. Adonis nodded. Tim did a quick count of the girls' names and checked the date on his watch. 'Ninety-eight, and it's only mid-May?' Again he paused to calculate. 'I'll tell you what,' he said slowly, in a state of total shock, 'Last season's record is looking mighty shaky.'

The incident put an immediate end to Tim and Budgie's now seemingly insignificant competition.

Mick took off in the Renault to complete the European junket by himself and Tim, Budgie and I drove out to Rome's Leonardo da Vinci-Fiumicino airport to meet the James Soh charter. We didn't have long to wait and as James Soh and I chatted in the terminal, his passengers regrouped and then made their way out towards the bus parking area. There were eighteen students in all, about nineteen or twenty years of age, with an equal number of boys and girls. They were quite small in stature, the girls in particular being very petite. They were extremely neat and well groomed; in fact it was embarrassing to learn later that our standards of personal hygiene and general cleanliness fell far short of their exacting standards. Their clothes were upmarket,

Martyrs on Charters – Europe 1980

designer labels. Many of the girls wore good leather shoes with little white socks. More than half of them carried suitcases, an absolute no-no for a double-decker as there was nowhere to store them. Departure information specifically requested that gear be brought in soft folding bags.

Tim had done a great job in preparing the double-decker, trying to create the best, possible impression for our newest agent. The inside had been scrubbed and polished until you could see your face in the varnish and even the tyres had been blackened and the rims painted silver.

We'd pulled up in the coach park behind two other buses that just happened to be the latest, most expensive double-deckers you could buy—'Highliners'—£500 000 worth of vehicle, one owned by American Express and the other by Tommy Cook. These vehicles were genuine engineering masterpieces, bristling with the latest technology, with double the internal space and comfort you would find on a regular single-decker coach. They also stood empty, awaiting the arrival of their passengers.

The Singaporean students reached the bus park and, without so much as a second thought, the leading group climbed straight on board the Amex Highliner. Mrs Oliver's Little Boy Tim, ensconced in the driver's cab of the Top Deck bus, had watched the group as they'd made their way across the car park. He saw the Singaporeans board the Highliner. Immediately, he jumped down onto the roadway and, as he did so, one couldn't help notice that he cut the classic figure of an Aussie camping-tour driver: A week's growth of stubble, a beloved Manly-Warringah footy jersey, baggy shorts (we called them Kathmandu flyers), poofter bag, and clogs. He pursed his lips and let out a shrill, sheepdog command whistle, then bawled, 'Oi. You lot. Over 'ere!'

The Singaporeans stopped in their tracks and turned their heads. We could see them sizing up the situation. They looked over and studied the Top Deck bus through squinting eyes then, slowly, they looked back towards the Highliner. With great reluctance and hesitancy, they made their way over to the much humbler of the two vehicles. I made a mental note to check what bus photos James Soh had been using for his sales presentations.

One of the students, a quite attractive girl called Susan, was clearly their unelected leader. She put her suitcase down and stood there, small and defiant-looking, with hands on hips, eyeing off Tim and the bus, while the others climbed on board with more than manifest reticence. Tim was one of the straightest talkers I'd ever met and he was never one to take a backward step. He and Susan were obviously two of a kind, and you could see the sparks flying before they'd even spoken.

'Don't like your caravan,' she said finally, in her typically stern, blunt Oriental manner. 'Don't like your caravan at all.'

Tim's look said, 'Well I don't like the look of you, lady,' but, fortunately, he held his tongue and just said, with forced bonhomie, 'Time to go then, eh?' and nodded for Susan to get on board and join her friends.

The first night in the campsite, Tim and Budgie gave the Singaporeans a rundown on how the trip would be organised, including the cooking roster, which they pasted up on the back wall. Like every Top Deck tour, passengers paid into a 'food kitty' over and above the regular tour price. Some of the kitty was spent on non-perishables before departure, and the balance was kept for fresh food en route. With astute budgeting, the kitty might allow for some national meals in restaurants. The passengers were put on a roster, one pair to do the cooking, another to wash and clean up. When Tim had finished his Churchillian oration (he loved an audience) he was met with blank, stony faces.

'We no cook,' said Susan finally. 'We all have servants at home. We no like cooking.' There was no doubt they came from well-off families and were pampered and indulged.

'Well, you'll just have to bloody-well starve then, won't you, sweetheart?' replied Tim diplomatically.

It was the first of many Mexican stand-offs between the two of them. More time passed before Susan finally relented.

'Where is the food then?'

Martyrs on Charters – Europe 1980

'If you'll move that friggen suitcase, I'll show you.' They'd already had a barney about Susan bringing her suitcase on board. Susan insisted on leaving her case on the front seat for the entire trip. Tim unceremoniously dumped the case on the floor and pulled up the seat-cover to show Susan the storage locker. 'There's your food. Now why don't you just cook it like the good lady you are, and stop complaining?'

Susan held up the seat-cover with one hand and, with the other, tried to pull up a large, five-kilo bag of rice. It was so heavy she needed assistance from one of the boys. Under that was another bag, and another, and another, all rice. Susan and the rest of the group then went around pulling up all the seat lockers. All rice. Tim must have spent the entire food kitty on ten tonnes of rice. There wasn't a morsel of anything else on board. Susan struggled to hold one of the bags at head height, studied it a moment, then dumped it back into the locker.

'I cannot eat this rice. This rice no good. Not fit for my chooks.'

'What do you mean, "Not fit for your chooks?"' said Tim in disgust. 'It's Uncle Ben's Long Grain?' That was obviously what Mrs Oliver had cooked for her 'Little Boy', and if it was good enough for him, well, Tim couldn't see the problem.

'Rice is rice, for God's sake.'

'Not fit for my chooks,' insisted Susan, and the stand-off continued.

We weren't sure what transpired the next day. Perhaps James Soh intervened and counselled Susan. He was a genuinely nice guy and we all got on well with him. He'd travelled extensively and was much more tolerant of our different ways than his student clients. Whatever, at eight o'clock the next night, the exotic smell of Asian cooking wafted from the bus. Whether they had brought the spices with them or found supplies in Rome, we never knew.

They may not have liked cooking, but they were experts at it. We found they cooked at least eight times a day. It was nothing for them to be in the kitchen at 4:00 a.m. with another brew of fried rice or noodles—hardly conducive to a good night's sleep.

Top Deck Daze

It didn't matter where we went, the Singaporean passengers were unimpressed. Budgie took them to the Vatican City and the Sistine Chapel.

'Not as good as Singapore,' they'd say. The Forum, the Colosseum, the Catacombs, the Piazza Navona, were, 'Not as good as Singapore.' By the time we reached Florence, Budgie was exasperated. He decided that no one, irrespective of race, creed or culture, could possibly be unimpressed with Michelangelo's David. He took all of them to the Accademia, stood them in front of the statue, and gave them the full incantation. He told them every detail of Michelangelo's life, the story of the 'Agony and the Ecstasy', the patronage of the Medici family, the classic portrayal of David as the Israelite king and the very embodiment of the ideal man. Again, all Budgie got was blank, stony expressions.

'So when do we see it?' said Susan after a pregnant pause.

'What do you mean, "When do you see it?" That's it. Right in front of you!' yelled the galled Budgie, pointing to the six-metre high monolith.

'Oh, is that it? We thought it was a painting,' said Susan, turning away without so much as a cursory look, and ticking it off her list.

They all had lists. They'd obviously been told of the 'one-hundred-must-see' sights in Europe and they ticked them off as we went along.

Things didn't improve. In Paris, the Eiffel Tower was, 'Not as big as Telecom Tower in Singapore,' and Susan asked, 'When do we see Champs Elysées?'

'The Champs Elysées? Good God, woman!' yelled Tim from the cab, trying the diplomatic approach once more, 'We've driven up and down the damn thing forty times in the last two days!' and so it too was ticked off the list.

And in Amsterdam, after a full day's sightseeing, Susan demanded, 'Now we go and see Anne and Frank?'

'We what?' asked Tim, bewildered.

Martyrs on Charters – Europe 1980

'Anne and Frank,' demanded Susan. 'Brochure says we go and see Anne and Frank's house now.'

'Look, you stupid …' he clenched his teeth so the words were mumbled while his cheeks turned blue and his knuckles turned white. 'Yes, yes. Of course,' he said, sucking in the air in great gulps, 'Anne and Frank. Anne and Frank. Of course. How silly of us to forget. We'll have a cup of tea with them too, shall we?'

On the last day, we dropped them at Schiphol Airport. Probably again because of James Soh's intervention, everyone was on their best behaviour so that at least the trip would end without any hint of animosity. We were quite impressed that the students had prepared a nice 'thank-you' card for the three of us and James Soh made a short, well-worded, farewell speech.

It was time for them to leave and we all shook hands, Tim included, and when he got around to Susan, it was obvious he wasn't sure what to do. Shake hands perhaps? Or should he even risk a peck on the cheek? After all, she was a very petite, attractive young girl with the most outgoing of personalities, and he wasn't the sort of guy to hold a grudge or feel the slightest bit of prejudice. He'd tried his absolute damnedest to ensure the trip went well, especially over the last week. Susan, too, seemed to hesitate. Tim was a handsome young man, destined for greater things. She looked up into Tim's eyes, and with a serene and gentle face, said softly, 'Just want to say one thing … Don't like you, and don't like your caravan.'

So much for Susan! Nevertheless, the trip was otherwise deemed to be moderately successful and the Singaporean bookings kept rolling in. Unfortunately, the trips were not at all popular with the crew. Like our colonial punters, they were motivated as much by the social interaction as anything else and as this was completely lacking on most charters, they considered being rostered on one as having drawn the short straw.

Asia wasn't the only place where Top Deck received unexpected support. Murgha Mack, the manager of the new charters division, had made contact with a company called Pan

Top Deck Daze

Trading that ran an outbound travel business based in Tel Aviv, Israel, and they also booked some European charters—three-weekers, into and out of Paris. The first group was due in at Charles De Gaulle Airport shortly after I returned from the James Soh episode. At the same time, Tim joined Dillon, playing 'silly buggers' (his description, not mine), as assistant operations manager at Kenway Road.

The Israelis were a special-interest group consisting of sculptors, artists and art historians on a cultural tour of Europe which, of course, was right down Top Deck's alley. We knew that this type of tour was going to have its own special demands but I doubt if anyone could have been prepared for what lay ahead.

The courier was Pauline 'Granny' Webb and we received her first distraught phone call from the Paris campsite on day one of the trip. The Israelis had told Granny that the cutlery and pots and pans were unacceptable for their special cooking requirements, as well as being unclean. The crew of another decker just departing London was organised to bring a complete replacement set out to them.

Granny was all set to hit the road the following morning but no, no one was going anywhere until the bus and its equipment had been properly blessed. More frantic phone calls to and from London managed to unearth a rabbi from some obscure Parisian synagogue. He was offered a substantial donation if he would go to the campsite and finally he and his cantor, after much singing of hymns, swinging of lamps, reading from Torahs and praying from siddurs, pronounced the bus, aptly named *Bollocks*, worthy enough to hit the 'frog and toad'.

No sooner had this little drama been resolved when, only an hour out of Paris, the Israeli tour leader ordered the driver to bring the bus to a screeching halt, right by the side of the motorway, only centimetres away from the great semitrailers hurtling along these stretches at their breakneck speeds. It was a Friday night and the sun had just gone down. This signified the start of the Sabbath, the holy day of rest, and so again, no

Martyrs on Charters - Europe 1980

one was going anywhere until three stars could be seen in the Saturday evening sky.

The organisation that went into the purchase, transportation, storage and cooking of the food to accord with the travellers' strictly kosher requirements was a logistics nightmare that would have sorely tested the British Army's quartermaster. It had been arranged that all the food would be flown in on their El-Al flight and be kept on the bus in insulated, polystyrene containers.

Much research had gone into where dry ice might and might not be obtained and so on but, of course, these complex types of arrangements always proved unworkable and by the fourth day the food wasn't fit enough to feed the fish under the Pont du Gard at Nimes, where it was jettisoned.

The nearest kosher restaurant the group could find was a silver-service job in Monte Carlo. The entire three weeks' food kitty was blown in the one evening's meal. Top Deck had to accept responsibility for the balls-up and feeding the group in restaurants for the remaining two-and-a-half weeks blew the trip's budget out the window. There were no bright ideas about how to resolve this issue short of doubling the contracted tour price and nobody at Kenway Road was willing to back their bargaining skills against the Jewish owner of Pan Trading. The pressure was mounting because more charters were banking up on the tarmac at Ben Gurion Airport as a result of Murgha Mack's overzealous marketing.

The other major problem Granny Webb encountered was that some of the Israelis proved to be deadset kleptomaniacs. They would steal anything and everything that wasn't bolted to the floor. It became quite serious when they were kicked out of a couple of campsites after being caught stealing from the shop.

When Tim finally went across to meet Granny he simply refused to believe her allegations. By all appearances the group was respectable and very well-to-do. It wasn't as if they were poor students who couldn't make ends meet. This was before we carried many more Israelis during subsequent years and found out that this was, indeed, an extraordinary characteristic of some of those punters. This was neither a biased nor bigoted opinion. It was a fact, and an experience shared by all our crews. No one has ever satisfactorily explained this odd phenomenon to us.

We got the final, distressed call from Granny in Amsterdam two days before the group was due to fly out. It was obvious she couldn't take it any more.

'It's either me or them,' she told Tim on the phone. 'Either I go or they go.' When Tim arrived that evening she was sitting by herself, a hundred or so metres away from the bus, puffing away on her roll-your-own cigarettes, swearing and talking to herself. 'I'm not going anywhere till they give 'em back,' she was mumbling, as Tim came near her.

'Give what back, Granny?' Tim asked, as gently as possible.

'Me undies. They've nicked me lovely undies, can you believe it? The tea-leaving sods, and I'm not going anywhere till they give 'em back.' Tim didn't know exactly why Granny was so attached to her undies, nor why she had chosen this particular issue on which to make her final stand—she'd had plenty of other opportunities to choose from—but Tim didn't dare ask, given her fragile emotional state.

Chapter 17
MATES IN THE STATES
(USA 1981)

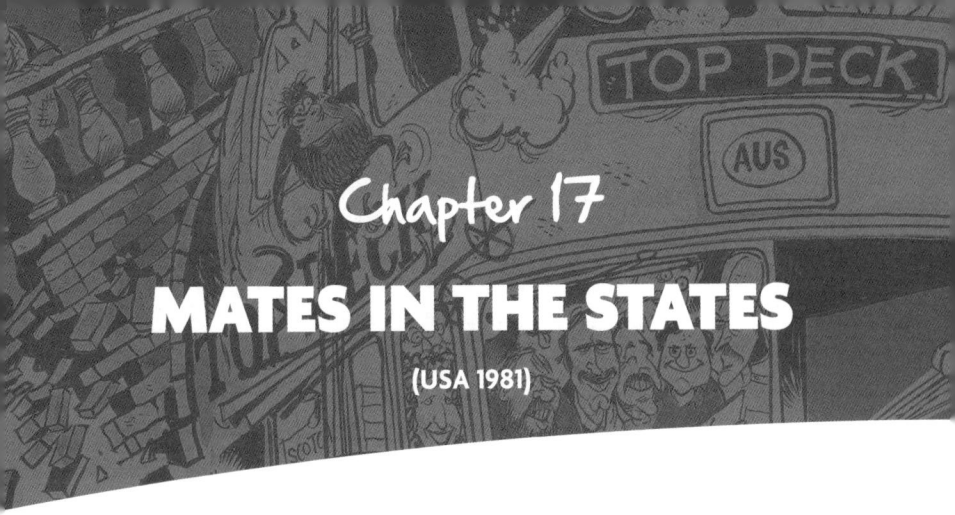

While Budgie, Tim and I had been on the James Soh charter, we'd spent two nights in Venice at Camping Fusina and had a chance meeting with a Mexican called Arnulfo which, by an interesting series of events, led directly to charters for Top Deck out of Mexico and, indirectly, to Budgie's idea of establishing Top Deck America. Arnulfo, a young, extroverted, twenty-two-year-old Mexican, had a father who was extremely wealthy, being a very successful businessman, and Arnulfo had made a bet with him that he, too, could make his fortune before he reached his twenty-fifth birthday.

Despite the fact he'd only been to Europe once before, as a ten-year-old, Arnulfo had placed ads in the Mexican newspapers for a series of European camping tours and had managed to book forty passengers on his first departure. He'd chartered a Spanish coach out of Madrid and was following his nose around the Continent. He had stumbled upon Camping Fusina.

Budgie could speak a little Spanish and French and Arnulfo began quizzing him in the campsite bar as to where to go and stay in Europe. Budgie had compiled a fantastic collection of trip notes, maps and city and country histories and he gave as much information as he could to Arnulfo. Arnulfo was so grateful he asked Budgie if he'd come to Mexico City later in the year to train some Mexican tour leaders for the following season which he hoped would be bigger and better than his first.

Errol Flynn *at the Freemantle.*

We'd forgotten all about this until the August of 1980 when, lo and behold, a fully refundable first-class air ticket arrived in the mail for Budgie. He cashed this in for five economy seats on an 'el cheapo' Braniff charter and gave two to Mick and me, kept one for himself, and gave the other two to his friends, Grant Hassell and Graham 'Silver Jacket' Holmes, who were also working for Top Deck at the time.

Budgie, Grant and Silver Jacket had a fabulous four weeks in Mexico coaching Arnulfo's couriers and then holidaying in Acapulco at Arnulfo's expense. The three of them decided to drive back to New York on a cheap hire-car relocation deal and it was during the idle hours chatting in the car that they hatched plans for a US operation.

Mick and I flew to Mexico City a few weeks later to meet Arnulfo and convince him to use Top Deck buses for his next season of charters. On our way back to London we had to transfer planes in Dallas, Texas. As we queued up to check-in again for the London leg, it was obvious that Braniff had way overbooked the flight. A barrel-chested, Texan cowboy, decked out in obligatory boots, Stetson and frilled-sleeve jacket was in front of us in the queue. He became more and more agitated as the waiting dragged on well past the scheduled time of departure.

Mates in the States - USA 1981

At last the Texan's patience ran out and he announced to the world at large that he wasn't, '… takin' no more o' this kinda shit.' He barged forward, elbowing aside the people in front of him, took a flying leap over the counter, pinned the poor check-in clerk against the rear wall by the scruff of the neck and demanded a seat on the flight. After a brawl with the clerk and several other airline staff, the Texan was finally dragged off by security guards.

Shortly thereafter, several of the Braniff management team appeared holding up great wads of cash and offering it to anyone who'd rebook on the following night's flight. Mick and I had never witnessed scenes like this before and we decided to take up the offer and spent the next day looking up friends that I'd met during my working holiday in Texas in 1973.

Budgie, Grant and Silver Jacket originally planned to operate in the USA with coaches and not to involve Top Deck at all but

Those at the launch of Top Deck America included Mick, Five-Eights, Chris Hyland, Dillon, Grant Hassell and Graham 'Silver Jacket' Holmes (standing) with Murgha and Budgie (in front).

after Screw got wind of this, he phoned Budgie and convinced him it should be a joint venture between the three of them and Top Deck. When it came down to actually forking out hard, cold cash to finance the venture, the three boys agreed. A decker was acquired in the UK, fitted out at the Woking farm, christened *Errol Flynn*, and shipped across to New York. Budgie and Mick Pepper, our sign-writer, came up with a new design for the bus' livery, which everybody agreed was pretty snazzy and the whole European fleet was repainted that year in the new style.

Screw came back to London for a few months in late 1980. I had agreed with Budgie that the US operation would be a fifty-fifty partnership but after Screw met with Budgie, he lived up to his name and reduced their shareholding to twenty-five per cent, take-it-or-leave-it. Things had progressed so far by this stage that Budgie and the other two boys had no option but to agree.

In the States, Budgie and Grant ran into a minefield of restrictive US Federal and State laws regulating transport

Errol Flynn *in New York, 1980, ready for its maiden voyage with a full deck.*

Mates in the States – USA 1981

operations. For example, the company had to be registered in every single State the tours intended to travel through; specific route licences had to be applied for and, if granted, fees paid; the buses required special registration and so on. Budgie and Grant hired some fancy New York lawyer to help them sort it all out. The lawyer charged like a wounded rhinoceros and would have enjoyed an early retirement if Screw hadn't found out what was happening shortly after his arrival in London. Screw exploded when he saw the pile of attorney's bills mounting up in the Kenway Road office.

'What do those idiots think they're trying to do over there? Run some sort of legal operation or something?' he thundered. He was obviously outraged at the thought of it. He managed to get hold of Budgie on the phone and gave him an earful. He then began to explain how to go about tackling these sorts of challenges Screw-Turner-Style. Some creative, lateral thinking resulted in Top Deck America Inc. being registered as a charitable club, with a US$10 joining fee deducted from every punter's fare, thereby circumventing all the onerous legislation. 'Screw the bureaucrats'—now that was the Screw-Turner-Style of operating a business.

In November 1980, a second bus, *Chips Rafferty*, was sent across the Atlantic. Mick and I applied to Document Handling Ltd (DHL) for airline tickets to New York, which came through in the first week of December. With a big base in London, DHL was an overnight air-courier company. If you managed to get onto DHL's courier list you could fly with them anywhere in the world, free. They'd check-in all their courier bags as excess luggage and all you had to do was hand the bag tags to their rep at the destination.

There was a surprise waiting for me when I checked in. My flight was to be on a Concorde, my only experience on the supersonic jet.

To see how things were progressing, Mick and I wanted to meet up with all the Top Deck crew in the States—which

Top Deck Daze

now included Andy Morgan, Mike Schweiger, Warwick 'Curly' Gladman and Tony 'Rat' Vanderway. Mick was a mad, keen country and western fan and the first night in New York, he took us all to the Lone Star Bar where one of his favourite singers, a big black momma called Greta James, was performing.

Mick and I stayed on till well after midnight before returning to our downmarket hotel, the George Washington. Budgie had returned a little earlier and was listening to the radio when he heard a newsflash—John Lennon had just been shot in front of his Central Park apartment. Budgie greeted us with the news as we came to our room.

We sat glued to the television for half-an-hour, all in a genuine state of shock that such a thing could happen—and just up the road from where we were, as well. While the Beatles had split up by this stage, everybody felt sure that they'd get back together again at some time. This then, really was the final curtain. The Beatles had been such a symbol of our generation that for the first time in my life, at the age of thirty-one, I felt really, really old. I guess I was thinking that part of my youth had died along with John that night.

Sleep was impossible so we donned our jackets and made our way up to Central Park. Hundreds of people with the same idea had gathered outside the Dakota apartment buildings where John had been shot and the crowd joined hands and sang songs like 'Give Peace a Chance'. We were still there at 3:00 a.m. when the first signs of weariness came over us. We decided we'd been out in the cold for long enough and headed off again in the direction of the hotel. It had only been four hours since the shooting and we couldn't believe our eyes when we saw two guys on Central Park corner selling T-shirts printed with 'John Lennon 1940–1980.' It was crass commercialism of the highest order, US style.

When we ventured outside our hotel the next morning queues of people, hundreds of metres long, lined the footpaths outside every music store in the city, waiting to buy any of the Beatles' records they could get their hands on, presumably as mementos of the end of an era.

Mick managed to get a flight back to London that evening but my booking wasn't for another few days so I decided to join Budgie and Grant on the *Errol Flynn* for the start of their coming tour. They were due to depart that day on the last trip for the season, a five-week 'Confederate' tour taking in all the southern States en route to LA.

The first day was spent sightseeing in New York itself. It was a full schedule and hard going for Grant, driving the big decker in the bustling city streets. New Yorkers are pretty blasé, most believing they've 'seen it all', but *Errol Flynn* turned many a head as it made its way around the Big Apple.

There was a full complement of punters on board, but two in particular stood out—a couple of gay Pommie guys who could have easily starred in Priscilla. One of them was named Derek and so the wags on board immediately nicknamed his mate 'Clive'. The gay guys completely ignored Budgie's pleading to be on time after each city sightseeing stop.

'Oooo, we just started chatting to the most wooonderful people,' Derek explained after holding us up for twenty minutes at the World Trade Centre and, 'Oooo, aren't the views just loverley,' after waiting half-an-hour for them at the Empire State Building. By the time we stopped mid-afternoon at the Guggenheim Museum, Grant was *trying* to lose them. It wasn't that Grant had anything against homosexuality (though it could leave a bad taste in your mouth), he simply ran out of patience. They'd been given sufficient warning and been told where to find us in the next city if they were late, and Grant ensured we were underway within thirty seconds of the specified departure time, minus our good pals Derek and Clive.

We headed south along the New Jersey freeway bound for our next stopover, Atlantic City. We'd been on the road for more than an hour when, out of the blue, we were overtaken by two police cars, sirens wailing and lights flashing, followed by a long, black stretch-limo. It was evident that the police wanted us to pull over and as we came to a halt behind the limo, who should pop out of its swinging rear doors but Derek and Clive! I expected them to be so outraged at being left behind they'd have their Polly Waffles stuck up the wrong doughnut, but, nothing of the sort. They fairly gushed with good spirits.

Mates in the States – USA 1981

'Oooooo, we never thought we'd ever seeeee you again, darlings,' they giggled, champagne glasses still in hand. The limo belonged to the State governor who, observing the unlikely lads trying to hitch a ride out of New York, decided to strike a blow for Anglo-American relations.

'We look after our guests in this here part of the world, darn right we do,' the governor said with a great smile, 'Y'all have a nice day now, yer hear?'

Atlantic City is the Las Vegas of the east, dominated by large casinos and hotel complexes. As far as Budgie was concerned, this was his kind of city. Like all the out-of-work or between-job entertainers back home, he'd learnt to supplement his income on the roulette and blackjack tables of the illegal gambling houses in Sydney, often working as a croupier himself or playing blackjack for the house.

It was my last night out before returning to New York to pick up my London flight, so Budgie and I went out for a night on the town. We started playing blackjack, very conservatively, limiting ourselves to two-and five-dollar bets. Our winnings mounted encouragingly and by midnight we were about US$500 up. The place was really buzzing by this stage and there was a great stir at our table when the famous singer Tony Bennett, who'd just finished his show, pulled up a chair to join us. He bought drinks for everyone, then started betting up big and throwing money around like confetti. We were joined by a few high rollers and before we knew it, not wanting to appear like novices, we too were betting with fifty-dollar chips.

It took an hour, but it seemed like the twinkling of an eye. By 1:00 a.m. not only our winnings but our entire stake had disappeared down the dealer's draw. Budgie had cashed-in the entire trip funds of US$2000, with my encouragement, and we were now left without a penny to our names. We couldn't believe how stupid we'd been. We were simply caught up in the hype of the moment. It was bad enough for me but for Budgie, his share of the losses amounted to six weeks wages.

Top Deck Daze

As we walked dejectedly to the doors of the casino, I rummaged through my wallet and found a spare twenty-dollar note and we decided to stop and have a quick cup of coffee in the lounge bar before we left. We sat there, sipping away in silence, ruminating on the night's events, inwardly cursing ourselves for our lack of responsibility and our bad luck. The change from the twenty-dollar bill lay on the table in front of us. We caught one another's eye as we stared at the money.

Without a word between us, we downed our coffees in one gulp, picked up the few remaining dollars, and headed for the quietest blackjack table in the room where we were the only two players.

Over the next three hours we built up our kitty to US$1950. We lashed out on the last hand. Had we won, we would have been all square. We lost, and finished the night seventy-five dollars down. It didn't matter. We rolled our eyes to heaven, blessed ourselves for good measure, cashed in the chips, and left. By the time we got back to the campsite the sun was coming up over the Atlantic and I only had time to pack my bag before catching a cab to the Greyhound terminal for the ride back to New York and the flight to London.

We shipped two more deckers to the States in 1981, the *Peter Finch* and the *Rod Taylor*, and later, set up a permanent office in LA on Sunset Boulevard. To have maximum use of the buses during winter, Budgie suggested that we should follow the sun south and do either a Mexican or perhaps a Central American program before the main USA season began in the spring. He even suggested that we attempt to take the buses all the way to South America. Lew Pulbrook, who had worked for Atrek and then Top Deck for several seasons, was already based there. He'd initially gone to work for Bruce Hodges' Goway together with another of our drivers, Denis Quinn, but had subsequently left and started up his own company, Inca Tours. Lew was well suited to this type of operation. He was more than a good mechanic, had a great affinity for South American history and culture, and

Mates in the States - USA 1981

learnt to speak passable Spanish, but we'd heard enough of his 'bandits in Bolivia'- and 'coups in Columbia'-type stories to question the wisdom of following in his footsteps. It didn't stop us trying.

In December 1981, twelve of the London-based crew flew to LA to team up with Gerry 'Puss Head' Watson and Gerard 'Geriatric' Rennie. The name 'The Two Gerries', as we called them, conjured up thoughts of a comic television duo rather than a driver and courier capable of taking a double-decker bus on an epic journey through Central and South America, but everyone in London was convinced that if anyone could get *Errol Flynn* to go where it wasn't suppose to go, the 'Two Gerries' could. Setting out from LA, the group travelled via Phoenix to the Rio Grand and then set the compass heading to 'South', through Mexico, El Salvador, Guatemala, Honduras, Nicaragua, Costa Rica and Panama.

Col Schirmer & Lew Pulbrook.

Meanwhile, Budgie had returned to London on a semi-permanent basis to take charge of marketing the US tours throughout the UK. Every night after work, Budgie, Mick and I would meet over at Dillon O'Sullivan's and Timmy Oliver's operations office to have a beer to cap off the day. Tim had a big map of Central and South America taped on a wall. We waited daily for news from the 'Two Gerries', as they would often report in at that time of night, if they could find a phone that worked. Tim charted their progress with red marker pins on the map.

'Gee, I hope they're not in El Salvador today,' Tim would say. 'The revolution's looking a bit nasty there at the moment,' or,

Flynn

FLYNN at Mt Rushmore

FLYNN

Mates in the States – USA 1981

'Struth, I hope they steer clear of Nicaragua. The war seems to have blown up there a bit lately,' and so on. Wars and revolutions seemed to be the flavour of the month in that part of the world at that particular time. At last the phone would ring.

'See San Jose in Costa Rica,' Puss Head would yell at Tim down the phone line.

'Yeeees,' Tim would say uncertainly, squinting at the map, and after a delay, 'Yeees, got that.'

'See that tiny town, Puerto Cortés, just below it?' Gerry would yell.

Pause, then, 'Yeeees, got that.'

'Well, that's where we are.'

After five weeks and 10 000 kilometres, they crossed the Panama Canal. They made it another 225 kilometres into the jungle, 'on the far side', until the road vanished into a green void of twisted vines and tangled undergrowth.

We had marketed the trip as 'The Last Great Adventure', and so it was. We decided to leave that part of the Americas to Lew Pulbrook, the Amazonians, the Incas, the Indians, and any other 'mad dogs' or 'Englishmen' who cared to go out there in the midday sun.

Chapter 18
WISE ENTERPRISE
(LONDON 1982)

The Fremantle Hotel in Cromwell Road, Earls Court, was Top Deck's social base in London and was where we booked passengers requiring pre-and post-tour accommodation. We held promotional film nights there during the week and the bar was regularly packed with crew, especially on Friday nights. In fact, the bar was so popular we reckoned that seventy per cent of Top Deck's wages bill passed over its counter. The Fremantle wasn't interested in any sort of a joint profit-share arrangement, so we went looking for a suitable alternative. We settled on the Enterprise Hotel in Hogarth Road, just behind our Kenway Road offices. It was owned by an Indian, Mr Madden, who was prepared to give us a share of the bar-takings, good accommodation rates, and office space for our newly-formed Deckers Club, modelled on the Walkabout Club and the old Overseas Visitors Club.

Madden was a very cluey businessman. He'd grown up in Kenya, as opposed to his native India, and had established a wide variety of successful businesses. He was aware of the Aussies' love of a drink and so, before we had transferred our patronage from the Fremantle, he had decided to renovate and quadruple the size of the Enterprise Hotel's bar, as well as locate a restaurant in the basement. He rented the restaurant area to Chris Jacobs, our Deckers Club manager, and Erin Hartley-Smith, who turned it into an Aussie-style charcoal grill-your-own-steak and wine bar called Swaggers. Increasing the size of the bar was a wise

Wise Enterprise – London 1982

Dave and Ellie Reed and Ackko.

move by Madden. Awarding the building contract to our crew from the farm wasn't. God only knows how they talked Madden into it but I was flabbergasted when I saw Five Eights and his offsiders hammering and sawing away there.

'I didn't know you were a builder, Five Eights?'

'I'm not, but the money's good and Madden opens the bar for us after work every night,' was the hard-to-argue-with reply.

Top Deck Daze

"Filthy"

Most of our crew would swim across shark-infested waters with cut legs if it meant free beers on the other side, so there was no shortage of apprentice labourers.

The opening night filled the Enterprise Hotel to overflowing. It was a success on all counts with the exception of a few minor hiccups. Five Eights' workers hadn't properly vented the barbecue grill in the basement restaurant and once the fire was well and truly stoked, ten by ten square metres of ceiling masonry swelled

Wise Enterprise – London 1982

and buckled with the heat, popped its rivets, and settled slowly on the diners. Upstairs, things fared slightly better. In the pursuit of higher profit margins, Madden had sourced the beer for the bar from one of his Kenyan trading companies. Despite the fact that it was some obscure Japanese brew, it had a great taste and was remarkably well received by the crowd. The only problem was that, unbeknown to us (because, not surprisingly, none of us could read the Japanese labels) it was more than double the strength of your average drop of Fosters and so, by nine o'clock, everyone in the bar was completely off their face. This inevitably led to a more-than-usual spate of strange occurrences.

Top Deck Daze

One of our drivers, Peter Browne, (aka 'Pierre', aka 'Dirty Pierre', aka 'Filthy Pierre', then just plain 'Filthy'), was having a drink at the bar when Five Eights gave him a playful clip over the ear. Filthy overbalanced on the bar stool, crashed to the floor, and split the back of his head open. He was told not to be a big girl's blouse until, finally, with blood spilling everywhere, some good, semi-sober soul recognised that Filthy was in need of stitches. The Transit van from the farm was outside and so the Good Samaritan and Five Eights took him to casualty at Kensington Hospital.

There was a wild pillow-fight going on in the crew rooms just at the time Filthy returned from the hospital and, immediately he walked through the door, he copped a tremendous backhander from Steve 'Hulk' Prosser that sent him cartwheeling across the floor, rupturing his freshly inserted stitches. Assisted by half-a-dozen of the crew, all of whom were making ambulance-siren-wailing noises, he was re-presented at Kensington Hospital casualty on an unhinged door, requisitioned from the hotel as a stretcher. When a request came over the intercom for anyone who could speak Spanish to please assist one of the doctors treating a Hispanic tourist, Hulk, Five Eights and the crew marched into the wards arm-in-arm singing Viva L'Espana, the Aussie signature tune from the Beerfest.

Back at the Enterprise again, the party continued in the crew rooms until 3:00 a.m. when Filthy finally staggered off alone into one of the darkened bedrooms to give his aching head a break. He undid his belt, dropped his jeans and, as he lifted a leg to drag off a boot, he lost his balance. Hobbled by the jeans, he stumbled backwards and crashed through the flimsy French doors. He then executed a perfect two-and-a-half backward somersault with pike, falling two floors from his third-floor balcony to a slightly enlarged first-floor balcony. Had Filthy missed that, he would have fallen a further two levels to the basement. He crawled into the room from the balcony he'd landed on, and collapsed unconscious on a spare bed.

Wise Enterprise - London 1982

Screeches and screams were heard at seven that morning when the room's single female occupant awoke to find a strange, deliriously-concussed, blood-soaked, multiply-fractured, half-naked man in the spare bed beside her. Filthy was off again to Kensington Hospital while the shocked girl tried to determine how the mangled stranger had entered through her securely locked door.

Filthy recovered after three months and was scheduled to go out as driver on a Russia/Scandi tour when he was run over outside the Prince of Teck pub in Earls Court and broke his leg. Two months later he broke the same leg slipping on the ice in Amsterdam.

When Filthy left to go on a skiing holiday to Andorra, Dillon O'Sullivan, our operations manager, pre-booked the Enterprise bar for a wake. We jumped the gun. Filthy was fortunate enough to break his arm on the footpath outside the Andorran Encamp Hotel Bar, before he could get anywhere near the ski slopes. We held the wake anyway when he got back, to celebrate his retirement to operations.

Chapter 19

REX'S RORTS

(RUSSIA 1982)

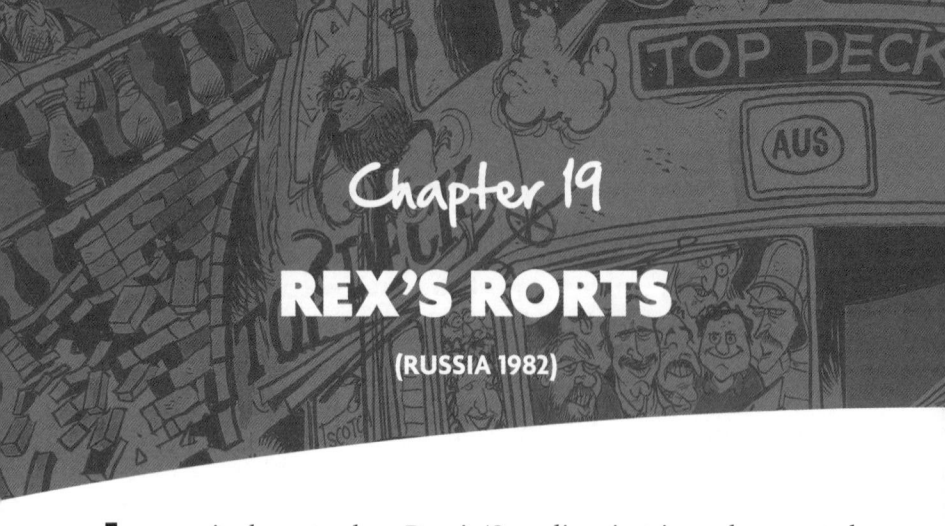

I was quite keen to do a Russia/Scandinavia trip and suggested to Liz that rather than go on a Top Deck tour, it might be good fun to be away from all the other people for a change and do a trip by ourselves—besides, sleeping in a tent never really appealed to Liz. She regarded camping as a slap in the face to three million years of human evolution. Consequently, I inherited an old ex-post-office Bedford van that had been bought by a friend, Rod McEwin, and it seemed to be the right sort of vehicle for that type of touring. It was diesel (more economical than petrol) with sturdy dual rear wheels and a large front and rear cabin. I began to fit it out at the bus yard but every single time I drove it to collect parts or equipment, it broke down. This became so frustrating that I was on the verge of giving the whole idea away. I didn't relish the prospect of spending half the holiday stuck under the engine bonnet, especially if we were to go as far as Russia.

An Aussie doctor friend of Liz's from uni college days had invited us to his wedding in Winchester and I said to Liz that this would be the final test for the Bedford. If it got us to and from Winchester, I would persist with the fit-out. If the slightest thing went wrong, well, that would be it. I'd simply forget the whole idea.

We took off for Winchester on a Friday evening after work. As we trundled down the M3, I thought I could smell something overheating or burning, but we made it by about 8:00 p.m. with

Rex's Rorts - Russia 1982

no real problems. Our friend Tony, the groom, had invited us to spend the night at his home, so we drove down the long front driveway, pulled off onto the lawn and parked parallel with the other guests' cars. We all took off to the pub and, after closing, returned to Tony's place to help him celebrate his last night as a single man.

Top Deck Daze

We were still drinking at 2:00 a.m. when I thought I could hear the sound of an engine trying to start in the front yard. No one had left the party and it suddenly occurred to me that someone was trying to steal one of the cars. I rushed onto the front veranda to be confronted by the sight of a huge shower of sparks billowing from underneath the Bedford van. The electrical system was short-circuiting and power was getting to the starter motor, turning the engine over. I'd left the van in gear and, as I watched in horror, the beast of a thing drove itself across the lawn and ploughed into the neighbour's paling fence. It knocked the fence over and with the engine still grinding away, it mounted the collapsed structure as if it were a monster on heat. The Guy Fawkes display ended with a final ejaculation of sparks and the van collapsed in exhaustion, front and rear wheels suspended over the supine body of the fence.

I was still watching in shock from Tony's veranda when the neighbour struggled onto his porch clutching his dressing gown.

'What in damnation's going on here?' he yelled at me as he surveyed the carnage.

'It's, it's my van. It, it, it just drove itself through your front fence, all by itself,' I dribbled, in my best Sir Les Patterson impersonation. The neighbour stared at me in palpable disbelief, but was too shocked to admonish me further.

The Bedford had done its dash. It was consigned to the 'Big Van Yard in the Sky'. If we were to do a Russia/Scandi, perhaps we were destined to do it with Top Deck.

The following week, in London, I was drinking in the Enterprise Hotel with Rex Julian and a dozen other Top Deck crew. Rex was king. He'd been couriering for eight years by this stage and knew everything and everybody. He was renowned for producing fantastic trips. I'd seen him firsthand in Andorra with 200 guests eating out of the palm of his hand as he hosted their various functions and later, in the bar, he'd had a special word for each individual, making them all feel special.

Rex's Rorts – Russia 1982

Rex had a uniquely animated way of talking, licking his lips with his protruding tongue while he gathered his thoughts, and gesticulating with his hands and pointing with his fingers when he spoke, which was always in rhyming slang.

'The bugs bunny you've got to Double Bay for an Aristotle of Germaine Greer at the rubbedy-dub is a bit butcher's hook if you ask me,' (the money you pay for beer at the pub is too expensive) or, 'I was having a billy-bat on the dog-and-bone with my skin-and-blister and tin-of-Spam and told 'em it was a bit Piccadilly for Elder Smith Goldsbrough Morts over here at the moment,' (he'd had a chat on the phone with his sister and old man to say it was a bit chilly for shorts). As a result of his legendary status, a hundred drivers and couriers became Rex clones, poking out their tongues and pointing with their fingers as they spoke, while any newcomer would need a dictionary of rhyming slang and Strine if they wanted to join in the conversation.

I was playing interpreter for some new crew when Mick raised the possibility of Rex and me doing a Russia/Scandi together. Mick had recently proposed the idea of chartering coaches from AMZ, a Dutch company, for our limited coach-camping program. It might well work out to be as cheap, if not cheaper, than using our own vehicles and operationally, it would be a breeze. We would supply our own drivers and couriers, but everything else would be AMZ's responsibility. If we broke down, AMZ would either repair or replace the vehicle immediately. Very appealing!

That night, I discussed with Liz the idea of going to Russia. We had recently established a retail travel agency called 'London Flight Centre' in a first floor office on Earls Court Road, opposite the tube station. Barbara Bates was the manager and Liz went to work there with another Australian girl, Anna Bowman. The business was doing extremely well and Liz felt it wasn't right to leave it for six weeks in the middle of its busiest season. She was quite happy for me to go to Russia with Rex because another opportunity like this might be rare.

Top Deck Daze

We were off again — this time to Russia/Scandinavia.

Bookings were so heavy for our 4 August 1982 departure that we felt we could easily fill a second coach. We came to an agreement to charter one of the AMZ vehicles on a trial basis and I chose to go as the driver. All I needed to do was get us there and back in one piece. Despite the usual hassles with Intourist and obtaining Russian visas, given all our late bookings, we got away on time.

As we waited at Dover to board the Townsend Thoresen ferry, Rex gave me the rundown on the trip. This was going to be different from any other trip I'd done, he explained. With a combination of planning, experience, contacts, and a dash of good old entrepreneurship, we could make some serious money along the way with very little risk of being caught. Was

Rex's Rorts – Russia 1982

I interested? Would I cooperate? Would I keep quiet about the experience after we returned? Of course I would. I was so intrigued I could hardly say no.

'Good,' said Rex, 'I'll explain things as we go. Timing will be critical. Now, this is how it works today …'

We had chosen the slightly longer channel route from Dover to Zeebrugge, to give us more time on the water. We synchronised watches. Rex embarked the punters on foot while I stowed the coach in the bowels of the ferry. I had no sooner turned off the motor than Rex reappeared with a bumbag full of pound notes. He had cashed the travellers' cheques for the entire food kitty of £3000. We had exactly seventy-four minutes to rearrange the luggage in the rear and side lockers and load the thirty-four crates (408 bottles) of Johnnie Walker Scotch Rex had ordered from the duty-free storeroom on the lower deck of the ferry.

Rex and Moose.

I hadn't understood why, on the way to Dover, Rex had told the passengers that they could only store one small suitcase each in the luggage lockers and that all their other gear would have be to stowed inside the bus. We could scarcely move down the aisle for all the excess gear. Even I had believed Rex when he'd proffered the explanation that the camping gear hadn't been economically stowed and that once we got to Scandinavia and weren't in such a rush, he and I would spend a day rearranging the luggage so that it would all fit snugly into the lockers. I now understood why we needed the extra space—for the whisky!

Top Deck Daze

We had stopovers in Amsterdam, Hamburg and Copenhagen before we were able to offload the whisky to Rex's contacts in Stockholm and Oslo, at more than double the price we had paid duty-free and so, on day ten, we had already made £4000 profit to share between us. We were able to announce to the punters that while they had been in the Kon-tiki Museum, we had spent hours rearranging the luggage for their comfort and that they were now able to walk freely up the aisle of the bus. I was embarrassed when they thanked us profusely for all our hard work.

We travelled along the Norwegian fjords from Trondheim to Hammerfest, through the land of the trolls and the midnight sun, into Finland and on to Helsinki, our last stopover before Russia. Rex had bought forty-five pairs of jeans in London before departure and these were now distributed to all the punters, one per suitcase. This was to avoid any suspicion at customs.

Happy in Hell.

Late in the afternoon we crossed the Finish/Russian frontier with no hassles and headed for a campsite to the north of Leningrad. We'd only been inside Russia for twenty minutes when some of Rex's mafia contacts passed the bus in their car, slowed, and flicked their indicators to acknowledge Rex's wave from the front window of the bus. The car sped on ahead and after a further kilometre, Rex tapped me on the shoulder and indicated that I should slow down as we approached a man strolling along the roadside. I opened the door of the coach and the fellow casually lobbed a fat envelope in Rex's direction.

Rex's Rorts - Russia 1982

We continued without further explanation until we pulled over at a large general store. Rex asked me and a few of the guys on board to come with him. He bought four crates of champagne, paying in Russian roubles, and the bottles were distributed to everyone on board as we made our way to the campsite. The envelope, Rex explained, which was full of roubles, had been a downpayment on the sale of the jeans.

After setting up camp we travelled a short distance to a restaurant that was relatively humble by comparison with those we were to experience every other night in Russia, but the caviar and quite magnificent champagne, heaped on every table in lavish quantities, more than made up for the drab surroundings. The gourmet food bore no resemblance to the basic camping fare we'd endured so far.

Leningrad (or St Petersburg, as it's now known) is a truly magnificent city with a rich cultural heritage and we spent the next day on a full city tour. We were assigned a Russian Intourist guide, as all foreign tourist groups were and, normally, these individuals proved to be unwelcome buttinskies to the harmony of the group. Ours, however, turned out to be a young, attractive blonde lady of handsome proportions whom Rex had befriended on an earlier tour. Rex decided to advance the causes of perestroika and glasnost by taking off with the guide every evening, much to the mutual satisfaction of all concerned because she gave our group free rein—allowing Rex to get on with running the tour in his own, inimitable style.

Rex's commentaries on all the sights were full of the most incredible facts, and all the history buffs were furiously writing up their diaries with details from Rex's extraordinary depth of knowledge. As we crossed the Neva River, Rex was in his usual, verbose form, '… and the most amazing feature of this river is how cold it gets in winter. You know, not only does it ice over, it freezes to its entire depth of 100 metres, and even the fish are frozen solid till the Spring thaw …,' and on and on he went to his spellbound audience.

Top Deck Daze

I stopped on the north bank of the river for everyone to alight and have a quick look at the Peter and Paul Fortress. As the last of the history-note-takers left the bus, I said to Rex, 'What you just said about the River Neva is just incredible. I had no idea a river could freeze to 100 metres!'

'Don't be a bloody idiot, Bill. Of course it doesn't freeze to that depth, but you have to understand that these punters have paid good money to come all this way. They want to be entertained; have the trip of their lifetime. They don't want some boring Intourist Guide's history of Russia.'

That evening, after an early but sumptuous meal, from which Rex suggested that he and I refrain, we announced that we were all going to the Bolshoi Ballet. To my surprise, everyone was keen to attend. The punters on the Russia/Scandi tours were, on average, a little older than those on the decker trips, with an even balance of guys and girls who were generally far more interested in history and culture than on other trips I'd done. There was a fair sprinkling of teachers among them as well, and I was fascinated to think of the new European history curricula that would be written as a result of Rex's dissertations.

While everyone was in the theatre, Rex and I waited on the bus and, true to form, it wasn't long before our mafia car showed up and we followed it in the bus at a gentle pace till we came to a quiet back street. We had gathered all the jeans together and the three large bags in which they were contained were exchanged for another lovely fat envelope.

It's difficult to understand why the jeans were so prized by the Russians but they were obviously an extremely sought-after status symbol in this still-backward but highly regulated and controlled society. I could hardly believe it when Rex explained that we had made £4000 profit on the sale of the jeans. What had cost £10 in London was worth an unbelievable £110 here.

Our profit to date was now a staggering £8000. I only had one major concern. The whisky had been sold for Swedish krona, which we could exchange back to English pounds, but the jeans were a different matter. They had been sold for roubles and I knew we couldn't exchange those for Western currency in Russia, and they were worthless even if we could get them out of the country. So were we really that well-off? I mean, one could only drink so much champagne and eat so much caviar in the ten days we were in Russia, and then what do we do with the thousands of roubles left over?

'No problems, Bill. Wait till tomorrow,' Rex reassured me.

For starters, Rex had explained to the punters that he was in the fortunate position of being able to act as banker for anyone wishing to exchange money. He could give them the roubles they would need for spending money in exchange for foreign cash. He could offer a far better rate than the banks and there was no chance of getting ripped off as you might well be if you changed money illegally on the black market. You may get a worse exchange rate or, worse still, counterfeit notes, so the punters were willing to take advantage of Rex's offer. We made £200 commission on the scheme and exchanged a third of our roubles this way.

We returned to the campsite immediately after the ballet and the punters were ready for a relatively early night. Having skipped the pre-theatre dinner, I was now ravenous. I was about to complain to Rex when he grabbed me by the arm and we drifted away to the main gates of the campsite. We were momentarily blinded by headlights that were suddenly beamed at us from 100 metres down the road. Slowly a big black car slid into view and the rear doors swung open to us in invitation.

Even the most-renowned restaurants in Russia were closed by midnight and it was already close to that by the time we arrived at the best one in the city. The last of the diners were being none-too-ceremoniously ushered to the door as our party was settled at a table. A bevy of formally clad waiters filled our glasses with Bollinger champagne and beautiful hors d'oeuvres were laid before us as our menus were brought.

'You like music?' Leonard, the mafia leader asked, and before either of us had time to reply, he turned and clapped his hands at the members of the eight-piece orchestra that still sat at their podium in the spacious but now, except for us, empty restaurant. Immediately they began a Viennese waltz. 'You like to dance?' Leonard asked, as he nodded to us and the two beautiful girls who had appeared from nowhere to sit beside us and again, before we had time to answer, the girls pulled us to our feet.

Waltzes were not one of my strong suits but I relaxed a little when I saw that the competition was hardly Fred Astaire and Ginger Rogers. Rex was getting right into it with his lady partner and it looked as if they were about to try the cucumber rumba. Presumably this is what Russians did when they went out to expensive restaurants so, when in Russia …

After dinner we were driven to Leonard's flat to view and possibly buy diamonds or religious icons; it was our choice. I was more than apprehensive when we arrived outside the flat. I thought they must have been leading us to an abandoned part of town from where we might never return. Not so much as a glimmer shone from the streetlights or from the outside of the building. The lifts were inoperable and as we groped our way up the external stairwell, the rusted-out metal railing almost gave way. There was an overpowering stench of sewerage coming from blocked drains.

The door of the flat opened into another universe. Plush white carpets enhanced the brilliant colours of the original works of art bedecking the walls. The latest multi-deck hi-fi equipment and oversized television unit stood out among the crystal and china artifacts. Rex had been here before, but Leonard enjoyed the stunned look on my face.

By the time we were back in our camp beds, we were the proud owners of an enormous diamond. The cost? All of our remaining roubles! It was now nearly 4:00 a.m. and despite the fact that I was exhausted, I couldn't sleep. I played the events of the night over in my mind. We could now smuggle the diamond out of Russia instead of the roubles and sell it for Western currency.

Rex's Rorts - Russia 1982

The rest of our tour took in Kalinin, Moscow and Smolensk. The last several hundred kilometres to the Polish border via Minsk were long, flat, and boring, and I drove as fast as I dare on the long, straight but poorly maintained highway. Rex kept us entertained. He had forewarned the punters that they needn't change much money into roubles but, inevitably, everyone had too many left over. As they were useless outside the country, Rex suggested what we might do with them before we hit the border. Every time we approached a group of peasants working the fields or near the road (and believe me, they are very, very poor in this part of the world) all forty-five punters threw a shower of rouble notes out the bus windows while bellowing a chorus of screams and yells. It was worth it just to watch the faces of the peasants as they realised what was happening—it was raining roubles! This idea of Rex's became a tradition for all Top Deck's Russian trips and the peasants on this stretch of road must have become the richest in the steppes.

Five days later we were outside a medieval shop in a narrow street in the Stare Mesto, the Old Town of Prague, overlooking the Vltava River. We were ushered into the rear of the shop by

Meeting up with other Top Deckers in Red Square, Moscow, with St Basil's in the background.

an equally medieval Jewish man. He peered at the diamond through his eyeglass under a brilliant light for several minutes. He turned slowly to Rex and mumbled something that neither of us understood. He scribbled the price on a piece of paper—the equivalent of £3000, in deutschmarks, cash. It was a modest profit on what we had paid for the diamond in Russia, but it was hard currency.

We'd done it—£8200 in krona and marks to be split between the two of us! That was the equivalent of a year's salary for an average Englishman. We burst out laughing as we walked from the shop. I thanked Rex profusely. On the one hand it was an extremely risky business but, then again, it was so easy, and no one was harmed. Also, I had an overriding feeling that had we been caught at any time, we could have bought our way out of trouble. In such corrupt systems, money speaks louder than the law. It had been too tempting not to give it a go.

On the forty-fourth day we arrived at Dunkirk. We were met on the docks by one of our own double-deckers, the UK licensed bus with all the seats that would take the passengers back to London. On this occasion it met us on the European side of the Channel. We had to deliver the coach to one of the AMZ drivers at the port, who was to take it on another job.

The decker driver (whom we called 'Slim Dusty') and the passengers helped us transfer all the luggage and camping gear from the coach to the decker. We had to give the coach a thorough cleaning before handing it over and Rex agreed to stay behind with me and help. We could do it in an hour or so and catch the next ferry and then a train from Dover back to London.

Rex pulled me aside. He still had the £8200 cash profits in an envelope. Currency restrictions were still in place in the UK and anything above £500 had to be declared. We discussed our options. Should we risk holding onto the cash and declare it? No. How could we explain where it had come from? Keep it with us and risk a search? No, I was too nervous for that. Okay, what about hiding it on the decker? We could retrieve it from the bus

Rex's Rorts – Russia 1982

that evening at the NCP car park in London. Yes. That was by far the best option.

Having bid our farewells to the punters who were now on board the ferry and with Slim in the driver's cab, we slipped upstairs on the decker. At the top of the stairwell was a little metal container with a small slit in the top that in the previous life of the bus had been used for the disposal of bus tickets. Unless you were looking for it, you'd hardly notice it was there. With a screwdriver you could open a small latch at the base of the box to clean it. Rex stuffed the envelope up into the box, closed the latch, gave me the thumbs up, and we jumped off as Slim pulled onto the ferry.

An-hour-and-a-half later we were on our way. We planned our celebration dinner and drinks. We would meet at Benito's Restaurant at 8:00 p.m. We'd get Liz and Mick to invite half-a-dozen of the boys and girls from the office to join us. From Victoria Station we jumped a cab straight for the NCP car park where Slim had parked the decker. Rex climbed in through the driver's cabin window. A minute passed before he reappeared, ghostlike, at the side window.

'It's gone. It's bloody-well gone!'

Even in our panic we realised immediately that a search was futile. The bus was as clean as a whistle. Someone had found our envelope of cash and taken it, as simple as that. If we were going to be able to find the driver, Slim Dusty, in a hurry, there was only one place to look—the bar at the Enterprise. I could tell by the look on Slim's face he was innocent.

'Wh … Wh … What are you talking about? Yeah. Sure I cleaned the bus. Looks great, doesn't it? Dillon said that if there was so much as a fingerprint on it when I got back I'd lose my bonus.'

'Okay. Okay, Slim. *Where* did you clean it?'

'Well, I started at a lay-by at Faversham when we stopped there for the loos, and then I finished her off at Farthings Corner Services when we stopped for dinner.'

Top Deck Daze

'Oh, Geezes. That means it could be in any of a dozen garbage bins between here and Faversham,' I said. I grabbed the keys to one of the Renaults from Mick, and Rex and I sped off in the direction of the M2. At 2:00 a.m. we were back on the decker in London. We were filthy from our fruitless rummaging through every garbage bin between London and Dover. We needed to settle our minds that we hadn't overlooked something obvious on the bus, like an un-emptied bin or the like. We hadn't. The only things on board were our own two luggage bags that, in our haste, we hadn't collected earlier in the evening. Rex pulled his open. He'd kept two bottles of champagne from the very first stop in Russia. He handed one to me and took the other for himself. We sat on the front seat upstairs, popped the corks, clinked the bottles, and drank in silence to the only thing we could think of to celebrate—our 'good health'. Some years before our tour, the crew of a rival camping-tour operator, Transit, were caught and jailed for selling jeans in Russia in circumstances identical to our own. The story was given major coverage in the London Sunday papers, particularly the Guardian, and all the camping-tour operators, including me, were contacted by reporters and, without exception, we all declared we had no knowledge of such 'goings-on' and did not believe that our companies would engage in such felonious activities.

Shortly after our return from Russia, Mick Wiles, one of the new Top Deck operations managers, received a phone call from the crew of one of our overland buses on the Iran/Pakistan border.

'It's Bruce Hall here, Wilesie. Brian and I are in the Go Slow.' Bruce, one of our most experienced drivers, had cut his teeth playing the black market as one of Rex's drivers on the Russia/Scandis, but had overplayed his hand one too many times. A Pakistani had agreed to buy all twelve-dozen bottles of whisky Bruce had on board and while the punters were off having an evening meal, Bruce and Brian Langbien, the courier, had backed their decker into a compound at the Pakistani's instruction.

Rex's Rorts – Russia 1982

They were just about to offload the whisky in the dark when the yard was suddenly floodlit. It was the police station's very own compound. The pair were sentenced to two years jail and the bus, *Belch*, was confiscated, never to be seen again. Johnno Wellington, who was also en route to Kathmandu on another decker, had to return from Lahore to retrieve the stranded punters.

For nine months we used every means known to try and extradite Bruce and Brian from the Pakistani jail. We'd almost given up hope when, one day, out of the blue and without explanation, the guards came along, unlocked the doors, and let them go. Both boys were badly shaken by the experience. The only relief they'd had during their long, mind-numbing incarceration was a more-than-occasional nip of Scotch. The guards sold them back forty-four bottles of their original haul of twelve-dozen. The system, of course, was totally corrupt.

To top it all, Bruce was searched thoroughly on his arrival back at Heathrow. In his poofter bag he still carried all the letters he'd received in Pakistan with the jail's address still clearly visible on all of them and to add insult to injury, he was thrown into the slammer at Heathrow for twenty-four hours before a series of representations to the Home Office secured his release.

Chapter 20
CONFERENCE NONSENSE
(SYDNEY 1982)

Back in Australia, Screw really started to crank up some good Top Deck bookings from our various State offices: Screw himself in Brisbane; Dave Reed who'd relocated to Sydney; Ray Smith and Brian 'Dark Blue' Coubrough in Melbourne; Erryn Wilson and Wombat, who had moved back to Perth; Ron Farrington, and later Colin Schirmer, who opened his own office at Norwood, in Adelaide. A company called Transglobal in New Zealand was also doing extremely well for us until, that is, it went broke a year or two later owing us $60 000 — a major blow to the already depleted London cash flow.

I flew back to Sydney in 1982 to attend what was Top Deck's first 'worldwide managers' conference,' held at a rather downmarket hotel in Kings Cross. For the Flight Centre managers of today, international company conferences are a common event but back in those days, it was a big deal to get everyone together for the first time. I remember the occasion more for the Seinfeld/Cosmo Kramer type personalities of the attendees rather than for any earth-shattering events that took place there.

Screw asked Ray Smith to give a presentation on various marketing ideas. Ever the showman, Ray was given to dramatic entrances and exits whenever called upon to talk. At the conclusion of this particular cameo performance, he bowed low to the audience, turned on his heel, and exited through a doorway. There was an almighty crash and bang behind the door. It was the broom cupboard. The short-sighted Ray reentered the

Conference Nonsense – Sydney 1982

conference room polishing his glasses, bowed gracefully once more, and exited through the correct doorway.

Later, discussion centred on which agents were responsible for which particular geographical areas. It was hardly the most-vexed problem facing the world on that particular day but, when the issue of the Northern Territory came up, Ron Farrington (from Adelaide) jumped to his feet, banged the table, and in a genuinely serious manner fairly yelled, 'The Northern Territory's my territory.'

Wombat and Ray had been close to dozing off up until this moment and the bang jolted them from their reverie. They looked at one another, wide-eyed, across the table. Wombat was on his feet first. In a mock, US Western gunslinger drawl, he too slapped the table, 'I say, I say, boy, the Northern Territory is myyyyah territory!' Ray, too, was now on his feet, slapping the table, 'Now you just lookie here, boy, you know that there territory is myaaah territory,' and they were off. No one could shut them up.

They were still rabbiting on about 'your territory and myaaah territory' when we all met in the hotel bar that evening for drinks. As they saw me approaching, they broke into the country and western ballad 'Don't Take Your Guns to Town', inserting their own words which finished with:

Don't bring your bus to town, Bill.
Leave your bus at home, Bill.
Don't bring your bus to town.

I didn't speak a word all night. I just stood there with tears of mirth rolling down my cheeks as Ray and Wombat regaled us with stories of their latest Top Deck business ventures in Australia. They told us of two characters I only ever knew of as 'the Animal' and 'Paddy' who'd bought a clapped-out Bedford bus from a collapsed travel company, Treasure Tours, and begun the first-ever express Budget Bus service between Perth, Melbourne and Sydney. Budget Bus had almost folded from lack of bookings before engaging Ray and Wombat (that is, Top

Top Deck Daze

Deck) as their principal agents. The latter pair could sell snow to the abominable snowman and Budget Bus bookings increased to the point where Wombat assumed genius status as far as the Animal was concerned.

Budget Bus experienced all sorts of operational and mechanical problems. The previous week the Animal had been heading out of Perth in the Bedford bus when he noticed a single wheel motoring along the highway beside him. On closer inspection, he recognised it as his own. He'd forgotten to tighten the rear wheel nuts, and one of the dual rear wheels had worked itself loose, and decided to head off with a mind of its own.

Wombat never paid any attention to silly concepts like 'load control'. If punters were willing to pay, he'd just keep booking them, selling as many seats as possible. The bus was always full to overflowing out of Perth and on one occasion, when one last punter turned up to pay on departure, Wombat sold him a seat at a five-dollar discount, then went back to the office, retrieved a castor-wheeled chair from behind one of the desks, and stuck it in the Bedford's aisle.

'But the passenger list says we've got another bloke to pick up in Norseman. Where's he going to sit?' asked the bewildered Animal.

'When you get there, just keep driving and pretend you didn't see him,' instructed Wombat. The Bedford motored through Norseman (the last major town before the Nullarbor) at top speed, leaving the squat-jumping, arm-flapping, would-be passenger in a cloud of dust. Not to be outdone, the Norseman passenger waved down a ute driven by his mate and then overhauled the bus and ran it off the road, hijack-style, and demanded to be taken on board. It was a Pyrrhic victory for the punter—he had to ride the several thousand kilometres to Melbourne sitting on the internal engine cowling, next to the Animal.

Poor Animal and Paddy were like zombies from too much driving and so Wombat organised some relief drivers from a group of Maoris he'd befriended at the local pub in Perth

Conference Nonsense - Sydney 1982

but, inevitably, one of the drivers failed to turn up as planned. Wombat convinced the Animal to head east regardless, and guaranteed him he'd get the relief driver to the bus one way or the other. After hours of driving, there was no sign of Wombat's car in the bus' rear-vision mirror and the Animal had all but given up hope of an extra pair of hands but, sure enough, with the sun setting slowly in the vast expanse of the Nullarbor, there was the long shadow of the relief driver, sitting on his suitcase in the middle of the empty highway, awaiting the arrival of the bus.

Wombat had wised up the relief driver and told him to play it cool when the bus arrived.

'Where've you been?' was all the relief driver said with a deadpan face as the wide-eyed, mouth-gaping Animal watched him mount the bus' stairs.

The Animal never found out how Wombat did it. In truth, he'd commandeered his father's Cessna from Perth's Jandakot Airport (he did have a pilot's licence), he then tracked down and overflew the Bedford as it sped east, set the driver down by landing in the middle of the Eyre Highway, and then flew back to Perth before the bus came into view. As a result of this miraculous feat, Wombat moved from genius to demi-god status in the eyes of the Animal.

At this time in Australia, the Government's anti-competitive 'two-airline policy' meant interstate airfares were too expensive for the bulk of the population. The market was ripe for some good, discount, intercity bus operators to compete head on with Greyhound Pioneer coaches that had the market to themselves and were relatively expensive. Budget Bus was the first intercity bus discounter (dozens sprang up later) and when the operation inevitably folded, Screw and Wombat bought a brand new Volvo coach for $85 000 and started their own interstate service, Across Australia Coachlines (AAC). The poor dealer who sold them the bus with a full warranty had no idea AAC would, in all seriousness, enter the *Guinness Book of Records* for the longest intercity coach service in the world, from Perth to Brisbane, travelling

650 000 kilometres in twelve months. Buying three more Volvos, AAC made $200 000 profit before Wombat bought Screw out eighteen months later and went his own way in business.

The managers' conference in Sydney was a great opportunity for me to learn more about all the other new business ventures we were developing in Australia at the time. One, in particular, proved to be absolutely crucial to our future success because it provided the blueprint on which the concept of the Flight Centre shops, as we know them today, was modelled. Dave Tonkin was only twenty-years-old, and fresh from Adelaide, when I employed him to sell flights in our London office in 1979. He did brilliantly well, due entirely to his own personality and initiative. He then left Top Deck and went on to manage 'The Flight Shop' in Kensington, London. This was a new concept in travel retailing; a highly proficient, professional, discount flight specialist — an upmarket version of the usually downmarket London 'bucket-shop' (cheap, unlicensed) travel agencies. The venture had been financed by a friend of ours in London, an expat Aussie by the name of Laurie Bongiorno.

When Dave returned to Australia in 1981, he approached Screw with the idea of establishing a similar venture in Sydney. They were both convinced the concept would work well in the then conservative environment of Sydney travel retailing. Top Deck put up all the money and took fifty per cent of the partnership. Dave was to do all the work, and he took the other fifty per cent. The business was called 'Sydney Flight Centre' and was originally located in the Carlton Arcade before moving to a very high-profile shop in Martin Place. How right Dave and Screw were about its prospects! It made more than A$100 000 profit in its first year of operation which, by any measure, was a remarkable achievement for a brand-new business. Dave bought out our fifty per cent interest soon after, and we went our own separate ways, but we always acknowledged that the thousand Flight Centre shops we went on to own were clones of Dave's original Flight Centre.

Conference Nonsense – Sydney 1982

Sydney Flight Centre remained in Dave Tonkin's hands, and he only ever had the one location. Top Deck, on the other hand, picked up on the 'Flight Centre' concept and continued to expand in Australia. Between 1981 and 1986, the Top Deck group grew to twenty travel agencies, either wholly-owned or in partnership with the various office managers. There was no common name (though some were called Flight Centres), nor common operating system, and everyone was pretty much doing their own thing. In 1986, Screw organised for all the shop managers to go to Bangkok for a conference. It was there that a common name and modus operandi was agreed upon. As soon as everyone returned to Australia, they changed their shop names to 'Flight Centre', refitted according to the agreed internal and external designs and colour schemes of red and white, and so on, and began to implement and conform to common operating systems. This was the real birth of Flight Centre.

It was also in 1981 that we struck up another fortuitous relationship, one that greatly assisted the above process. As well as Dave Tonkin, we also met Geoff Harris in London in 1979 when he'd approached us for a job as marketing manager at Top Deck. Geoff had grown up in Melbourne and after studying marketing at the Melbourne Institute of Technology (MIT), he'd set off overseas at about the same time that Screw and I had. He travelled all the way from Melbourne to London overland by public transport on the old hippie trail, via Darwin, Bali, South-East Asia, India, Nepal, etc. on an epic six-month saga. He then worked for NAT camping tours as a courier in Europe. We were keen for him to join Top Deck in 1979 as marketing manager but he received a better offer and went to work for Contiki instead.

Back in Australia in 1981, Geoff made contact with Screw again and wanted Top Deck to join him in a Club 18–35-style tour operation to the Barrier Reef islands, but Screw had other ideas. Tour operations could be great fun, as we all knew, but fun doesn't always pay the bills. From that time onwards we saw retailing as our future. Screw convinced Geoff to go fifty-fifty

Top Deck Daze

with us in a retail travel shop and try and emulate Dave Tonkin's success in Geoff's own hometown of Melbourne. Geoff proved to have the same rare, genuinely entrepreneurial flair that Dave Tonkin possessed. That is, he had vision, passion, ability, and great ethics but, most importantly, like Dave, he could translate these qualities into tangible, cash profits—rare qualities indeed.

Geoff opened a small travel agency in Little Bourke Street, in the heart of Melbourne city, called The Flight Shop (modelled on Dave Tonkin's Sydney Flight Centre). With no retail experience, no trained staff, pitifully few resources, and facing antagonistic competition and suppliers (read Qantas in particular), he also made more than $100 000 profit in his first year of trading! To put this into context, thirty years later it is still considered quite an achievement for a Flight Centre shop to make $100 000 profit in one year. For Geoff to have done this in his first year, especially under the circumstances described, was phenomenal. Shortly thereafter he opened two more shops, both equally successful. Geoff was formally brought into the Top Deck group as a partner. He owned fifty per cent of his Melbourne shops and twenty-five per cent of all the other Top Deck shops that had opened, or would open in the future.

Screw's expansion of Top Deck Australia to twenty travel agencies by 1986 would not have been possible without the fifty per cent share of profits Geoff was contributing to the group from his three Melbourne outlets. Screw was not really motivated by profits at this stage, in fact, he never has been. He regarded this phase as one of purely rapid expansion. Screw knew the profits would come later. His philosophy has always been that profits are only a means of measuring how well a business is run. Profits represent the qualitative things that are being done properly. Screw is not materialistic. Money, as such, has no intrinsic worth to him. Perhaps that is why he has become one of Australia's richest men and has influenced and inspired so many others!

On many occasions, in those very early days, Geoff openly questioned the wisdom of his arrangement with Top Deck.

Conference Nonsense – Sydney 1982

While, on paper, he owned a quarter of all the new shops Screw was opening, would they ever turn in a sizeable profit? What did the future hold? Why not make hay now, while the sun shone? Why share his $300 000 annual profit with Top Deck? Why not do as Dave Tonkin had done — split with Top Deck, go it alone, and pocket the lot? He would have been set for life. I guess Geoff harboured the same gut feeling that I did — that is, with Screw's foresight, passion and ambition, combined with our own joint endeavours, one day the whole might exceed the sum of the individual parts.

The Sydney managers' conference concluded with a dinner out at the cheapest Chinese restaurant we could find. Of course we were still there well past the normal closing time and nowhere near finished our supply of BYO drinks when Screw started to hand out some awards for assorted achievements. Steve 'Hulk' Prosser was in attendance from London, representing the Top Deck overland program and, when Screw had finished, he, too, decided some awards from the London head office might be appropriate. However, having failed to prepare anything beforehand, Hulk starting taking down the pictures from the wall of the restaurant and presenting these to the various recipients.

Having well-and-truly worn out our welcome by this stage, mine host, a Mr Wong, was desperately trying to find someone to settle the bill. No matter who he gave it to, they pointed to someone else. Around and around the table

Steve 'Hulk' Prosser

went Mr Wong for five minutes in a fruitless search for a payer until the saucer with the bill on it ended up in front of Hulk Prosser. Without taking his eyes off the person who was talking to him, Hulk picked up the bill, screwed it up into a small ball, put it in his mouth, and ate it. It disappeared without a trace.

Mr Wong couldn't contain himself any longer.

'Get out, you hear! Get out, get out of my westaurant!' he screamed, jumping up and down on the spot in total exasperation.

He was utterly and completely ignored as everyone, engrossed in their conversations, continued until all the alcohol had been consumed. When everyone finally filed out twenty minutes later, they all shook Mr Wong's hand vigorously, smiling, and thanking him profusely for a wonderful evening. Screw had finally paid the bill, and probably tipped Mr Wong more than necessary, and poor Mr Wong fought back tears of frustration as he tried to return everyone's thank-yous and goodnights. In other words, the whole event had set the tone for the countless conferences that followed.

Chapter 21
STRINE STEINS
(MUNICH 1982)

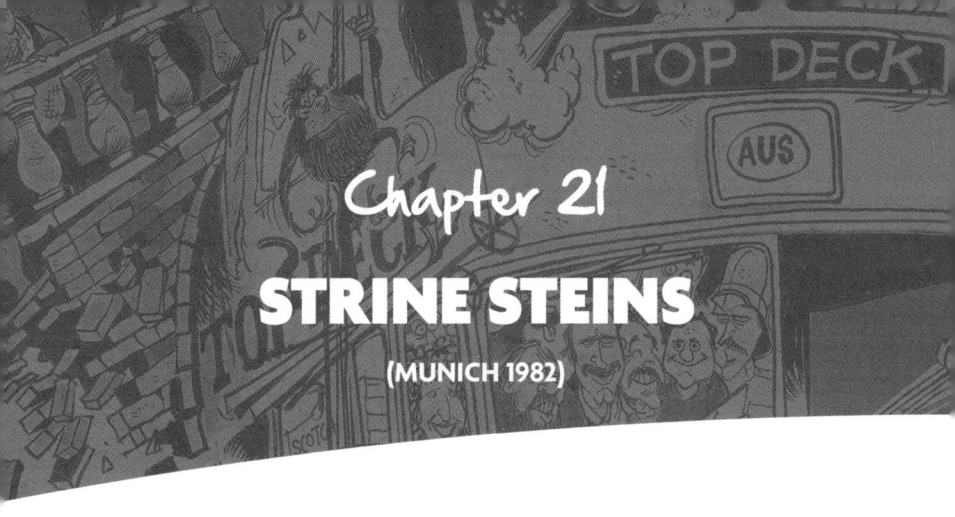

At the conclusion of the Sydney conference, Liz stayed on in Australia for several weeks to spend time with her family and friends. I returned to London immediately and was joined a week later by Screw who wanted to check-up on developments in London. Mick, Screw and I were together again for the first time in nearly a year. Over dinner at our Ealing home, having just collected Screw from the airport, our talk centred on the parlous state of Top Deck's finances, especially with the dreaded winter months fast approaching and the seasonal drying up of our cash-flow.

The conversation was depressing. It frustrated me enormously that on the one hand, the company could be so successful, with trips full and operations as well-managed as ever but, on the other hand, we just couldn't translate all this into bottom-line profits. It was like managing a runaway locomotive or, at other times, like stuffing feathers into a bag full of holes. We just couldn't seem to get a handle on things and exercise effective financial control.

Screw suggested that we go to the Enterprise for a bit of Friday night cheer. It might put us in a better frame of mind. 'Sure, Screw. Check your watch, mate.' His body clock was still on Brisbane time. It was nearly 2:00 a.m. in London.

'Well, let's go to a bar then,' he insisted. Even in London it was nigh-on impossible to find a regular bar open at 2:00 a.m. Screw looked at his watch again. 'I know a place,' he said. 'They're definitely open now. Come on, hurry up. Oh, and bring your passports. They may need some ID.'

We headed for the West End where all the bars we knew were located, but Screw kept driving through to the East End, then on to Bromley, then out onto the M20. I was in a rotten mood as a result of our conversation, and keen for another drink. Screw was openly critical of Mick and me and the way we were running, or at times not running, the company. We are more tactful these days but back then, we openly carped and criticised one another.

'This is ridiculous,' I said. 'Are you lost or something? Where the hell is this bar, Screw? It's three o'clock in the morning, for God's sake,' but he just kept driving purposefully, ignoring my questions in his typically exasperating manner as he pontificated on how to run the business, '… and if I was in London …,' he'd say, and on and on the monologue would go.

We found the bar, eventually. It was just off Marien Place, or Marienplatz to be exact, Munich. It was definitely open and foreign visitors were welcome, but we'd missed the Grand Parade. It was Beerfest time.

The lord mayor had already tapped the first keg with his traditional exclamation of, 'O'zapft is!'—which I always took to mean, 'Up yours,' or something similar, because the mayor immediately raised his stein in salute and upended his beer in one swig. The Fest was officially open. We'd driven non-stop from London to find our bar, the Hofbräuhaus—not the big tent in the grounds of the Oktoberfest itself but the old one that's been in town since 1897. Six of the Top Deck crew were there with sixty of their passengers, and the fräuleins with their steins of beer were doing a brisk trade. One of the crew, on turning around and seeing Screw, said, 'Fancy seeing you here, you old …,' and, with that, tipped a full stein of beer over Screw's head.

We took the car to Camping Thalkirchen and met up with the rest of the crews and all our other buses that were there. That year, Top Deck had a record twenty-two double-deckers at the Beerfest for the opening day and the sight of all of them lined

Strine Steins – Munich 1982

up, side-by-side in the camping ground, was quite astonishing. Top Deck would bring more than 1000 passengers to Munich in several shifts during the next sixteen days.

I walked along the row of deckers and there was dear old *Grunt*, my first bus, dusted off and spruced up for the occasion, possibly making her last trip. I hopped on board and all the memories came flooding back: the Moroccan trip when I'd met Liz in 1974, the overland in 1975 when we'd pushed the old girl beyond her limits but she'd still seen us safely home; and what about the first Beerfest in 1974?

I walked along the aisle and lay on the big triple bunk downstairs, behind the driver's cab, where I used to sleep. I thought of the Beerfest I'd come to with Wombat, Kevin 'Rev Head' Mooney, and Bruce 'Moose' Maloney. Rev Head had flaked out on this bunk, sprawled across it, dead to the world. No one could ever wake Rev Head after a night on the turps. Moose had returned to the bus with a lady in tow. The only bunk not occupied by paying passengers was this one and so Moose set about commandeering it for his own use. Even a fire-hose wouldn't have disturbed the comatose Rev Head and try as he

In 1982, a record twenty-two double-deckers were at the Beerfest in Munich for the opening day.

317

might, there was no way Moose could roll him over to one side. Not wanting to miss the opportunity, and never a man to give up easily, Moose took off his belt, tied it to Rev Head's ankles, hoisted him up and secured him to the ceiling handrail. I came back to the bus from the beerhalls at 5:00 a.m. to discover the moaning, groaning Rev Head, still suspended from the ceiling in the vertical position.

'I'm paralysed, I'm paralysed. Somebody help me please, I'm paralysed,' pleaded the poor, barely conscious, Rev Head.

After recalling many more hilarious incidents we'd experienced, I must have drifted off to the land of Nod. Screw roused me with a rude shake. We rode into the Theresienwiese, the grounds where the Oktoberfest is held, in one of the Top Deck coaches and made straight for the Hofbräuhaus marquee.

You came to Munich to be with friends, drink beer, and generally have the time of your life. I was miserable. I couldn't get the state of the company off my mind. I was dogtired from the drive. I was hungry. Screw's criticisms were still ringing in my ears. To top it all off, five of the crew turned on me the minute I joined their table. It was always the same, or at least, always when they'd had too much to drink. They would start criticising us and the company for things they perceived to be wrong, sometimes with great justification but at other times unfairly. This was the price you paid for being in such a position but in Top Deck's case, there was very little opportunity to escape. The truth was that the company was not well-managed. We were still very much in our learning phase and any disquiet among the crew was ultimately our responsibility. I was, therefore, more defensive than I should have been. The stein over Screw's head had been in jest but there was just that little hint of provocation. It really shouldn't have bothered me as it was all part of the job but, sometimes, in these situations, I just needed to get away.

It wasn't as if I hadn't been to the Beerfest before; I'd been half-a-dozen times. I wandered around the sideshows and joyrides. The smell of the roasted meats on the open spits was

Strine Steins – Munich 1982

irresistible and I scoffed some pork sausages on fresh bread rolls with mustard. The oom-pa-pa bands in the six other beer palaces, set up by the major breweries, all played as the drinkers sang traditional beerhall songs.

In the Hofbräuhaus, the rowdy colonials displayed their imported 'culcha' to the Germans with rousing renditions of 'The Wood Pecker's Hole', 'The Good Ship Venus', 'Swing Low Sweet Chariot' and 'Singing in the Rain … a roo cha cha, a roo cha cha, a roo cha cha char …' They would only pay attention to the band when 'Viva L'Espana' was played or their other favourite, 'The Mexican Hat Song', and then a thousand voices would sing

Eye, eye, eye-eye,
Si, si, Señora,

Top Deck Daze

The Aussies always took over the Hofbräuhaus at the Munich Beerfest.

My sister Belinda she pissed out the winda
All over my new sombrero ...
I like the whisky
It makes me feel frisky,
But give me the good old vino.
I like the vino, the vino is so supremo,
Eye, eye, eye-eye ...'

When the band finished, some Aussie dingbat would jump up on a table and yell at the top of his voice, 'Ziggy zaggy, Ziggy zaggy,' and the colonial crowd would reply, 'Oi, Oi, Oi.'

Then, caller: 'Ziggy zaggy, Ziggy zaggy.'
Crowd: 'Oi, Oi, Oi.'
Caller: 'Ziggy.'
Crowd: 'Zaggy.'
Caller: 'Ziggy.'
Crowd: 'Zaggy.'
Caller: 'Ziggy zaggy, Ziggy zaggy.'
Crowd: 'Oi, Oi, Oi.'

Strine Steins – Munich 1982

The caller would then conclude his performance by doing a suicidal stage-dive into the drunken crowd. These days, at international sporting events in which Australia participates, you'll hear the Australian crowd yell the same chant, but the caller yells, 'Aussie, Aussie, Aussie,' and the crowd responds with, 'Oi, Oi, Oi,' and so on but, for all the trivia buffs, this is a corruption of the original chant from the Aussies in the Munich beerhalls.

I didn't feel like going back to Camping Thalkirchen that night, not that anyone would notice as most people didn't wander back until morning. The campsite gave me bad vibes and I did my best to avoid it. Munich was one of the few European cities to be openly hospitable to young travellers backpacking on a budget. Each summer, from June through to September (and, this year, till the end of the Beerfest), the city erected a massive circus tent at Jugendlager Kapuzinerhölzl, known to all of us as simply 'the Tent,' where 400 young travellers bedded down together in the one spot. I caught streetcar 17 from the Hauptbahnhof to the Botanic Gardens and walked to den Kirschen where 'the Tent' was located. I paid my few deutschmarks and just like on the weekend sojourns with Liz in the English countryside, I had the soundest night's sleep I'd had in months.

The reason I disliked Camping Thalkirchen dated back to an incident that had occurred there during Top Deck's very first Beerfest in 1974. Screw and I had arrived with *Grunt* and *Tuft*. The following day we undertook the mandatory city tour, including the Glockenspiel, Deutsches Museum, the BMW factory, and the 1972 Olympic Stadium, before ending the day at Dachau. The visit to the World War II concentration camp with its infamous gate, barbed-wire fence, huts and gas ovens, still intact, had been a chilling experience. The museum with its photographs, letters from internees, and other disturbing displays, further detailed the terrifying horrors committed there. You couldn't have left without questioning what it was in the German character that had allowed such barbarity to occur. It was obviously not possible to make broad generalisations, after all, Australia had been guilty of the genocide of Tasmanian Aborigines and many other atrocities but, nevertheless, the sometimes-blind authoritarianism of the German people, still evident to this day, was often hard to accept.

All these thoughts of Dachau had filled my mind that evening back at the campsite. On my way to the shower block, I had mulled over the metal disks we'd had to buy to insert in the gas hot-water heaters. Somehow I'd had a premonition that something sinister was about to occur, just how it must have felt for those poor people on their way to the showers in the camps during the latter years of the war, knowing, deep down, that their lives hung in the balance.

Just at that moment, I'd seen a young couple scaling the fence of the camping ground with all their gear. It had cost the equivalent of six or seven dollars per person, per night, to camp and these two had obviously decided to skip without paying. The twenty-year-old son of the German camping ground manager had caught sight of the couple and come racing across, grabbing them by the legs and hauling them back to the ground. I'd seen this young guy before and thought he was a bit schizo. He had a long, thick rubber lash and had started belting the hell out of the couple. You could hear the whack a hundred metres away and the screams of the girl and the yells for help from the boy had added to the drama.

Without thinking, I'd run over to the three of them and yelled at the German boy to stop the beating. The couple were a quivering mess on the ground and going nowhere, but the young German wouldn't stop until, eventually, he'd turned on me and screamed, 'Vot's it got to do wizz you?'

'You fucking Nazi,' I'd screamed back at him. 'Hitler had nothing on you, you little prick.'

The words had just spilled out. I hadn't been able to help myself. I had been so worked up I just hadn't thought about what I was saying. The wildest, most ferocious look had come into his eyes. It was obviously the most provocative thing I could have said. He'd lunged at me with an almighty swish of the lash.

Strine Steins - Munich 1982

I'd thrown my shower gear and towel in his face and started running. In the twelve years I'd played rugby, I was such a slow runner I'd only ever beaten one player once over fifty metres in all that time. I'm sure I gave a great display at Thalkirkchen that day but, basically, I was dead meat. The German boy had caught me and started lashing my back and I'd turned on him and started belting him with all the strength I could muster. Eventually, bruised and bloodied, we'd been dragged apart by the other campers, and then his father and camping ground assistants arrived and frogmarched me off to the camp commandant's office. I was then in more trouble than the would-be absconders.

After an hour's interrogation the police had arrived to charge me with assault. Whether I was to be fined as well as arrested and thrown into jail they hadn't decided but, in any event, I was told to prepare to leave the camping ground immediately.

'I can't leave,' I said. 'I'm the driver of that double-decker bus over there.' It was *Grunt*. They could see Screw working away under the bonnet. The possibility of my imminent death at the hands of the Gestapo had prompted Screw to lift his head for a few minutes to watch the hostilities, but he'd since turned back to work on the motor (Screw was never one to confuse his priorities). '... And it's broken down (which was true), and I'm the only one who can drive it (which was a lie). That mechanic over there (pointing at Screw) drives the other bus. If you take me away, my bus and twenty Australians stay.' Now that was a dilemma for them to stew on. It was a minor victory, certainly the only one I'd had all evening.

I was taken to the police station but let off with a fine. That had been eight years ago and ever since then, I'd done my best to avoid Thalkirchen as much as possible, if for no other reason than I was officially banned from ever setting foot there again. On the odd occasions I returned, I had to be smuggled in. Unfortunately, as far as campsites were concerned, there were no real alternatives, so I made the Hofbräuhaus and 'the Tent' my temporary base.

Chapter 22

PAY DAY

(LONDON 1983)

Screw stayed on in London for a few weeks after our Munich jaunt. Despite endless discussions, we had no concrete plans about how we might improve the way Top Deck operated. Eighty per cent of all small businesses go broke and of those that survive, most struggle and cause immeasurable heartache to their owners. Employees sometimes feel pressured and stressed at work, but nothing compares with the anguish a struggling business-owner experiences. Staff can't conceive of what it's like to have everything you've ever worked for and everything you own 'on the line' while you struggle for survival.

When we started Top Deck, we were only twenty-three-years-old. We had no families to support, no assets, and no responsibilities, unlike most people who establish their businesses a little later in life. We charged headlong into Top Deck's expansion without a care for the consequences, because we had nothing to lose. Now, after nine years, to lose everything would have been a traumatic experience, not only for the hurt we would cause our creditors and passengers who'd lose their money, but also for the irreparable damage it would do to our reputations and self-confidence.

I knew we were entering a watershed in our history and while I tossed and turned in bed at night, searching for a solution, nothing seemed to fall into place. The pieces of the puzzle, and how they all fitted together, continued to elude me.

Pay Day – London 1983

Mick seemed to handle the pressure much better than I did. It was pointless for him to watch television on the rare nights he'd spend at home; he'd be asleep within seconds. Liz and I bought a great little tenement in Shepherds Bush but we regularly ate out, often in company with Mick and his successive girlfriends. His routine at restaurants was as regular as clockwork. Dead on 10:00 p.m. the eyelids would flutter, the head would bobble a few times and then, 'plonk', he'd be face down, sprawled across the dinner table, nose in the soup bowl, snoring away to his heart's content. Diners at nearby tables would glance askew with astonishment at the Monty Pythonesque scene as the rest of us leisurely finished our dinner with a deliberate lack of concern while the waiter hovered around the snorting, lolling head, wondering about the etiquette such a situation might demand.

When it was time to leave the restaurant, we'd always slip the bill under Mick's nose and quickly and quietly sneak outside, then stop and watch through the window as the waiter came and woke him up, demanding payment for the meal. Mick probably thought it was funny, once, but we never tired of the prank and it was an endless source of amusement for us.

Next morning, Mick would bound out of bed at the crack of dawn, bright-eyed and bushy-tailed, full of energy, anxious to meet the challenges of the new day. I hated people like that. I would have endured a restless, fitful night, having lapsed into a dream-filled coma an hour before we were due to rise, and then would have cursed the buzzing alarm clock and the daylight peeking through the blinds.

Mick left for holidays in Australia on the second Thursday in December 1982, just before Rex and the first coachload of passengers departed for the Andorran ski season the following day. I was just about to leave the Kenway Road office late on the Saturday when the phone rang. It was Rex, calling from the Hotel Encamp in Andorra where he'd just arrived. He was angry. Very angry. He reeled off a litany of complaints he'd been hit with during the first few hours at the resort. The ski school,

Top Deck Daze

the ski hire company, the lift operators and the hotels all had outstanding accounts from the previous season, and not small amounts either, more than £10 000 worth.

'How can you allow this to go on?' Rex demanded. 'How can you expect me to run the Andorran operations under these conditions? It's outrageous. Can't you get your act together up there?'

I tried to reply as calmly as I could. The Andorrans' accounting was hopeless, I said. If they'd keep proper invoices and could add up, I'd pay, but you couldn't expect me to pay on guesses. Rex was unconvinced. The coach was just about to leave Encamp for its return to London and he'd be on it, he said. If the issue wasn't resolved there and then, I'd better find another courier to replace him. And bang, down went the phone.

I replaced my receiver slowly. I opened the top drawer of my desk. There were all the bills from each of the Andorran operators, all neatly tallied, all checked and double-checked in red pen, in Mick's meticulous handwriting. I added up the bills again, to the penny. I checked our bank statements again—£80 000 overdrawn. The bank had already refused to honour the cheques we'd issued the previous week. We'd manage to contain that news but if word leaked out that Top Deck was in a cash crisis, it would spread like wildfire throughout the Australasian community in London and ski bookings would dry up overnight.

This was it then. It was exactly the same as when the 1976 overlands were held up on the docks at Dover. How was I going to handle the collapse of the company and the mental and physical trauma that would follow? I sucked in the air slowly, in long, deep breaths while my head started spinning. I had to grab the desk to steady myself while mentally, I tried to steel myself for the weeks that lay ahead.

I forget exactly what I said to Rex. The only thing I can remember, vividly, was the look he gave me when he left. I remember I stuck to the story I'd given him on the phone but as we talked, his anger gradually subsided. I think he began to understand the truth behind my lies and the unenviable position in which I found myself. He obviously had mixed emotions too. Okay, he said. He would go back to Andorra and try and sort out the accounts one more time, playing along with my story, but the final look he gave me said it all. This was the last throw of the dice. If I couldn't pull a rabbit out of the hat this time, it was all over, and he would be unable to support me any longer. I shook his hand and thanked him sincerely, struggling to keep my composure.

Somehow, by shuffling money here and transferring money there, we managed to scrape through by the skin of our teeth, week by week, for the next two months. The night Rex had left again for Andorra I'd phoned Screw in Brisbane and laid it on the line. We were going under, and in a big way. There were no spare funds in Australia, so how was I going to handle it? We had talked on the phone again every few days.

In the first week of January 1983, the phone next to my bed rang at 3:00 a.m.

'Bill, I've got it, I think. Listen.' For half-an-hour Screw outlined his thoughts. London was going badly, he said but in Australia, all, or at least most, of our shops were doing well. Why? What were the fundamental reasons for this? First, in Australia, the shops were obviously all small-business units. We could easily account for their profits or losses. If there were losses, the problems could be immediately identified and, usually, be resolved. Second, each Australian manager had a share of their business. Each had a strong sense of moral ownership which was reinforced by some form of equity participation by way of shares or partnership agreement. The managers were empowered to make decisions that directly impacted on their profits. Irrespective of the talents of the individual, so long as they were reasonably competent and followed the right business formula (we had enough successful managers to act as role models), then total commitment and hard work was often enough to ensure that the business pulled through and eventually prospered.

Top Deck Daze

Top Deck London wasn't like our Australian operations. It was one big amorphous blob. Some sections probably made profits and some made big losses, but which ones? We couldn't tell. Screw went on to explain that he'd just read about TNT, the big Australian transport company, in an Australian business magazine. It had been a bit like Top Deck—big and unwieldy and in financial difficulties. However, TNT had divisionalised—that is, divided itself into separate, logical business units to improve its accountability. As a result of these changes, TNT had managed to transform itself and dramatically improve its profits, almost overnight. Couldn't we learn something from all these experiences and examples and reorganise Top Deck on similar lines to TNT?

I said very little as Screw talked, just the occasional, 'Yes,' and, 'Thanks,' when we hung up, with the promise that I'd call him the next day but, already, my mind was working overtime. He'd done it, the bastard! He was brilliant! Of course that was the answer. I had formulated a rough outline of how it could all work even as he'd spoken to me on the phone. Even though it was the middle of the night, I raced to the fridge and opened a beer. I took out a notepad and diary and started writing furiously, drawing up all sorts of organisational diagrams, flow charts, management positions and personnel to fill them.

Poor Liz thought I'd lost it completely and she wasn't alone. Mick was only back in London from his holidays for a few days before I was on a plane to Australia. Mick had been out of touch and knew nothing of what Screw and I had discussed on the phone. I was so excited about the plans I'd drawn up and talked so effusively and quickly (most unlike me), Mick found it almost impossible to follow what I was on about. I'd obviously undergone a personality change and as he'd never seen me acting like this before, he obviously thought the pressure of it all had gotten to me and I'd finally flipped completely. Neither Liz nor Mick was sure whether they should share my enthusiasm and excitement or phone for the men in the little white coats.

Pay Day – London 1983

On my arrival in Australia, I discussed all my plans with Screw, taking on board his suggestions, and then I went to see our accountant in Sydney, Peter Barrow. Pete was an old schoolmate of mine and knew our businesses well as he'd been doing our accounts in Australia since day one. I gave him an overview of what I was trying to achieve and he said the ideas sounded great. I asked him if he would consider coming to London to help me implement the new plan and get our accounts department in order. He agreed. In fact, he would come for six weeks and stay with Liz and me at Shepherds Bush. I was ecstatic.

We split the company into ten separate divisions: Europe (John O'Donnell), Asia (Hulk Prosser), America (Dillon O'Sullivan), Ski (Chris Greive and Andy Morgan), Charters

London 1983
(L to R) Andy Morgan, Bruce Cherry, Chris Jacobs, Hulk Prosser, Jeff Skinner, Screw, Diesel Morse, Filthy Browne, Johno O'Donnell, Mick, Bill Speaking, Murgha Mack, Graham Sewell.

Top Deck Daze

(Murgha Mack), the Kenway Road sales office and marketing department (Graham Sewell), accounts (Graham Hammond), the Deckers Club (Chris Jacobs), London Flight Centre (Barbara Bates) and the workshop at the farm (Diesel Dave Morse). The physical assets and liabilities of the original company were divided among these areas. The workshop inherited the buses and hired them out to the operating divisions.

Each major division became a separate proprietary company with its own managing director. Up to this point, fifty per cent of the shares had been held by Screw, with Mick and me holding twenty-five per cent each. Screw gave half of his shareholding away to the new shareholders so that the three of us now held twenty-five per cent each of the new subsidiary companies while the individual managers held twenty five per cent of the company they managed. This proved to be a very generous gesture by Screw because it made all the new managers very rich shortly thereafter, but Screw was comfortable with his decision.

'I'd rather have twenty-five per cent of a profit than fifty per cent of a loss,' was his fairly sound logic.

The companies bought and sold services to and from one another. For example, the Europe 'division' would sell a tour and receive money from a client, give ten per cent commission to the sales office, then pay the marketing and accounts companies a service fee, and then hire the buses it needed from the workshop on a weekly hire charge. So each subsidiary company had its own income and expenses. If the managers could make a profit in their company they would get a twenty-five per cent share of it, above their salary package.

We set the date for the changeover to this new set-up for 1 May 1983. Each of those I approached to take over a company had a different reaction. Some, like Murgha and Andy, were very enthusiastic. Others were noncommittal. We'd made promises in the past about profit-sharing but nothing had come of it, they said. Why should this arrangement be any different? Of all the people in London, the one I most admired and respected was

Pay Day - London 1983

Chris Greive. Unfortunately for me, he was downright scathing in his criticism.

'Top Deck has huge debts and this is just a way of shovelling some of the responsibility onto us,' he claimed. Perhaps he was right? I was genuinely enthusiastic about the company's future but it was hard for me to refute Chris' criticism. It wasn't as if my form guide suggested I should have been a redhot favourite.

Top Deck Daze

Chris had been perceptive enough to think through all the possibilities and he always spoke his mind. Despite all of this, I asked him to have faith and give me his full support and one final opportunity to make it all work. To his credit, and with my continued gratitude, Chris agreed.

Our 'management accounting', up until this stage, had been nonexistent. We only did statutory end-of-year accounts and by the time these were prepared, they were so far out of date they were useless for management decision-making purposes. We used a small accounting firm run by two Indian gentlemen, Mr Gupta and Mr Mystry. The firm was aptly named because the accounts they produced were a complete mystery to all of us and to anyone else who tried to read them. Not that it was Gupta and Mystry's fault. Our record keeping was hopeless and with the limited money we paid them and their limited resources, it was no wonder their work wasn't up to scratch.

Peter Barrow drew up the first accurate balance sheet just before the changeover. A balance sheet lists all the things of value a company owns (its assets) and deducts all the things it owes to outsiders (its liabilities — such as loans, overdrafts, and the like). The balance between the two is the company's net worth. Obviously, this net worth should be positive, with the value of the assets exceeding the liabilities (this equates to the initial capital plus any accumulated profits). However, in Top Deck's case, we had a negative net worth, that is, our liabilities exceeded our assets — by a staggering £250 000, nearly A$700 000! This negative net worth represented our accumulated losses through the years.

I couldn't believe it. We were seriously insolvent. It's illegal for directors to allow a company to continue trading under these circumstances and we really should have called in the receivers. I panicked and was ready to jump on a plane the next day and fly home to Sydney in disguise. Peter Barrow calmed me down and counselled me.

Thankfully, Peter can play any role demanded of him. He is a businessman first and the cautious accountant side of him only surfaces when he wants to ensure you have sufficient accurate information on which to base your decisions or when he is acting as an auditor and, as such, is legally and morally bound to play it 'by the book'. In this instance he was engaged as a consultant and so his advice was pragmatic and commercially-based.

'You can't run away, Bill. It's too late for that. You've been trading while insolvent for years, probably, so the crime's already been committed. Hang in there. Have faith. It'll work.'

Our plan for Top Deck did work, brilliantly. Fifteen months after it was introduced — that is, by August 1984, Top Deck's combined assets exceeded its liabilities by £300 000. In other words, we'd made profits of £550 000 in that short time, a colossal amount of money given our earlier losses.

Outwardly, no one would have recognised the changes to the company but, internally, the transformation was like turning night into day. Previously, Mick and I thought we were exercising 'management control' simply because we held the chequebook. Nothing could have been further from the truth. Countless decisions were being made by middle management without any regard or knowledge as to how these were impacting on profits. After the divisionalisation, these same managers were now highly accountable and every decision they took was with an eye as to how it impacted on the bottom line. Therefore 'accountability', and 'rewards and recognition' combined with 'moral and actual ownership' became the catchcries of our future management philosophies.

There was an interesting sidelight to all of this. London Flight Centre, which we'd established in early 1982 in a low rental, first-floor, walk-up office in Earls Court Road, had already been operating for a year as a separate business unit. In the first twelve months under the new Top Deck structure in 1983–4, this London Flight Centre made £60 000 profit. This was with Barb Bates as manager and five other consultants, including Liz, with no management input from either Mick or me. Additionally, it was a nine-to-five, five-and-a-half-days-a-week type of business,

Top Deck Daze

with very little initial capital expenditure required. Meanwhile, for example, Johnno O'Donnell who was running the Top Deck Europe company with eighty buses, 150 road crew, and all the hassles in the world, twenty-four-hours-a-day, seven-days-a-week, only made £50 000 profit in the corresponding twelve-month period. Johnno was doing a great job—it was just the nature of the business. If we needed any further convincing that our future lay in travel retailing rather than tour operating (which we didn't), we'd just found it.

During the year I noticed a small shop for sale at 131 Earls Court Road. There were some complications relating to its sale which no other buyer wanted to cope with and so I managed to negotiate a bargain price with the vendor. We moved London Flight Centre into this shop and with the fantastic walk-past and drive-past exposure, given the busy road, the business improved even more and was soon making £80 000 to £90 000 profit a year. A short time later, the freehold on the shop next door at

A far cry from our first office in Fulham, 131–135 Earls Court Road gave Top Deck prominent exposure in London.

Pay Day – London 1983

133 Earls Court Road came up for sale, and we bought that building as well. It was much bigger than number 131 and so we relocated Top Deck's main booking office from Kenway Road up to 133 Earls Court Road. A year after I left London, Top Deck bought 135 Earls Court Road as well. The three sites were then consolidated and painted pillar-box red and this gave the Top Deck name huge exposure in London.

The true test of success for any manager is when they realise they have done themselves out of a job. That is, having employed people smarter and more capable than themselves and having given those people the opportunity to grow and develop and accept responsibility, they find it's time to step back, move on, or retire. That's exactly what happened with Mick and me in London in 1984. The managers of all the subsidiary companies were doing such a great job under their own direction they, more or less, made both of us redundant.

In January 1985, Liz and I moved back to Sydney in time for the greatest event in our lives, the birth of our twin sons, Richard and Andrew. It was time for a new lifestyle and new business challenges. The Top Deck managers in London had come up with a new advertising slogan that proved to be very popular and successful in their marketing campaigns. It read: 'Some day you'll have a nice, sensible family, live in a nice, sensible house and have a nice, sensible holiday ... Some day.'

That 'Some day' had arrived for Liz and me.

I failed to heed my own advice. I did go back.

CRUSADER GASWELL

TADPOLES

last SPM 96

Modern Coach

TOP DECK'S RECENT HISTORY

In 1986, John Anderson, the founder of Contiki Travel, expressed interest in buying Top Deck (UK) with funds raised by a New Zealand investment company of which he was a director. The sale never proceeded, but our willingness to entertain a prospective buyer raised the interest of our London managers who proposed a management buy-out. In 1986, Murgha Mack, Chris Greive, John O'Donnell, Dave Morse and Graham Sewell bought the seventy-five percent shareholding held by Mick, Screw and me.

In 1989, Murgha bought out the other four boys. They did well for themselves, pocketing a cool million dollars each from the sale proceeds. Not a bad return on the sixty-thousand-pound mortgage they'd each had to arrange to finance their purchase two years earlier!

The next seven years proved to be a bumpy ride for Murgha. In addition to the stress of being the sole owner of such a diverse operation, a series of outside events compounded the pressures. For example, a fire at the farm destroyed the workshop. Then there was the Gulf War in 1991, followed by several poor snow seasons. These events occurred against the background of soaring interest rates, followed by the worst recession since the 1930s.

Murgha progressively sold off equity in the company until finally, in 1997, he sold out completely. The buyers were the Kuwaiti Algerian

Top Deck Daze

Investment Company (KAIC). Based in Luxembourg, this company was made up of government officials with investments in everything from oil pipelines to fish processing plants. (I'm not sure where double-decker bus tours fitted into their investment strategy.) Top Deck was still managed by Aussies and Kiwis, Dennis Jack and Paul Ludemann being two of the key personnel.

In May 1997, *Tadpoles* was the last double-decker to complete an overland tour and the remaining double-deckers were sold or scrapped later that year.

The 2003 season proved to be one of the toughest in Top Deck's history with the company on the verge of bankruptcy. A partnership made up of Geoff McGeary's Australian Pacific Group (APT) (30%), Dick Porter from STA Travel (20%), Screw Turner, Peter Barrow, Geoff Harris, Chris Greive, and me (4% each), and Jimmy Nathan, founder of Connections Adventures (30%), who came on board as Chief Executive Officer, took control of the company

Contiki had come to totally dominate the market but after several months of research, Jimmy believed that while Contiki was a household name it had become overly commercialised and most importantly 'was no longer cool' as far as the younger travellers were concerned: so the challenge was to re-invent Top Deck and fill this gap. The look and feel of everything changed: from brochures to websites, from the coaches' livery to the company name—and so Top Deck became *Topdeck*.

Taking professionalism to new heights, the company gradually began to build momentum so that by 2007 Flight Centre, Australia's largest retail travel agency, replaced Contiki with Topdeck as their Preferred Global Youth Touring Operator, and that year Topdeck outsold Contiki in Australia for the first time! In November 2008, Jimmy, Screw, Geoff, Chris, Peter and I bought Connections Adventures from APT and re-named it Topdeck so that now, our coaches can proudly be seen in Australia and New Zealand. The company also operates in Egypt, Turkey, Morocco, Syria, Jordan and ... Iceland. Profits and client numbers have soared.

The year 2014 marked another major milestone in the company's history. Flight Centre purchased 90% of Topdeck's shares, valuing the company at £22 million (A$39 million). Jimmy Nathan retains 10% of the company and oversees the management. During the current year Topdeck will carry 28 000 clients in the Northern Hemisphere and 6000 in Australia and NZ.

Epilogue

THE ESTABLISHMENT OF FLIGHT CENTRE

By the time we sold out of Top Deck in 1986, Screw, Geoff Harris and I had established about twenty-five travel agencies throughout Australia, principally in Brisbane, Sydney and Melbourne. However, there was no common name, logo or operating system. There was a general consensus that this should change in order that we establish a strong brand, enabling us to expand and become a major force in travel retailing. So, in 1986, Screw organised a conference in Bangkok for all the agency managers. Over several days we hammered out our new modus operandi. We agreed that we would rename all our agencies 'Flight Centre' and conform to all the agreed shop designs, signage, colour schemes and management and operating systems that we had drawn up at the conference. This was the real birth of 'Flight Centre'.

The management and leadership philosophies that evolved during our latter days with Top Deck enabled us to develop a business formula that we were able to successfully apply to our new Australian company. 'Flight Centre Limited' listed on the Australian Stock Exchange in November 1995. The shares were originally valued at ninety-five cents. They now trade in a range from A$35 to A$55. The company has 17 000 staff, annual sales of A$16 Billion and annual pre-tax profits of A$380 Million. It is the largest travel agency group in Australasia and the country's fourth largest retailer. Screw is still the company's Chief Executive Officer. I retired in 1997 to spend more time with family and pursue other interests.

I first trekked the Kokoda Track in 1999. The lack of research on the Track was the inspiration for extensive ground research to uncover the 'lost battlefields'. This led to my next book in 2006, *The Field Guide to the Kokoda Track*.

Top Deck Daze

HONOUR ROLL

Following are the names of many of the crew who have worked for Top Deck since its inception. It has been updated since the first edition, with the help of Lew Cody, Dave Reed and Peter Yates and now includes an additional 678 people. Unfortunately, few of the old company records remain and so, inevitably, it is far from complete. Please write to the publisher if you can add to this list.

A

Noel Abraham
Craig Ackland
Anita Adamek
Andrea Adams
Kevin Adams
Bruce Adamson
Bessie Addicott
Chris Agnew
Ros Ainley
Rachelle Alderton
Ang Alexander
Carla Aliphon
Brett Allan
Fiona Allan
Megan Allard
Christopher Allatt
Jonathan Allen
Mark Alsop
Joe Anderson
Tina Anderson
Matthew Andrews
Susan Andrews
Craig Anquetil
Sally Anscombe
Mark Arbuthnot
Aiva Arminas
Mark Armstrong
Neil Armstrong
Tim Arnold
Jo Arundale
Gary Aschenberger
Heath Ashcroft
Brendan Atkinson
Mark 'Acko' Atkinson
Judy Ayres
Vanessa Ayres

B

Rosco Bain
Glenn Baines
Ross Baines
Catherine Baker
Julie Baker
Melanie Baker
Peter Baker
Scott Baker
Justin Ball
Matthew Bangma
Mark 'Cassanova' & Kerry Bannerman
Pat Barden
Carolyn Barker
Daniel 'Red' Barker
Nial Barker
Laurie James Barnhill
Gary 'Mouse' Barnier
Roger Barr
Rosemary Barrett
Patrick 'Paddy' Barrow
Todd 'Biscuits' Barry
Dave 'Dehy' Bartley
Diane Bartley
Brendon Basten
Barbara Bates
Stephen Bates
Merrin Bath
Ken & Dot Batton
Joanna Baudinet
Jason Baxter
Stuart Bayley
Michael Beadle
Paul Beames
Oliver Beasley
Amanda Beer

Marina Begolo
Ric Belcher
Alistair Bell
Brent Bell
Erin Bell
Jenny Bell
Kathryn Bell
Kylie Bell
Mike Bell
Niki Bell
Peter Benne
Martin Bennett
Bennie Benson
Virginie Bertomeu
Sue Berwick
Lance Best
Raelene Beynon
Thomas Bimrose
Brook Bindley
Anne Birch
Brad Birch
Katrina Birmingham
Ashley Bishop
Andrew Black
Brendon Black
Janet Blair
Lisa Blake
Karen Blanchette
Dan Blatch
Nial Bleakley
Nicholas Bloom
Norman Blunck
Milton Blythe
Zak 'Ritchie' Bodgema
Jenny Bond
Dave Bood
James Booth

Honour Roll

Greg	Boquet	Nicky	Buchman	Mick 'Carrot'	Carroll
Roger 'Pretty Boy'	Borthwick	Simon 'Moose'	Buckley	Trevor 'Tricky One'	Carroll
Boz & Ellen	Boskma	Dwain	Buffett	Brian	Casey
Brad	Bouquet	Terry	Bugden	Pat 'Psycho'	Casey
John 'Timbo'	Bourke	Ivan	Buktenica	Richard	Casey
Justin	Bourke	Anna	Bulleid	Wayne 'Waggs'	Casey
Tim	Bourke	Annie	Bulmer	Craig	Cassidy
Geoff	Bowden	Cally	Burke	John 'Santa'	Catt
Ric 'Whisper'	Bowen	Declan	Burke	Roger	Catton
Anna	Bowman	Alister	Burn	Owen	Caufield
Mick 'Mario'	Bowman	Kevin	Burn	Scott	Caulfield
Filip	Braams	Craig	Burns	Peter 'Spike'	Cawthorn
Paul	Bracken	John 'Burnzy'	Burns	Raitis	Cerkasovs
Shayne	Bradley	Rebecca	Burns	Laura	Chamberlain
David	Braid	Stuart	Burns	Andrew	Chapman
Charles 'Bob'	Brailsford	Andy 'Budda'	Burrell	Alan	Chappin
Ken	Brathwaite	Polly	Burrowes	Lia	Checkett
Ashley	Bray	Tim	Burt	Kelly	Checketts
Emma	Bray	Andrew	Burton	Bruce	Cherry
Ross	Brayshaw	Mick 'Walla'	Burton	Julie	Chesterfield
Dan	Breeden	Ashley	Burton-Brown	Diana	Chiene
John	Bremner	Allan 'Knuckle'	Butler	Elyse	Childs
John & Lynda	Bremner Harrison	Eric		Nigel	Childs
Hayley	Brennan	'Dirtbag'	Butler	Terrance	Chilton
Molly	Bresnahan	Steve	Butler	Mark	Chisholm
Peter 'Brewmaster'	Brew	Jarrod	Buxton	Adam	Christensen
Corrie	Bridgeman		**C**	Ellen	Clancy
Barry	Brien	Nicki	Cairns	Lindy	Clarbull
Dianne	Brock	Allan	Caldwell	Dominic	Claridge
Kathleen	Brockway	Andrew	Caldwell	Cameron	Clark
Kimba	Brookes	Mark	Callega	Sarah	Clark
Barbara	Brown	Victoria 'Tori'	Calver	Andrew	Clarke
Geoff	Brown	Claire	Camazon	Lawrence 'Flo'	Clarke
Jeff	Brown	Jenny	Cameron	Peter	Clarke
Lesley & Steve	Brown	Julia	Cameron	Tim	Clarke
Mary-Lynn	Brown	Adrian	Campbell	Jeff	Clarkson
Roger	Brown	Allan	Campbell	Richard	Clifton
Steve 'Bombardier'	Brown	Fyfe	Campbell	Peter	Clooney
Todd	Brown	Marissa	Campbell	Paul	Cobbit
Tracey	Brown	Peter	Campbell	Pete	Cochrane
Veronica	Brown	Derek	Cane	Robert	Cochrane
Yvonne 'Ya Pants'	Brown	Pat	Cantwell	Ross	Cochrane
Jennifer	Browne	Dave	Caon	William	Cochrane
Peter 'Filthy'	Browne	Aoife	Carbin	Ty	Cockburn
Dennis 'Dbk'	Brown-Kenyon	Russell	Cargill	Nicholas 'Rooster'	Cockerell
Paul 'Toot'	Brunton	John	Carnibella	Leanne 'Headless'	Cockle
Lisa	Bruton	Robert	Carr	Colin	Codlin
Paula	Bryon	Libby	Carroll	Lew	Cody
Shaun	Bucci			Joe 'Jag'	Coelli

Top Deck Daze

Michelle	Coetzee	Ron 'Darlo'	Darlington	Jax	Drummond
Mark	Colhoun	Rachel	Davey	Anthony	Drury
Simon	Collins	Chris	Davies	Nick	Duce
Paul	Collishaw	Karen	Davies	Phil	Duce
Warren	Collits	Matt	Davies	Louise	Duffy
Daryl 'Condo'	Condon	Phil	Davies	Nancy	Duffy
Danielle	Connelly	Ben	Davis	Simon	Duffy
Charlotte	Cook	Bev	Davis	Kevin	Duggan
Ed	Cook	Paul	Davis	Julian	Duncan
Peter	Cook	Peter	Dawes	Murray 'Tyres'	Dunlop
Sheralyn	Cook	Rhiannon	Dawes	Bradley	Dunn
Steve 'Cookie'	Cook	Ken	Dawson	Christine	Dunn
Dorothy	Cooke	Charlotte	Day	Jeff & Cheryl	Dunn
Martin 'Maggot'	Cool	Chris	Day	Paul	Durrell
Kate	Copley	Matt	Day	Terry	Dwyer
Pamela	Copsey	Monique	de Haan	Mark	Dykes
Debbie	Corbett	Renee	De Silva	Narelle	Dyson
Jade	Corby	Allen	Deans		**E**
Bags	Corcoran	Ric	Delaney	John	Eagleton
Nadine	Cordery	Scott	Dennon	Laura	Earl
Fiona	Corsie	Elizabeth	Dent	Sarah	Eastes
Suzanne	Cossey	Eoin-Pol	Denton	Wayne	Edlin
Gabrielle	Costin	Ashish	Desai	Brett	Edmonds
Jo-Anne	Cottle	Brent	Devetak	Tom	Edwards
Brian 'Dark Blue'	Coubrough	Carmel	Devine	Michelle 'Rivet'	Elia
Ian	Coulter	Robert		Martin	Elliott
Jude	Coulter	'Two Sheds'	Dickinson	Paul 'Rip'	Elliott
Amanda	Cowie	Lucretia	Dijkstra	Dianne	Ellis
Trevor	Cox	Craig	Dillon	Geoff	Ellis
Evana	Coyne	Liz	Diprose	Lisa Jane	Else
Gillian	Craig	Ros	Diprose	Paul	Emery
Jackie	Crase	Colin 'Dobbie'	Dobson	Kathleen	England
Chris	Craven	Grant 'Dog'	Doherty	Peter	Englefield
Greg 'Backdoor'	Craven	Liz	Doherty	Pgilip	English
Jeness	Crawford	Janelle	Dollery	Mark	Enright
Billy 'Stumpy'	Crawshaw	Jimmy	Donaldson	Greg 'Wombat'	Ettridge
Mandy	Creed	Peter	Donkin	Richard	Euston
Mark	Creed	Helen	Donnell-Gledhill	Dave 'Dinga'	Evans
Melissa 'Chook'	Cribb	Pat	Doolan	Deborah	Evans
Pete	Crochrane	Jason	Dowling	David	Eves
Malcolm 'Crim'	Crook	Rebecca	Downs	Nicola	Eyles
James	Crosby	L.D.	Doyle		**F**
Brendan	Crosswell	Owen	Doyle	Russell 'Dial'	Facer
Scott	Crowe	Robert	Doyle	Paul	Fallon
Eric	Culpan	Vanessa	Doyle	Janelle	Farley
Michelle	Curran	Chris	Drage	John	Farley
	D	Dee	Draper	Clayton	Farr
Samantha	Dalla	Mark 'Bobby Sands'	Draper	Dave	Farrell
Julie	Darling	Wayne	Dreher		

Honour Roll

Ron	Farrington	Glenn 'Homer'	Gamble	Rod	Grenda
Dave 'Spud'	Fauves	Vicki	Gane	Kiri	Grennell
Rhys	Fell	Matt	Gannan	Amanda	Grentell
Steven	Fensom	Andy	Gardner	John	Grey
Jane	Fenton	Roxanne	Garner	Mark	Griffin
Allan 'Nugget'	Ferguson	Graham 'Boof'	Garside	Jimmy	Griffith
Mark	Ferguson	Kerry 'Scruff'	Garside	Shirley	Griffiths
Marie	Field	Julie	Gates	Randall	Griggs
David	Filmer	Mike & Marie	Gaudin	Ben	Groundwater
Tracy	Finch	Phil	Gazzard	Peter	Gulliver
Antonia	Fincham	Pete	Geale		**H**
Ron	Finlayson	Suzanne	Geary	Rachael	Haase
Bruce	Fitzgerald	Natasha	George	Jacqueline	Hain
Trudy	Fitzgerald	Zoe	Georgiou	Sarah	Hale
Tim 'Sniffer'	Fitzpatrick	Jean	Gereme	Bruce	Hall
Kane	Fletcher	Patricia	Gerigk	Craig	Hall
Adrian	Flint	Peter	Gerrick	Ian	Hall
Pamela	Flockhart	Trish	Gersbach	Sharelle	Hall
Mark	Floyd	Nicky	Gibbs	Minna	Hamalainen
Daniel	Fluker	Julie	Giblett	Brian	Hamilton
Amanda	Flynn	Gary & Liz	Gibson	Tom	Hamilton
Craig	Foote	Mark	Gibson	Graham	Hammond
Anne	Ford	Chris 'Prong'	Gilbert-Wilson	Jilli	Handley
Garry	Ford	Frank	Giles	John	Hansard
Martin	Ford	Teresa	Giuseppina	Jane	Hanson
Heather	Forshaw	Warwick 'Curly'	Gladman	Gavin	Hardcastle
Aaron	Forster	Amanda	Glassop	Margot	Hardgrave
Gary	Forsyth	Alison 'Petal'	Glen	David	Hards
Doug	Foskett	Victoria	Glenn	Lance	Hardy
Louise	Fowler	Peter 'Monk'	Goddard	Craig	Hare
Felix	Fox	David	Godfrey	Paul	Hargraves
Jane	Francis	Darryl	Goldstone	Mona	Haria
Rebecca	Francis	Robby	Goodall	Barbara	Harkness
Hamish	Fraser	Margaret	Goodhew	David	Harrison
Stuart & Deb	Frater	Natalia	Goodwin	Garry	
Rob	Frazier	Sjef	Goossens	'Harry Gartley'	Hartley
Guy	Freeman	Luke	Gordon	Erin	Hartley-Smith
Wayne	Freeman	Jason	Grady	Rachel	Hartwig
Kathee	Frohn	Anthony	Graham	Grant	Hassell
Bridget	Frost	Richard	Graham	Dave	Hatfield
Elizabeth	Frost	Nikki	Grant	Chris & Nicky	Hay
Lauren	Fuller	Bronwyn	Gray	Jennifer	Hayden
Peter	Fuller	Emma	Gray	Chris	Hayes
Gary 'Fuzz'	Furey	John 'Bloody'	Gray	Mark 'Rat'	Hayes
	G	Fiona	Greaves	Matthew 'Napoleon'	Hayward-Ryan
Karly	Gallagher	Antoinette	Gredig	Gaye	Hazlett
Peter	Gallagher	Mike	Greenwood	Ryan	Heath
Shane	Galvin	David	Gregg	Jennifer	Hedge
		Chris & Liz	Greive		

Top Deck Daze

John	Heffernan	Andrew	Hughes	Stuart	Johansen
Tim	Heffernan	Peter 'Pedro'	Hughes	Chris 'Curly'	Johns
Wayne	Heggarty	Rory	Hulse	Bill	Johnson
Brian	Henderson	David	Hulton	Deb	Johnson
Kate	Henderson	Angus	Humphries	Lawrence	Johnson
Casey	Henney	Cliff	Hunt	Mandy	Johnson
Melinda	Heron	Nicole	Hunt	Mark 'Brocky'	Johnson
John	Herrick	Antony	Hunt	Stephen	Johnson
Tony	Hessen	Andrew	Hunter	Stuart	Johnson
Richard 'The Unmentionable'	Hewitt	Sally	Hunter	Terry	Johnson
		Stuart	Hurst	Tony	Johnson
Jason	Higgot	Merinda	Hutchison	Sam	Johnston
Justin	Hill	Grant	Hutton	Meegan	Johnstone
Louise	Hill	Chris	Hyland	Sharon	Johnstone
Ray 'Mumbles'	Hill	Ivan	Hyslop	Alex	Jones
Rod	Hillman	**I**		Belinda	Jones
Shaun	Hilton	Ruth	Ingerson	Bridget	Jones
Simon	Hilyer	Barry 'Bulawayo'	Innes	Caroline	Jones
Anthony 'Tony'	Hinton	Cam	Insull	Chris	Jones
Kathy	Hinwood	Karen	Inwood	Kym	Jones
Melanie	Hitchens	Phil	Irons	Peter	Jones
Pauline	Hoban	Cecilia	Ituralde	Peter 'PJ'	Jones
Adam	Hodge	Gary	Ivulich	Raechel	Jones
rachel	Hodson	Sam	Izatt	Ross	Jones
Phil	Hogan			Sharon	Jones
Luke	Holcombe	**J**		Shelly	Jones
Cameron	Holden	Dennis	Jack	Sennet 'Now Now'	Jordan
Timothy	Holden	Arja	Jacob	Per	Jorgensen
Lisa 'Doris'	Holder	Chris	Jacobs	Brooke	Judd
Brenda	Holding	Erin	Jacobs	Rod	Judge
Matthew 'Husky'	Holland	Jens	Jacobsen	Hannah	Jukes
Bruce & Jenny	Holmes	Lisa	Jacobsen	Rex 'Sexy Rexy'	Julian
Graham 'Silver Jacket'	Holmes	Bill	James	**K**	
Nicholas	Holmes	Chris	James	Vickie	Kane
Jean	Holtom	Heather	James	Apa	Karis
Ray	Hookam	Keri	James	Kosta	Karis
Carolyn	Hope	Peter	James	John	Keefe
Trevor	Hope	Alan	Jamieson	Mark	Keenan
Claudia	Hopkins	Glenn	Jamieson	Nigel	Keenan
Sarah	Hopkins	Phil	Janene	Jude	Keighley
Milton	Hornhardt	Brian	Jarvis	Russell 'Rusty'	Kelaart
Beverly	Hornibrook	Amanda	Jelley	Andrew	Kelleher
Glen	Hoskins	David	Jenkins	Jane	Kelly
Mathew	Housden	Wendy	Jenner	James 'Blurter'	Kemsley
Paul	Houston	Andrew	Jennings	Leigh 'Donk'	Kennett
Deborah	Howe	Sharon	Jennings	Al 'The Vicar'	Kenny
Ian 'Hak'	Howell	Grange	Jephcott	Robert	Kercher
Amanda	Huckstadt	Istvan	Jere	Nicola	Kerr
John 'Hugeore'	Hughan	Stephanie	Jervis	Sean	Kershaw

Honour Roll

San 'Sandshoe' Khoo
Lauren Kidd
Richard Kilbride
Anouk Killestein
Neil Kimmel
Heather King
Leslie King
Roger Kirkwood
Melissa Klinge
Adam Knight
Megan Knight
Tony Knowlson
Cornelius 'Maggot' Kool
Martin Kool
Johan Koorevaar
Karinya Kosh
Paul 'Toby' Kundycki

L

David Lafferty
Mellissa Lafferty
Diane Lai
Trudie Laidlaw
Brad Lamb
Marlene Landon
Steve Lane
Brian Langbein
Thomas Langston
Nick Larsen
Stuart Lavender
Nix Lavin
Amelia Lawrence
Darren Lawrence
Tracey Laxon
Dean Leedham
Kees Leenman
Brent Leggert
Kerrie Leifels
Brett Lemin
Lisa Lennox
Tracey Levendal
Gerrard Lewis
Jonathon Lewis
Malcolm Lewis
Shelley Lewis
Pierre Leyser
Greg Liddington
Sandy 'Madam Lash' Lillecrapp
Krzysztof Lindner
Darren Lindsay

Amanda Lipscombe
Dennis 'Lippo' Lipscombe
Magdalena Lirova
Gareth Liscoe
Darren Lively
Glenn Livingstone
Greg 'Five Eights' Lloyd
Kristine Lockwood
Niki Logan
Tara Logan
Neal Lohse
Geoff 'Spy' Lomas
Matthew 'Foggy' Lord
Thomas Lott
Les Love
Tracey Love
Paul Ludemann
Richard Lugg
Alan Luke
Gilbert Luke
Rohan Lumley
Erik Lundquist
Jamie Lynch

M

John & Bronwyn MacDiarmid
Christina Macdonald
Ian Macdonald
Georgina Macfarlane
Alison '99' MacGregor
Kirsty Macgregor
Murgha Mack
Scott & Kay Mackay
Robert Mackenzie
Roma Mackeviciute
Ian Mackinnon
Sandra 'Sandy' Macklin
Alan MacLeod
Stewart 'Birdbrain' Macpherson
Marcus Macrury
Akos Madacsi
Raelene Madden
Roz Madden
Gail Maddox
Tate Madgwick
Michelle Magee
Laurie Maguire
Barry Mahon
Lindy Mahon
Sam Maller

Alison Malone
Bruce 'Moose' Maloney
Maurice Maloney
Tony Maloney
Morris Malony
Crenagh Manion
Gabrielle Manion
Christian Manley
David Mann
Rachel Mann
David Manners
Chelsea Mannix
Paul Mansfield
Philip Mansfield
James Marchant
Sally Margen
Peter Markey
Greg & Ala Marks
Angelo Marras
Ian 'Swampy' Marsh
David Marshall
Jessye Marshall
Kelvin Marshall
Michael Martin
Wayne Mason
William Massart
Brent Masters
Ian Mather
Emily Mathew
Nathan Mathews
Adrian Matthews
Edan Matthews
Max Matthews
Trevor 'Tricky' Matthews
Heather Maxwell
Allira Mayr
Julian 'Yappa' McAll
Linda McAskill
Shelley McBride
Rebecca McCaig
David Mccallum
Jo McClaren
Jane McClymont
Gerard McCormack
Julie McCormack
Rebecca McCoy
Karen McDonald
Lisa McDonald
Sue Mcelroy

Top Deck Daze

Brian	McFadden	Craig	Mitchell	Lyndsay	Mylan
Bruce	Mcfarlane	Daryl 'Animal'	Mitchell		**N**
Shelley	McGlashan	Deanne	Mitchell	Brent 'Ferret'	Naish
Sue	Mcgovern	Christelle	Moller	Bradley	Nardi
Gordon	Mcgowan	Maurice	Moloney	James	Nathan
Lewis	McGrail	Tony	Moloney	Sally	Nathan
Bradley 'Filthy Low'	McGrath	Cameron	Monaghan	Tiggy	Nathan
Rodney	McInerney	Katie	Montgomery	Ann	Neeley
Lynda	McKee	Penny	Moody	Peta 'Mav'	Nelson
Leasa	McKenzie	Brian	Mooney	Raewyn	Nelson
Matt 'Little Mattie'	McKerrow	Kevin 'Rev Head'	Mooney	Bruce 'Bear'	Nemer
Jo	McLaren	Rick	Mooney	Michael	Nesdale
Penny	McLean	Alison	Moore	Jan	Newby
Bradley	McLeod	Debbie	Moore	Marie	Newby
Shelley	McLure	Sharon	Moore	Kim	Newman
Kylie	McMahon	Stephen	Moore	Alan	Ng
Ben	McMaster	Jan	Mora	Anne	Nicoll
Chris	McMiken	Diane	Morel	Bradley	Nielson
Tija	McMullen	Andy		Toni	Nightingale
Craig	McNaught	'Randy Organ'	Morgan	Steve	Noakes
Shona	McPherson	Jane	Morgan	Sarah	Nock
Garry	McSkimming	Shane	Morgan	Pam	Nolan
Martin	McSkimming	Steve	Morgan	Adam	Norman
Steve 'Nose' 'Derv'	McSkimming	Teresa	Morgan	Hydie	Normington
Mike	McWha	Andrew	Morley	Ian	North
Rex	Mealey	Sam	Morrah	Laurence	Norton
Sonya	Meehan	Nadine	Morris	Viviana	Novelli
Helga	Mehandiratta	Tessa	Morris	Brent	Nunns
Kerrie	Mellick	Steve	Morrish		**O**
Lisa	Melvin	Owen	Morrison	Basil	O'Boyle
Gavin	Menzies	'Diesel' Dave	Morse	Stephen	O'Brien
Gordon	Menzies	Keith	Morse	Anthony	O'Callaghan
Kirsty	Menzies	Marilyn	Morse	Tim	O'Callaghan
Victoria	Messer	Brett	Mugford	Tricia	O'Connell
Trevor	Mews	Blake	Muir	Kate	O'Connor
Russell	Miatke	Brett	Muir	Sean	O'Connor
Larry & Geraldine	Michell	Robyn	Muir	Eris	O'Donell
Nev	Michell	Gerry 'Smurf'	Murphy	Johnno	O'Donnell
Sail	Michell	Keith	Murphy	Ann	O'Halloran
Rowan	Michelle	Rachel	Murphy	John	O'Keefe
Howard	Milham	Stephen	Murphy	Paul	O'Mahoney
Bruce	Millar	John	Murray	John	O'Neill
Tanya	Millar	Kim	Murray	Brian 'Dillon'	O'Sullivan
Candice	Miller	Steve 'Whirlwind'	Murray	Michelle	O'Sullivan
Dave	Miller	Jason	Murrell	Dennis 'Havachat'	O'Toole
Hayden	Miller	Lyndsey	Mutch	Charmagne	Oakley
Scott	Miller	Derek	Myers	David	O'Brien
Janice	Mills	Jane	Mylan		

Honour Roll

Kerrie	Obst	Mark	Paton	Gavin	Porthouse
Darcy	ODonnell	Tracey	Paton	Greg	Potter
Pete	Officer	Andrew	Patterson	Dale	Potts
Robert	Offner	Don	Patterson	Ellie	Pouls
Sky	Ogier	Rochelle	Patterson	John 'Powelly'	Powell
Gillian	Olive	Greg	Paul	Sebastian	Powell
Tim 'Mrs Oliver'	Oliver	Sunjeev & Margie	Paul	Sara	Pratt
Kevin		Tracy	Paul	Amy	Preece
'Tiny' & Yvonne	Olliff	Anita	Pavulins	Chanelle	Preiato
Katrina	O'Malley	Joanna	Pazowski	Sarah	Prentice
Kym	OMeara	Cameron	Pearce	Kristine	Preston
Belleta	Ormsby	Grant	Pearce	Stacey	Price
Alexander	Osborne	Clem	Pearson	Garth	Prichard
Courtney	Osborne	Robert	Peart	Ian 'Snake'	Prichard
Judi	Oswin	David	Peck	Terry	Pride
Sophie	Othenin-Girard	Graham	Peek	Leticia	Prieto
Ainslie	Otto	Holly	Peel	Shelley	Pritchard
Ainslie	Owen	Ron	Peggs	Steve 'Hulk'	Prosser
Nick	Owen	Robbi	Pell	Herwig	Puchberger

P

		Marion	Penard	Lew	Pulbrook
		John James	Pentland	Greg	Pullen
Brad	Page	Mick	Pepper	Steve 'Krypto'	Pyatt
Matt	Page	Alex	Pereira		

Q

Lisa	Pagotto	Andrea	Peterson	Benny	Quayle
Harold	Paice	Ray	Petts	Anita	Quigley
Jennifer	Palframan	Alan	Phillips	Cath	Quinn
Craig	Palmer	Gavin	Phillips	Denis	Quinn
Gary	Palmer	John	Phillips	Peter	Quinn
Andrew	Paltridge	Tom	Phillips		

R

Michela	Pantini	Kirstin	Phillipson	Kath	Rabbidge
Ourania	Pantopolis	Marg	Philp	Paul	Rahill
Nicholas	Pantopoulos	John	Pickering	Daniela	Ramondino
Evan	Pardington	Natalie	Pickett	Bryan 'Light Blue'	Ramsey
Roslyn	Park	Karen	Pierce	Martina	Rangihuna
Alison	Parker	Jade	Pieterman	Monika	Rasenen
Antoinette	Parker	Natalie	Piggott	John	Rattigan
Dan	Parker	Shelly 'George'	Piggott	Damien	Rawlings
David	Parker	Andrew	Pilkington	Judith	Raynor
Lance	Parker	Raui	Pirake	Kevin	Reddy
Mark	Parker	Bec	Pleasant	Dave	Reed
Terry	Parker	Jodie	Plum	Warren	Reid
Steve 'Tom the Pom'	Parkhill	Sandie	Plunkett	Jasmine	Remy
		Sandy	Plunkett	Andrea	Rennie
Keith	Parkin	Dave	Pocklington	Gerard 'Geriatric'	Rennie
Andy	Parkinson	Pete	Pocock	Allison	Rich
Martin	Parnell	Greg 'Grog'	Pollard	Eugene	Richards
Gav 'Parto'	Partington	Clare	Poole	Kerry	Richards
Andrew	Partridge	Terry	Porter	Brenda	Richardson
Danyil	Pascoe				

Top Deck Daze

Mark	Richardson	Stewart	Rust	Paul	Seymor
Ross & Irene	Richardson	Alexis	Ruth	Jamie	Seymour
Neville	Riley	Abbie	Ruttelle	Bob 'Uncle'	Shadforth
Steve 'Magoo'	Riley	Bill	Ryan	Jodie	Shanks
Debra	Rimington	Marlene & Mark	Ryan	Janine	Shanley
Sophie	Rist	Michelle	Ryan	Helen	Shannon
Bradley	Ritchie			Howard	Sharp
Ross	Ritchie		**S**	Nigel	Sharp
Murray	Robb	Greg	Saggers	Louise	Shaw
Katrina	Robbie	Stephen	Sai-Louie	Sally	Shaw
Amanda	Robbilliard	Failagi Joe	Saipele	Carl	Shearer
Eoin	Robbins	Charlie	Sales	Tina 'Tines'	Sheehan
Jeff	Robers	Fleur	Salter	Sophie	Sheilds-Brown
Geoff	Roberts	Dave 'Aqua Man'	Salvemini	Robert	
John	Roberts	Bob 'Bob-A-Job'	Sanderson	'Moonflower'	Sheldrick
Tim	Roberts	Janelle	Sands	John	Shephard
Amanda	Robilliard	Bob	Saunders	Carla	Sheridan
Ray 'Prawn'	Robinson	Craig	Saunders	Philip	Shires
Carla	Robson	Andrew	Savage	Rebeka	Shorland
Michelle	Robson	John	Savage	Jason	Shugg
Selena	Robson	Elinor-Jane	Sawyer	Dave 'Worm'	Silk
Michael 'Mad Max'	Roche	Dario	Scafasci	Brenda	Simonsen
Gary	Rodgers	Kevin	Scaife	Karen	Simpson
Greg	Rodgers	Adrian	Scarlett	Julie	Sims
John	Rodgers	Jennifer	Schaefer	Mark	Sims
Michelle	Rodney	Janelle	Schembri	Jennifer	Sisson
Mark	Rodwell	Colin	Schirmer	Jess	Skepper
Robert 'Tumbles'	Roel	Refo	Schmidger	Jeff 'Skin'	Skinner
Thomas	Rogers	Muzza & Lou	Schofield	Mark	Skurr
Sam	Rohan	Linley	Scholes	Ronald	Slatcher
Leanne	Rohde	Kym	Schracler	Susie	Small
Ian	Rolland	Mike	Schweiger	Trudi	Small
Margaret	Rollinson	Al	Scott	Kim	Smart
Kerry	Rollo	Damian	Scott	Maria	Smart
Philip	Ronald	Kerryann 'Scruff'	Scully	Russell	Smart
Annie	Roper Coutts	Cassandra	Searle	Tom	Smethurst
Alan 'Camel'	Rose	Peter	Searle	Brad	Smith
Kim	Rosenthal	Martina	Sebova	Carl	Smith
Derek	Rossiter	Loxley 'Cocksley		Carmel	Smith
Nadine	Rowan-Thomson	Sucker'	Secker	Christa	Smith
Alan	Rowe	Steve	Sedgmen	Christine	Smith
Emma	Rowe	Greg	Seggars	Diane	Smith
Rachel	Rowley	Dave	Sellers	Fiona	Smith
Trevor	Rowston	David	Sellers	Jeff	Smith
Luke	Ruby	Alison	Selman	Merryn	Smith
Alan	Rukuwai	Nino	Servedio	Michael	Smith
Gavin 'Doctor'	Rush	Yasmine	Sethna	Mick 'Slippers',	
Kara	Rushton	Dennis	Sewell	'The Reverend'	Smith
Kay	Russell	Graham	Sewell	Paul	Smith

Honour Roll

Polly	Smith	Brent	Sutherland	Bill	Trengove
Ray	Smith	Greg	Sutherland	Rachel	Trew
Robert	Smith	John	Sutherland	Seamus	Trodden
Russell	Smith	John 'Slutty'	Sutton	Peter	Trotman
Tina	Smith	Helena	Swan	Grahan	Trubuhovich
Scott	Smyth	Cherie	Swanepoel	Graham 'Screw'	Turner
Glen	Smythe	Danae	Swinburne	Jude	Turner
Brian	Snape	Amanda	Syddall	Kevin 'Tich'	Turner
Robert	Snelling	Dave 'Dingo'	Symons	Liz	Turner
Keith	Somers	Zoltan	Szalay	Paul	Turner
Margaret	Spargo	David	Szeibert	Drewe	Twine
Mark	Spearpoint		**T**	Jessica	Tye
Grant	Spedding	Brian	Tanner	Pip & Liliana	Tyler
Carolyn	Spicer	Nicole	Tanner		**V**
Libby	Staggs	Eddie	Tarau	Alison	Vagg
Robyn	Staples	Justin	Tarpey	Jakoba	Van der Linden
Megan	Starr-Thomas	Nial	Tarrant	Frank	Van Dijk
Steedy	Stedman	Amber	Taylor	Wendy	van Dijk
Guy	Steedman	Candice	Taylor	Evelien	Van Vliet
Craig	Steele	Darryl	Taylor	Michael	Van Werkhoven
Cheryl	Steer	Denise	Taylor	Tony 'Rat'	Vanderway
Mike	Stent	James	Taylor	Alan	Vant
Anthony	Stephens	Judi	Taylor	Byron 'Mattress'	Varney
Dale	Stephens	Melanie	Taylor	Garry	Vaughan
Phillipa	Stephens	Neal	Taylor	Maxie	Veale
Sandra	Stephens	Robert	Teune	Aurelian	Veaux
Eden	Stevenson	Brian	Thacker	Jacqueline	Veldhuis
Jude	Stevenson	Kerry	Thomas	Alan 'Paddington'	Vent
Lisa	Stevenson	Mark	Thomas	Leen	Verhaeghe
Suze	Stevenson	Richard	Thomas	Andrew	Verryt
Ken	Stewart	Alison	Thomassen	Arian	Vitali
Matthew	Stewart	Henry 'Malaria'	Thompson		**W**
Joey	Stockman	Michele	Thompson	Tony	Waldron
Lauren	Stokes	Nick	Thompson	Chris 'Muttley'	Walker
Michael	Stormon	Stewart	Thompson	Jason	Walker
Chrissy	Stowe	Deryn	Thorpe	Neri	Walker
Sue	Strain	Jody	Thorpe	Pamela	Walker
Craig	Street	Darren	Timms	Warren	Walker
Bianca	Stringer	Roger	Timms	Fiona	Wallace
Les	Stringer	Ivan	Tolj	Sally	Wallace
Mark	Studd	Alison	Tolley	Anthony	Waloron
Marta	Sturmey	Jeremy	Tolmie	Benjamin	Walsh
Dean	Sullivan	Dave	Tonkin	Ben 'Nummy'	Walters
Kate	Sullivan	Kate	Toohey	Wayne	Walton
Louise	Sullivan	Tonya 'Toe'	Toomey	Craig	Ward
Mark	Sullivan	Richard	Townsend	Mal	Ward
Melissa	Sullivan	Rosie	Treasure	Samantha	Ward
Harry 'Spaceman'	Sutcliffe	Amanda	Tremeer	Michael	Wardley

Top Deck Daze

Kerrie 'Kessa'	Ware	Grant	Wheeler	Nicola	Wilson
Jenny	Warren	Rebecca	Whiffin	Linda	Windsor
Mike	Warren	Natalie	Whiston	Cameron	Winduss
Amy	Waterhouse	Cathy	White	Kate	Winley
Valerie	Waterson	Chris 'Critter'	White	Denise	Wittke
David	Watson	Ian	White	Alina	Wojcik
Gerry 'Puss Head'	Watson	Jeremy 'Jezza'	White	Annie	Wood
Gianluca	Watson	Tracey	White	Ian 'Perfecto'	Wood
John	Watson	Chris	Whitehouse	Robyn	Woodburn
Andrew	Weatheroy	Claire	Whiteman	Maria	Woodend
Darryn	Webb	Rodney	Whitney	Gavin	Woodfield
Pauline 'Granny'	Webb	Warren	Whitney	Billy 'Darky'	Woodhouse
Angela 'Flange'	Webber	Kate	Whittaker	Michael	Wordky
Jenny	Webster	Jeremy	Wiles	Robyn	Wright
James	Weeding	Mick 'Willys' &			
Regina	Weedon	Rosie	Wiles	**Y**	
Julie	Weir	David	Wilkins	Peter	Yates
Danielle	Weisse	Christopher 'Welshy'	Wilkinson	Samantha	Yates
Barry	Welch	Paul	Willcocks	Malcolm	Yeates
Peter	Welch	Nerida	Willenbrock-Walker	Michael	Yeates
Erin	Welgus	Alison	Williams	Belinda	Young
Timothy	Welling	Lyndal	Williams	Chris	Young
John & Barbs	Wellington	Megan	Williams	Hayley	Young
John 'Grilly'	Wells	Sonya	Williams	Jonathan	Young
John	Welsh	Sue	Williams	Neil	Young
Nathan	West	Tim	Williams	**Z**	
Jennifer	Westbrook	Trevor	Williams	James	Zambrano
Tony 'Beaka'	Western	Jeremy	Willis	Jeroen	Zwartsenburg
Matthew	Westmore	Alan	Wilson	Pieter	Zweemer
Timothy	Weston	Erryn	Wilson		

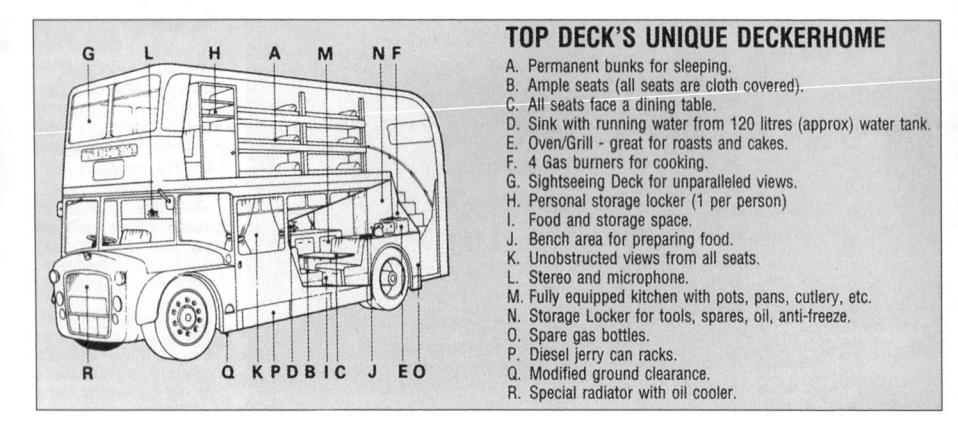

TOP DECK'S UNIQUE DECKERHOME

A. Permanent bunks for sleeping.
B. Ample seats (all seats are cloth covered).
C. All seats face a dining table.
D. Sink with running water from 120 litres (approx) water tank.
E. Oven/Grill - great for roasts and cakes.
F. 4 Gas burners for cooking.
G. Sightseeing Deck for unparalleled views.
H. Personal storage locker (1 per person)
I. Food and storage space.
J. Bench area for preparing food.
K. Unobstructed views from all seats.
L. Stereo and microphone.
M. Fully equipped kitchen with pots, pans, cutlery, etc.
N. Storage Locker for tools, spares, oil, anti-freeze.
O. Spare gas bottles.
P. Diesel jerry can racks.
Q. Modified ground clearance.
R. Special radiator with oil cooler.

How the double-decker buses were named:

1. ACKO — after Mark Atkinson
2. ARGAS — From Argas Persicus, the turkey tick (our first bus)
3. ARTHUR — after the boss of the Richmond yard
4. BEFA — 'B for' bus
5. BELCH — slang
6. BEN — after 'Diesel' Dave Morse's dog
7. BILLY DUNK — ask Tim 'Sniffer' Fitzpatrick
8. BLOATA — slang
9. BOLLOCKS — slang
10. BOOBS — after a well-endowed crew member
11. BOOGIE — up your nose
12. CAMEL — after Alan 'Camel' Rose
13. CASPER — ghost if I know
14. CHUNDER — Liquid laugh
15. COSTA — it 'cost a' lot to fit out
16. CRUNCH — it had a buggered gear box
17. CRUSADER — was bought from a scout group
18. DA BUS — phrase 'da'
19. DINGA — after Dave 'Dinga' Evans
20. DROUGHT BREAKER — after one of the crew
21. DEEP PURPLE — was singed in a fire at the bus yard (recalling the band and their hit song 'Smoke on the Water')
22. DRAB — after one of the crew
23. EDGAR — rhyming slang, 'Edgar Britt'
24. EDNA — after Dame Edna Everage
25. FIIK — acronym 'Fucked if I Know'
26. FINCH — after the Australian Hollywood actor Peter Finch
27. FIVE EIGHT — after Greg 'Five Eights' Lloyd
28. FLANGE — slang
29. FLAPS — slang
30. FLYNN — after the Australian Hollywood actor Errol Flynn
31. FROGGIN — rhyming slang, 'frog and toad' (road)
32. FRECKLE — James 'Budgie' Kemsley's cartoon character
33. FUUH — acronym 'Fucking Useless Up Hills'
34. GASWELL — after 'Diesel' 'Gasoil' Morse
35. GOBI — reference to the desert; dry as

Top Deck Daze

36 GOLLY—slang (our first FLF model)
37 GORDON—after Bryan 'Gordon Blue' Ramsey
38 GRUNT—slang (our second bus)
39 HANNIBAL—destroyed all that lay before it
40 HARDY—first VR model, twin of LAUREL
41 HULK—after Steve 'Hulk' Prosser
42 INTER—'into' this and 'into' that
43 KNACKERS—slang
44 KHYBER—rhyming slang, 'up the Khyber Pass'
45 LAUREL—twin of HARDY
46 LEMMING—followed everyone else
47 LEYLANDI—noxious South African weed
48 LOFT—acronym 'Lots of Fun on Top'
49 MOOSE—after Bruce 'Moose' Maloney
50 NAFAI—acronym 'No Ambition, Fuck All Interest'
51 NERO—acronym 'Never Ending Raging Orgy'
52 NARELLE—after Diesel's sheep at the farm
53 PHOENIX—replaced a bus burnt at the farm
54 PIG PEN—transported Diesel's pigs to market
55 PLATT—rhyming slang, 'platypus'
56 PLOD—Pissed and Lost On Drugs
57 RAFFERTY—after Australian Hollywood actor 'Chips' Rafferty
58 RAGS—slang
59 REX—after Rex Julian
60 ROXANNE—after Roxanne Garner
61 RUSH—the subject of a record fit-out, in one week
62 SCROTE—slang
63 6p—sixpence was found on board during fit-out
64 SLIPPERS—after Mick 'Slippers' Smith
65 SLUG—slang
66 SNAFU—acronym 'Situation Normal, All Fucked Up'
67 SNIFFER—after Tim 'Sniffer' Fitzpatrick
68 SNORT—slang
69 SNOT—slang
70 STEW—registration number
71 STRETCH—long wheel based VR
72 TADPOLES—slang
73 TAYLOR—after Australian Hollywood actor Rod Taylor
74 T.C.—after Diesel's cat at the farm
75 TEKI—(ask a Maori)
76 TROUBLE—broke down before fit-out
77 TUFT—'Get stuffed' (our third bus)
78 TUTAI—(find that Maori again)
79 VIKING—a rival company that folded
80 WOFTAM—acronym 'Waste of Fucking Time and Money'
81 WINO—its engine whined

Names of the single-decker coaches:

82 CITY OF LEETON— small Riverina town
83 CITY OF DURBAN
84 CITY OF TAKAPUNA—a New Zealand North Island suburb
85 CITY OF KAWERAU—a New Zealand North Island town
86 CHAOS
87 DAFFY
88 DEVIL
89 GONOR— refer Rhea
90 GASH—as in "drop kick & punt"
91 GROYTER
92 RAFT— acronym Rex and Andy's Fuck Truck
93 RHEA— refer GONOR
94 TROLLOP
95 UWE—first part of registration plate of this vehicle

Australian Buses (both Leylands)

96 BRUCE—first Australian bus
97 PEANUTS—used to advertise peanuts